READING SHAKESPEARE READING ME

Reading Shakespeare Reading Me

Leonard Barkan

FORDHAM UNIVERSITY PRESS   NEW YORK   2022

Fordham University Press has no responsibility for the persistence or accuracy of URLs for external or third-party Internet websites referred to in this publication and does not guarantee that any content on such websites is, or will remain, accurate or appropriate.

Fordham University Press also publishes its books in a variety of electronic formats. Some content that appears in print may not be available in electronic books.

Visit us online at www.fordhampress.com.

Library of Congress Cataloging-in-Publication Data available online at https://catalog.loc.gov.

Printed in the United States of America

24 23 22   5 4 3 2 1

First edition

for Benjamin Taylor, friend and inspiration

To read, v. transitive: To make out, discover, or expound the meaning or significance of.

—OXFORD ENGLISH DICTIONARY

To read, v. To wittily and incisively expose a person's flaws (*i.e.* "reading them like a book"), often exaggerating or elaborating on them; an advanced format of the insult.

—RUPAUL'S DRAG RACE DICTIONARY

Contents

Photographs follow page 104

Preface

At some point in the mid-1950s, my mother started buying antiques, and I tagged along with her. Among the pleasures of this undertaking was the fact that it was a little bit clandestine, or at least vaguely subversive, as regards my father, who possessed an ineradicable sense that he had come from poverty and might easily return there. The scene for much of this slightly furtive activity was a combined used furniture/antique store/auction house in downtown Yonkers, run by a pair of scary brothers, loud, gruff, suspicious, dour, openly unashamed of looking only for their own advantage in any transaction. Yet they presided over what became for me a treasure house, something that in the Renaissance would be called a *Wunderkammer*, a cabinet of curiosities filled with marvelous things.

Marvelous, but of very uneven quality. Often, while my mother studied the English china in the part of the shop where the high-end stuff was to be found, I rummaged around among the dust-covered secondhand items in the rear. On one occasion I found what seemed to me the perfect bookcase for my incipient home library. The price was duly bargained down by my mother, and it was delivered to our house, igniting—unforgettably, to my delicate psyche—a terrifying performance of rage from my father. Fortunately, the object in question was so bulky that it had barely been made to squeeze into the winding staircases of our Victorian house (also something of a wreck); as a result, threats of sending it back to the shop, and recouping the fifteen or twenty bucks that it cost, were in vain.

On a later occasion, again poking about in the dusty back room of the shop, I noticed an oak chair that in the dim light looked like something out of a haunted castle or a European beer hall. Nowadays I would know from its shape to call it a Savonarola chair, the kind where the two arms and the legs form a sort of curved X shape, as though it could all be folded up into a neat package, if the seat and back were made of fabric. Neither was made of fabric in this case, and it was the seatback that I fixated upon. As I did so, Alfred Cooper, one of the proprietor brothers, sauntered up to me. "You like that piece?" he asked. I'd been well taught, so I said something coolly like, "It's cool." I kept staring at the scene on the chair back. I had a sudden recognition and completely lost my cool, "You know what it is?" I gushed. "It's the scene in *Henry IV, Part One* where Prince Hal has been summoned to the royal palace; Falstaff says he'll play the king so that Hal can rehearse his visit to see his father, who really *is* king. Falstaff puts a cushion on his head that's supposed to be the crown and holds up a dagger as his scepter. The young guy kneeling—that's Prince Hal." "Twenty-five bucks," was the reply. I thought far too briefly about my hopelessly insufficient piggy bank and cried, "Sure." Soon, in fact, there were further negotiations out of my earshot; I suspected my mother was managing to get a better price. She was a good customer, after all, and a good mother.

It was all very well to stand there being dazzled by the idea of Shakespeare-memorializing furniture, by the clarity of the scene depicted on the chair back, the details of the beer tankard, the prince's boots, the leaded windows, the door half ajar, the way the ceiling beams and the floorboards provide linear perspective. Only once the chair was loaded into the trunk of our Studebaker did my consciousness shift focus to the inevitable rage of my father once it got home, given that it was far too bulky to hide. And the anxiety level rose when the chair was placed in the front hall of our house, where I knew my father would encounter it upon his return from work. At the usual time, I heard the front door open, then shut. There was conversation between my parents, but the sound did not carry upstairs—a good sign. My mother called me, I came slowly down the staircase, saw both my parents. "Don't you want to take the chair up to your room?" my mother asked. My father was smiling, "So you knew enough about Shakespeare to get that *gonif* Alfred Cooper to sell you this chair for fifteen bucks? I guess that private school tuition money isn't a waste after all."

Only now, in recollecting this, do I realize that I was myself playing out the role of Prince Hal before a menacing, if ultimately indulgent, father. That may be the most important signpost to the rest of this book: Not only was I in love with Shakespeare, but I also found in his work the key to my own life. But with that observation we get ahead of ourselves.

This is a book about a lifelong love affair. I can't recall far enough into childhood to trace the beginning of my Shakespeare obsession. Like the Prince

Hal chair, which has followed me through some sixty years of my life, it just seems to have always been there. Other pieces of furniture get replaced, go out of style, need refinishing, find themselves in storage, but Falstaff with the crown-cushion on his head remains. Eventually Shakespeare became my profession, with years of study and research. I became a professor who was employed as the "Shakespeare person" in several English departments; I tried out my own theoretical approaches to literature by testing them against the works of Shakespeare; I directed productions of Shakespeare and performed as an actor in other productions of Shakespeare. But it's not just about my professional résumé. Wherever I have turned in life, Shakespeare has popped up, not the historical man or the cultural icon; rather, the life inside the work has seemed to me something like an undifferentiated extension of real experience, a guide to living and to my own life.

I have touched upon two of the three key words in this book's title: *Shakespeare* and *me*. But the most important word, the thread that will become this book's fabric, is *reading*. As I write this, I am in my fiftieth year as a professor of literature. What that profession means to me, above all, is that I teach people how to read. I began to exercise this calling in early 1970s surfside Southern California, in a milieu where (at least as it seemed to this newly transplanted and highly prejudiced aspiring professional literary scholar) my students seemed to take it for granted that the purpose of reading, if it had any, was to aid and abet their continuing efforts at self-realization. Looking back on it, it all seems like the perfect setup for one of those classroom movies—Sidney Poitier, Robin Williams—where the teacher comes upon the scene with tons of superior ideas and ends up learning some ideas of his own.

What happened in *my* movie, though, was that I hunkered down on everything I had brought with me. Reading—particularly when the material in question is as remote in time and place from the reader as my reading materials are—needs to be the discovery of the Other. After all, whatever one's literary methodology may be, the profession in which I was trained and which I still practice hands out frequent signals that some sort of scientific detachment is the badge of seriousness in professing literature. When I lecture, when I write, the job is to hand my audience an authentic Shakespeare. Of course, I know that more than one authentic Shakespeare is possible, but I have reasons—in the text, in the context, in history, in the history of interpretation—for preferring mine and selling that product to my students and readers, though with all due open-mindedness toward other people's Shakespeares.

I am heavily invested in that enterprise, and happily so. But all serious readers know that this business of reading-as-analysis is a quite artificial, technical, even (in the most restrictive sense) scientific enterprise. The true, the inveterate reader enters the worlds of fictions and experiences them page by page as person-to-person encounters. I read Shakespeare, and I am Cleopatra, I am Mercutio, I am Othello at the same time as I am Iago. Or at the very least, I am in a small room alone with them, and they are speaking to me, to my life, to my sensibility, to my experience.

Reading Shakespeare Reading Me aims to bring this closeted process out into the open, at least regarding one particular reader. In the pages that follow, I am summoned by Bottom wearing an ass's head, by Lady Macbeth when she says she'd cheerfully bash her baby's brains out, by the marble statue that turns out to be the revived Hermione in *The Winter's Tale*, by the sonnet speaker who is tortured by the sense that a man he loves is also having sex with a woman he loves. I violate the rules that I was taught and have taught: I ask, Where does this brilliantly contrived fiction actually touch me in *my* life? Where is Shakespeare in effect telling the story of my life?

Imagine me, in other words, as a somewhat less delusional Don Quixote. The madness of Cervantes's hero (and this is one of the very few works I count as equal to Shakespeare's) consists of the fact that he obsessively reads chivalric romances, which are in themselves as fanciful and unreal as any literature can possibly be, and he construes them as real. He is just sane enough to know that life in his God-forsaken village doesn't resemble the world of chivalric romance, so he rides off in search of worlds that *do*, and, when he doesn't find such worlds, he invents them around himself. Now, Shakespeare's works are a whole lot better, a quantum leap better, than the books in Don Quixote's library, so I don't need to seek out exotic and alien realms in order to share the Don's sense that the literature I read can be understood as raw experience. Whatever it is I do when I reflect on my own past or make moves toward my own future, the works of Shakespeare count as life experience, as data.

Scholar that I am, I have to introduce a few more authorities. This is a book about Shakespeare, but there are a number of offstage presences who deserve to be acknowledged. The pivot is the Montaigne who has in his back pocket the examples of St. Augustine and Dante. In other words, the radical who dares to say, "I am writing about *myself.*" Yes, yes, he says in effect, "I've absorbed the corpus of classical wisdom and its narratives, I support all the ethical teachings of both bibles, I believe in every detail of orthodox Christianity. . . . *But now let's talk about me.*" St. Augustine, inspired by the new religion's emphasis on the soul of the individual believer, says, "I am so important that I'll subject the reader to agonies about how as a teenager I stole some fruit off a tree." Dante, following in those footsteps, says, "I am so important that I'm going to invent a fable in which I was permitted while still alive to see with my own eyes everything from hell to purgatory to heaven." Montaigne reaches an even higher level of chutzpah: "I am so important that I'm going to cover a thousand pages with my every thought and the entire range of my experiences, from the sublimity of a sacred friendship, now ended in death, to the precise sensations of passing a kidney stone." "Authors communicate with the people by some special extrinsic mark," says Montaigne. "I am the first to do so by my entire being, as Michel de Montaigne." And, most succinctly at the very opening of his vast volume: "I am the material of my book." I don't claim to have Montaigne's material, but that's quite all right, since I am borrowing Shakespeare's material and making it mine. I am the material of *this* book, but—cheer up, dear reader—so is Shakespeare.

READING SHAKESPEARE READING ME

1

Father Uncertain

I can't claim to understand exactly what Keats is talking about in his sonnet entitled "On Sitting Down to Read *King Lear* Once Again," but a couple of things about it strike me forcibly. First of all, he may be reading Shakespeare, but he's mostly thinking about Keats: what kind of literature he should, or should not, be reading (hence writing), and what his chances for poetic immortality are. That matter of readerly narcissism (is that too strong a word? I don't think so) is, of course, the matter of this book, as has already been suggested, and I am thankful to the great Romantic poet for clearing out some of the underbrush on this pathway. The second thing, which seizes my imagination even more, is that *once again*. What is Keats trying to tell us, trying to advertise, when he broadcasts his extensive experience with the play? After all, he died at age twenty-five: How many times *could* he have read *King Lear*? Samuel Johnson, who possessed the proper geriatric credentials, also trumpeted his dense and repeated experience of the play: Burdened with the task of producing his Shakespeare edition, he declared, "I was many years ago so shocked by Cordelia's death that I know not whether I ever endured to read again the last scenes of the play." Why, I ask, must we always be reading this play *again*?

Of course, for each of us there has to be, technically, a first time (doubtless, first and only for many beleaguered youngsters), yet for the kind of reader who is liable to make many future visits—Johnson, Keats, me—it's quite likely that the long-brewing cultural noise emanating from this literary object, quite independent of actual reading, makes it almost impossible for there to be a maiden voyage, a tabula rasa moment generating the kind of receptivity, the sense of open-ended possibility, that the viewer of the merest TV cop show enjoys.

For me, and throughout this book, there is a great deal at stake in the idea of a first-time reader, even though I have long since failed to qualify as such, and I have to summon it back as one might summon Adam and Eve back to the state of innocence. In the most extreme case, the first-time reader would actually be a first-night (possibly, afternoon) viewer of the play at the beginning of the seventeenth century. That is the viewer who possesses no playbill, no plot summary, no knowledge during the first scene of what will happen in the second scene, and so on and so on. That is the viewer who is working hard to grasp the fundamentals of the fiction and—for me, this is the most important thing—who is demanding to know, *what's in it for me?* That is the supremely egocentric viewer who says, "I'm not a prehistoric king of Britain, I'm not on the payroll as a full-time fool whose job is to be some kind of truth-teller, I'm not a lofty peer of the realm who has his eyes gouged out, so, once again, what's in it for me?"

Of course, for a twenty-first-century professional Shakespeare scholar to play the part of this naïve reader is a pretty questionable piece of casting, and a recent chance discovery brought home to me the challenges of postulating my own state of innocence. I possess, have often used, and recently reopened the excellent Kenneth Muir Arden edition of the play (the publication date 1959, and the price on the dust jacket—surprisingly, also preserved—$3.85); the pages sport some deliciously naïve reader's comments of my own, some of them even (horrors!) in pen. What literally fell into my hands, though, when I recently opened this volume was a sheet from a notepad with the printed header "The Elizabethan Club of Yale University." Both sides of the page are covered with a list of shorthand quotations and paraphrases from the play, in minuscule but quite readable hand, all attesting to one particular theme. There are seventy-two of these references moving chronologically through the first four acts, and they are headed by the simple title "KL—NOTHING." So, circa 1967, I was sipping tea at the Lizzy, availing myself of a bit of free stationery, and summing up *King Lear* under the rubric NOTHING.

It's a good rubric for understanding this work, and, truth to tell, the same throughline, NOTHING, gets quite a lot of air time in my classroom lectures on the play more than half a century later. But there is nothing naïve about finding NOTHING in the play; distilling that essence from the text reeks of reading *King Lear* not just "once again" but many times and feeling quite confident about a summing up. What it reeks of in particular is a reader/viewer who knows what is going to happen next, and after that, and after that . . . and through to the unbearable final nihilism that Dr. Johnson, when preparing his edition of the play, couldn't bear to read . . . *again*. Knowing that I had already ceased to be that innocent reader on the eve of my very first practice appearance before undergraduate English majors, the best I can do, in regard to *Lear* and all the other works that are treated in these pages, is to weave innocence with experience, attempting to recapture the condition in which one lives guilelessly inside a set of artificial lives while at the same time offering to present it as the impossibly many-layered creations of a genius whose work, to quote from a play that will soon grace these pages, "hath no bottom."

Two men are in conversation; a third, younger, man is standing, probably, off to the side. The two who are speaking must be grandees of some sort, since they seem to be privy to significant matters at the court. Or not quite so privy as might be imagined from their lofty titles, since what their conversation actually records is their former misapprehension about the king's intentions, which has now been corrected.

KENT I thought the king had more affected the Duke of Albany than Cornwall.

GLOUCESTER It did always seem so to us, but now in the division of the kingdoms it appears not which of the dukes he values most; for equalities are so weighed that curiosity in neither can make choice of either's moiety.

(1.1.1–6)

Much to chew on here. The kingdom is being divided, which is quite a shocker in its own right, since it presumes (without saying it explicitly) some form of royal retirement. Particles of the realm are being assigned to a pair of high noblemen. Both our informants had previously believed that the division would be determined along the lines of the king's preference for one of the noblemen (the "right" one, as it happens, though it will be a long time before we know that), but the king has surprised them and therefore accomplished what we have to assume is a brilliant piece of governance. Perfect equality of gifted land, after all, affords some kind of assurance that the transition will be peaceful. No reference is made to a third particle or to the fact that Albany and Cornwall are the king's sons-in-law. In fact, no indication at all that the king is a father, a circumstance that screams out to be mentioned if the subject is royal succession. The narrative, in short, is scrupulously cleansed of anything personal; it's all top-down politics.

What kind of tragedy do you think will follow from this? Surely, this perfect division is headed for trouble. Perhaps the division wasn't so equal after all; more likely, there will be lethal rivalry between these recipients of Lear's carefully apportioned largesse. Kent and Gloucester may have cleared up their misunderstanding, but Shakespeare will be stringing us along a bit further in ours. A few scenes later, a messenger, who by ancient theatrical tradition has no other purpose than to instruct the audience accurately, informs Edmund of "likely wars toward" between the two dukes. And almost immediately thereafter, Edmund, feigning concern, uses this piece of supposed information as the opening move in marginalizing Edgar:

> Have you not spoken 'gainst the Duke of Cornwall aught? . . .
>   Have you nothing said
> Upon his party 'gainst the Duke of Albany?

> (2.1.23–24)

It is slightly absurd to think that somehow Edgar might have been so lacking in political astuteness as to have spoken against *both* Cornwall *and* Albany, if that's what Edmund means; it feels more like a hastily concocted stratagem on Edmund's part, with no more validity than anything else he says. But then, at the beginning of the next act, it is Kent, the very emblem of trustworthiness, who picks up this thread. By way of prelude to announcing the arrival of the king of France's army, he brings up, once more, the prospect of intra-British warfare:

>   There is division,
> Although as yet the face of it be cover'd
> With mutual cunning, 'twixt Albany and Cornwall;
> But true it is.

> (3.1.18–21)

Despite the reliability of Kent as an information source and despite the forceful monosyllabic spondees of "But true it is," coming from a self-defined simple truth-telling individual, the play, it turns out, is never about war between Albany and Cornwall. Like Kent and Gloucester, we (briefly) got it wrong. The play is going to be about something else, but what, exactly?

There is, as mentioned earlier, a third character on the stage, off to the side; he wouldn't seem to be a suitable auditor for a discussion concerning lofty matters of state. For the first couple minutes of the play he is a question mark. Then Kent asks Gloucester the question that will provide us all with an answer: "Is not this your son, my lord?" In the premodern world (or should we say the pre–DNA testing world?), this is not so innocent a question as it may seem; it is indeed a question that rumbles through whole worlds of history, tragedy, and comedy, not to mention real life: *mater semper certa, pater semper incertus est.* The principle derives from Roman law as invoked to determine rights of inheritance. Childbirth establishes ironclad bloodlines; impregnation doesn't. Notoriously, in *Lear* as well as many other Shakespeare plays, fathers are everywhere whereas mothers are scarce, which means that parentage itself is nearly always subject to instability.

Gloucester's answer to Kent's (innocent?) question does little to render the matter more stable.

GLOUCESTER   His breeding, sir, hath been at my charge. I have so often
   blushed to acknowledge him, that now I am brazed to it.

(1.1.8–10)

A simple yes-or-no apparently will not suffice. *Breeding* could mean either *begetting* or *financially supporting* (a separation that itself speaks volumes), and via this ambiguity Gloucester reports his own process of transitioning from, formerly, embarrassment concerning this past sexual indiscretion to his current attitude of something like outright shamelessness on the subject. He is not, however, so brazen as to deliver an unambiguous answer, as is evident from the fact that Kent (again, the plainspoken man) has no idea what Gloucester means. It's a confusion that the befuddled Kent communicates in—dare we say?—pregnant language:

   I cannot conceive you.

At which point, audience members may well be thinking that they've stumbled into a comedy. The pun itself is joke material, and Gloucester's whole devil-may-care attitude offers at least temporary assurance that grave matters of legitimacy may be given a pass in this play. The promise of the pun is soon fulfilled:

KENT   I cannot conceive you.
GLOUCESTER   Sir, this young fellow's mother could, whereupon she
   grew round-wombed and had indeed, sir, a son for her cradle ere she
   had a husband for her bed. Do you smell a fault?

(1.1.11–15)

Have these dangerous subjects ever been treated so cavalierly—by an earl and in a tragedy, yet? How shall we understand the extraordinary nonchalance with which this grand nobleman advertises his transgression and its consequence, itself embodied and visibly loitering before us? Much later in the play, Gloucester's legitimate son, who by that time has suffered unspeakably as a direct result of this amusing peccadillo of his father's, will put a quite different construction upon the matter:

EDGAR (to **EDMUND**)
> The gods are just, and of our pleasant vices
> Make instruments to scourge us
> The dark and vicious place where thee he got
> Cost him his eyes.

(5.3.166–69)

Gloucester's susceptibility to sexual attraction, construed traditionally as entering through the eyes, explains it all—and in no flippant manner. Of course, by the play's final scene, in which Edgar speaks those lines, we may have become skeptical about the justice of the gods, no matter what Edgar says about them, and we may feel—at least I do—that this is a rather savage judgment in response to a relatively venial misstep. But even without four acts of hindsight, is it quite as venial as Gloucester presents it back in the play's first five minutes?

The self-excusing goes several steps further than the mere admission to fatherhood out of wedlock:

GLOUCESTER   I have, sir, a son by order of law, some year elder than this, who yet is no dearer in my account. Though this knave came something saucily into the world before he was sent for, yet was his mother fair, there was good sport at his making, and the whoreson must be acknowledged.

(1.1.18–23)

Note, first of all, that Gloucester has added adultery to his list of transgressions (assuming, at any rate, that his lady hadn't died in the months after the birth of Edgar). It is difficult to be certain whether a seventeenth-century audience would, as I would, find something admirable in the equal treatment of the two differently begotten sons such as Gloucester proudly enunciates it here; quite possibly they wouldn't. What is not so equivocal is the extraordinary claim, asserted in the presence of the Earl of Kent *and* of the bastard in question, that Edmund should be recognized on equal terms with his legitimate brother because the sex was so good when he was being conceived. And Kent is entirely on board with this: "I cannot wish the fault undone, the issue of it being so proper."

So, whereas Lear's fatherhood is, as one might say, under erasure in this scene—present only via the extratextual fame of the work but utterly absent from the actual conversation during these opening minutes—the notion of fatherhood itself is boldly, even bizarrely, exposed at the center of things. With hindsight, or with knowledge gained (again) by the text's cultural noise, it becomes easy enough to say that something is going on in *King Lear* about parents and children as well as about dynasties, but the differences between the cases of the two families are so striking that it becomes difficult to line up the Gloucester story and the Lear story as anything more than a tissue of oppositions. Gloucester loves his son despite the circumstances of the boy's conception, for which the boy can scarcely be held responsible; Lear comes to hate his (legitimate) daughter, on grounds for which he (illegitimately) holds her responsible: For the moment, that's about all we have to go on. The best we can do—and I think it's pretty good—is to say that there is something very complicated about being a father (indeed, about *having* a father), and it ramifies all the way from sexual intercourse to . . . what? Beyond that, what precisely does a father *do*? But that's exactly a question for the rest of the play. Along with the question: What do the offspring do in response?

In October 1921, my father married a woman who, like him, had emigrated as a small child from the shtetls of Eastern Europe. Even for that day and age, they were marrying young: he was twenty-one; she was nineteen. Judging from the dozens of photographs that ended up in a secret cache that has come down to me, she wasn't a great beauty, but her luxuriant wavy blond hair, bobbed in the style of the day, gives her a golden gleam and a certain presence.

The photographs, taken some twenty or so years before I was born, emerge from a world I never inhabited. The individuals memorialized here seem to have been living the American Dream of family glamour. Ben and Pauline in plus-fours for country walks, in evening attire for New Year's 1925, and in modish onesies for lounging at the beach. Their son—they had only one child at the time—is a fashion plate in his own right: an aviator suit complete with goggles (à la Lucky Lindy before his romance with Hitler?), three-piece dress-up tweeds, a sporting ensemble that wouldn't look out of place on the playing fields of Eton. In my lifetime I never witnessed a single member of my family dressed to kill in this particular way. It's not just the up-to-the-minute stylishness or even the expenditure (though both surprise me); it's the wish of a family of immigrants who, as a matter of certain fact, had not struck it especially rich yet chose collectively to exhibit themselves publicly in the costume of Vanderbilts.

Between that moment and, say, 1940, something happened. I'm not talking about the stock market crash or the rise of the Nazis, but something more local to these nattily attired seekers of the brass ring. It starts much earlier in the old country, with one of those demon matriarchs who fought off pogroms and defended her offspring with savage intensity. Chaia, the daughter of this formidable lady, had married a *monster*: cruel, abusive, a sexual outlaw. His escapades among the women of the shtetl netted a terrible result: Their first child was born with congenital syphilis. Let us stop right there to state the obvious: We enter here a phase of the story that has passed through several hands, none of which belonged to anyone with reliable medical expertise. Whatever the telltale signs at birth of Chaia's newborn are purported to have been, the story goes on to say that the ever-busy grandmother immediately seized the infant, rode through the night to the nearest center of medical care, and thus brought about a miraculous intervention that saved the child's life and—the medical plausibility is getting even more folkloric here—her eyesight. This is the child who grew up to marry my father.

At some point, even perhaps during the period memorialized in the photographic idyll, Pauline began to show symptoms of mental illness. Details about obsessive-compulsive behavior, again without the stamp of scientific authority, circulated among the cousins. There was a second- or third-hand story that Pauline's second child—born fully twelve years after the first—was conceived on the premise that her psychiatric condition would benefit from a pregnancy. This narrative was accompanied by a sad shake of the head and the assertion that no such beneficial effect was produced; quite the contrary.

The photographs themselves ought to tell us something beyond the opulence of the garments. It's clear that the dozen years in which this was a family of three coincide with the riot of picture taking. The baby in an infant frock, less than a year old, a radiantly smiling Pauline; my father has not yet grown the moustache that remained with him the rest of his life, and he has a full head of hair. The child, now three or four, wears a grown-up little overcoat; once again the parents sheltering him, Pauline embracing both husband and child. My father has lost some hair but gained the moustache. The child is having a birthday party; there seem to be five candles on the cake. Another birthday party, and there are seven or possibly eight candles. Another snapshot and the child is perhaps twelve and playing an accordion that dwarfs him. My father has lost more hair, grown a shade thinner, and his moustache is taking on the contours that I remember. Then the photographs stop—or at least my archive stops. Out of some two hundred family pictures, there is only one in which the second child, the one whose appearance on the scene was supposed to possess therapeutic powers, appears. The elder is maybe eighteen and is seated next to his future wife; the younger is a slender five-year-old; my father has lost yet more hair and is alarmingly thin, such as I never saw him until the end; Pauline is a plump middle-aged woman staring abstractedly into the middle distance.

And that's what one really seeks from these fading images: a photographic record of a mental breakdown. It's not to be found there, at least not for certain. A different sort of record proves to be quite accessible via Google, however. Working out dates and numbers from such scant family lore as there was, I hypothesized that Pauline had probably died around 1942, almost certainly in the state of New York. With minimal difficulty it is possible to access state death records for every year from 1880 to 1956. The challenges begin once one has broached these documents, however. There are, of course, thousands of names ("who would have thought death could have undone so many": so, Dante upon first entering Hell). The alphabetics are imperfect, as is the typography. Only a tiny fraction of the names are actually legible; for some unknown reason, they have been inked in, whereas the others have faded. Luckily (for me, not perhaps for her), hers was one of the inked: Pauline Barkan, died 4/24/42, age 40. Plus one more piece of information. Place of death: Dover, New York.

This came as a surprise. I was quite certain that the family lived in the Bronx. Thanks to census records, I even had the address: 763 Fox St. But Dover rang a distant bell (and not just because of Gloucester and Poor Tom, though it's not the only time that the uncanny enters these braided narratives). This time the internet search was not laborious at all. Dover, it turns out, was the site of the Harlem Valley State Psychiatric Hospital, which operated from 1924 to 1974. It reached its peak of occupancy—over five thousand residents—in exactly the years when Pauline was committed there. That moment also represented the pinnacle of its original contributions to the science, or rather technology, of treating the mentally ill. In 1936, Dr. Manfred Sakal, a refugee from Vienna, came to Harlem Valley to demonstrate the effectiveness of insulin shock therapy on the mentally ill, thus rendering the place a launching pad and showplace for this technique. Five years later, electroconvulsive shock therapy was added to the arsenal of procedures in use at the facility. Lobotomies flourished there as well, but they were only instituted in the 1950s, after Pauline's time.

Regarding this particular forty-year-old woman, can we connect the dots and declare with certainty that she died as a result of one of these therapies? We know that fatalities in such treatment centers were of a number that was not insignificant statistically, and one paper (W. S. Maclay, *Proceedings of the Royal Society of Medicine*, 1952) places lobotomies, electroconvulsive therapy, and insulin shock treatment in that order as the top three causes of what Dr. Maclay refers to in his title as "Death Due to Treatment." Harlem Valley maintained its own graveyard (along with its own golf course and its own bowling alley), whose entrance sported an iron arch with the rather crudely carved words GATE OF HEAVEN inscribed upon it. The individual markers of the dead, apparently in keeping with the practice of cemeteries for mental patients, bore no names, just numbers, so that the living relatives of the mentally ill would not be embarrassed by association.

Pauline Barkan did not pass through the Gate of Heaven; she was buried in more middle-class fashion at a Jewish cemetery in New Jersey. A little less than five months later, her widowed husband, the father of her two children, married my mother. And now that she enters the story, it's time to reveal that she—and therefore I—have actually been in the story all along. Pauline's high-functioning grandmother had another problematic son-in-law. Her elder daughter's husband had gone off to America, as so many shtetl husbands did, to establish residency and income in order eventually to send for his wife and children. But the all-seeing, all-knowing grandmother got wind of the fact— True? False? Who knows?—that he had taken up with another woman in New York. This time she didn't ride through the night, but, without warning the possibly wayward husband, she dispatched her daughter and that little subset of her grandchildren posthaste on the arduous journey that would take them to Ellis Island and beyond.

The littlest of that subset was my mother. She was Pauline's first cousin. The 1920 census in fact reveals that as teenagers they lived in the same crowded tenement flat at 182 Henry Street on the Lower East Side. Pauline's grandmother was my great-grandmother. My mother was marrying her cousin's widowed husband, and she married him just four months after his wife's death, quite possibly "due to treatment." Pauline's children are my second cousins as well as my half brothers; we share, in other words, that indomitable great-grandmother who, back in the Old Country, traveled through the night so that the infant Pauline might be saved.

What does a father do after planting the seed? In this play, it seems that a father suffers from the consequences of having planted that seed. Consequences of a very specific kind: a radical difference of moral character among the same father's offspring. Nothing new about this problem; it goes back to Genesis. The story of Cain and Abel in Genesis 4 is, like so many Bible stories, infuriatingly evasive on questions of cause and motivation, both as regards human beings and, even more, as regards the deity. "The Lord had respect unto Abel and his offering. But unto Cain and his offering he had not respect" (Genesis 4:4–5). Despite efforts to moralize Cain versus Abel, the text launches the radical opposition as something not in the acts themselves but rather enfolded in the mysteries of God, who expressed his foreknowledge of Cain's nature by refusing his sacrifice. It's that enfolding, in fact, which tells us that the author of this story doesn't know how to explain two brothers of opposite dispositions and thus relegates it to the divinely unknowable. As is often the case among such theological paradoxes, this foreknowledge is also a cause, since it's God's refusal of Cain's sacrifice that provides the only motivation we have for his (subsequent) crime. God knows how the brothers came to be so different—and He isn't telling.

King Lear is a grand document of this fundamental human enigma: Why is my sister, why is my brother so different from me, and what does that mean about who I am? But on this weighty theme, the play starts us off easy. The curious piece of family history that Gloucester narrates in the opening scenes is not just a story about adultery, bastardy, and legitimacy; it's also, as one might say, Cain and Abel 2.0. As of this moment, we have no idea what kind of character these two sons have or how they will turn out. What we are given, though, is a circumstance that places sibling difference in its simplest and most explicable form. Whatever may become of Gloucester's two sons will be ascribable to the fact that they have different mothers; half the enigma of sibling difference, in other words, can be explained away and therefore need not be enigmatic anymore.

With the next phase of the action, Shakespeare ups the Cain-and-Abel difficulty factor. As we have seen already, when Shakespeare introduces the theme of dividing the kingdom at the play's opening, he withholds any reference to daughters, in other words, any reference to family, to siblings, or indeed to females, rendering it for the moment a matter of pure royal politics. Now, however, it turns sharply in a different direction:

LEAR
Attend my lords of France and Burgundy, Gloucester.
GLOUCESTER   I shall, my liege.
LEAR
Meantime we shall express our darker purpose.
The map there. Know we have divided
In three our kingdom: and 'tis our fast intent
To shake all cares and business off our state,
Confirming them on younger years.
The two great princes, France and Burgundy—
Great rivals in our youngest daughter's love—
Long in our court have made their amorous sojourn,
And here are to be answered. Tell me, my daughters,

Which of you shall we say doth love us most,
That we our largest bounty may extend
Where merit most doth challenge it?

(1.1.36–47)*

"Our darker purpose." Darker than what? Presumably than whatever it was that involved France and Burgundy. Abdicating and dividing the kingdom certainly qualify as darker than almost anything. That being the case, Lear certainly passes quickly to what was evidently the *lighter* purpose, which is, in a word, love. First, the love that, as he expects, will be expressed in some sort of debate or challenge between Cordelia's two suitors, and second, far more important, the love that the daughters will express for him.

The establishment of difference between two suitors for the same lady's hand—a poetic genre that Shakespeare alludes to (it was the subject of what is commonly considered the first piece of Elizabethan secular drama, *Fulgens and Lucrece*)—does not detain us for long. The real contest, as we soon see, is intrafamilial. Endogamy, as one might say, outperforms exogamy on Shakespeare's stage. And as soon as it is turned into a contest ("which of you shall we say doth love us most?"), it becomes essential that the daughters distinguish themselves from one another. This is their chance to exhibit sibling difference, but the first two sisters do not rise to the occasion. Goneril covers what appears to be the whole field of filial devotion, leaving Regan to say, essentially, "me, too, but with sprinkles on it." We may not like these sisters, but, comfortingly, they appear to be cut from the same cloth. No need for the kind of genealogical background that we've been given as regards Gloucester's two children.

Not yet, at any rate. The system is about to crash and burn, but the change will be signaled by Lear before Cordelia even opens her mouth.

LEAR (to **CORDELIA**)
But now, our joy,

Although the last, not least in our dear love:
What can you say to win a third more opulent
Than your sisters?

(1.1.76–79)

---

*As with many crucial passages in the play, there are radical differences in these lines between the Quartos of 1608 and the Folio of 1623, and one cannot always make arguments that apply identically to the two versions. I have chosen the Gary Taylor text as presented in the Oxford edition, and I proceed with that as the document upon which I base my reading.

By this time it has become explicit that love is being equated with the winning of territory. It should also be clear that Lear has staged this whole contest with a view toward a dramatic climax. Which takes us toward a significant dimension as regards sibling difference that has been notably absent so far in the play: the issue of birth order. Not just in the case of monarchs but well down the social scale, the most obvious matter of sibling difference in Shakespeare's society would not be internal to individual character; rather, it would be imposed by the rule of primogeniture.

Whatever the presumed dynastic practices of this shadowy prehistoric world, Goneril has the priority of being first, but, via Lear's staging of "which of you doth love us most," the real priority turns out to be that of the baby in the family, daughter number three. Which, as it turns out, is as time-honored a sweet spot as that which is conveyed by primogeniture. Not in kingdoms but in fairy tales. The three-child paradigm in fairy tales invariably establishes the youngest as the winner of whatever is at stake, quite possibly as a compensation on the level of fantasy for the disadvantages of being the youngest child on the level of reality. However we may understand the folkloric dimension here, we are certainly witnessing an aspect of sibling difference as culturally prominent in its own way as that of primogeniture. Whatever qualifies the youngest as the best, it is another vivid form of sibling difference that, unlike the privilege of the eldest, which is given from the outside, may express itself as individual character. What it also contains traditionally, and it will be of spectacular significance in this play's sibling difference, is another quality that comes from outside: The youngest is loved the most.

And the fairy tale best beloved will provide a climax, but it's Shakespeare's climax and not Lear's. Cordelia's answer to her father's request that she say something sufficient to win the best third of the kingdom is, famously, "Nothing." Sibling difference is installed as the central principle of the narrative. The plot of the two interwoven families becomes a study in the permutations of individual identity as it follows, or fails to follow, the circumstances of birth. In the traditional manner of subplots, the story of the Gloucester family lays out the terms in a more straightforward manner, allowing the main plot to be, by comparison, mysterious and occulted. We've already observed how the opening scene presents us with complementary surprises: In the Gloucester family, where there is ample grounding for sibling difference, the father vows to treat his offspring identically; in the Lear family, where there is every expectation of both equality and equity, catastrophic and (so far) inexplicable difference erupts.

When I look at one particular way that Shakespeare places this issue of difference on the play's map, I ask myself how it is that, growing up in my own laminated family circumstances, I never had recourse to what must count historically as one of the most attractive schemes for explaining the inexplicables in human personality. Shakespeare was way ahead of me, it turns out.

Gloucester, quite legitimately, has trouble coping with the sudden changes that have taken place at Lear's court, and he has an app for it:

GLOUCESTER   These late eclipses in the sun and moon portend no
   good to us. Though the wisdom of nature can reason it thus and
   thus, yet nature finds itself scourged by the sequent effects. Love
   cools, friendship falls off, brothers divide; in cities mutinies; in
   countries discords, palaces, treason, the bond cracked between son
   and father.

(1.2.101–7)

Forget heredity, forget parents: It's the stars that determine our natures, not just the circumstances of family. Once astrology gets introduced by Gloucester, it becomes a sort of plaything within his clan. Edmund will parrot it in conversation with his brother, much as he will parrot the supposed Albany-Cornwall division: "I am thinking, brother, of a prediction I read this other day, what should follow these eclipses . . ." (1.2.130), to which Edgar's dismissive reply suggests that this whole line of thinking is not taken seriously by cool members of the younger generation.

It's Edmund, however, who delivers the appropriately cynical verdict on astrology as a scheme whereby we make the heavenly bodies, and not ourselves, "guilty of our disasters, as if we were villains by necessity" (1.2.110). The real payoff, though, comes at the end of this great prose soliloquy:

My father compounded with my mother under the Dragon's tale and
   my nativity was under Ursa Major, so that it follows I am rough and
   lecherous. Fut! I should have been that I am had the maidenliest star
   of the firmament twinkled on my bastardy.

(1.2.120–24)

Edmund's claim is that astrology is nothing but a scheme to deflect personal responsibility. It is a feature of his magnetic personality—the man you love to hate—that he does not deploy it for that self-excusing purpose in his own case. It wouldn't suit him, after all, to claim any explanatory origin of his own character except himself, his own nature, which in effect he worships as his goddess. Yet, whether in his time or mine, what else is there but the stars to explain the radical difference between persons with (to use our terminology) the same heredity and the same upbringing?

It's an appropriate question regarding the Lear children, as becomes explicit late in the play when Kent, looking upon the moral gulf between Cordelia and her sisters, declares,

> It is the stars,
> The stars above us govern our conditions,
> Else one self mate and make could not beget
> Such different issues.

(4.3.32–35)

But in Edmund's case, the prospects for this kind of explanation are murky at best. The Gloucester children share only half of what we would call their DNA. And, so far as upbringing is concerned, one might have thought that an early modern bastard in a noble family would not have been treated the same as a legitimate heir. Yet, as we have seen, the play opens with the seemingly unnecessary piece of information that no such inequality was practiced. We're left in a quandary about sibling difference. The stars may have played a role: Edmund discounts astrology but declares that "my father compounded with my mother under the Dragon's tail and my nativity was under Ursa Major" (1.2.120–21), circumstances that would, in astrological terms, have been accurate predictors of his character. On the other hand, a plot summary such as offered by the Hebrew Bible—"For I the Lord your God am a jealous God, visiting the iniquity of the fathers upon the sons to the third and fourth generation" (Exodus 20:5)—seems to fit the case best, except that the iniquity of the sons has found a way to be visited back on the father, who in this case launched the process with a relatively small (or was it?) iniquity of his own.

Speaking as a fifty-percenter myself, with brothers from another mother, I'm not sure that I needed either astrology or DNA or Exodus to explain why I was different from my brothers. I had—and have—Shakespeare.

•

> Have more than thou showest,
> Speak less than thou knowest,
> Lend less than thou owest,
> Ride more than thou goest,
> Learn more than thou trowest,
> Set less than thou throwest;
> Leave thy drink and thy whore,
> And keep in-a-door,
> And thou shalt have more
> Than two tens to a score.

(1.4.112–21)

This series of admonitions forms part of a thread early in the play when the Fool pronounces quite savagely upon Lear's error of surrendering power and land to his daughters. The Fool finds several ways of "proving" that Lear, and not he himself, is the fool, and he offers a little parable about having two coxcombs and giving neither of them to his daughters. Though these critiques tend to be in the form of enigmas, their purport is easily deduced. The Fool's jingle quoted here, however, seems less obvious in its relevance to Lear's current situation; hence, presumably, Kent's dissatisfaction with it: "This is nothing, Fool." Essentially: I expected a rousing condemnation of Lear's mistakes, like that stuff about the two coxcombs, but instead I got a little jigging rhyme with a series of oblique directives concluding in a nonsensical punch line.

It meant something to me, though, from my very first reading of the play. For Lear, it can be boiled down to the Fool's usual mantra: The king was imprudent; he did not sufficiently look after his own interests. For me, it pinpointed an ideology to which I seemed to owe the sorrows of my childhood, such as they were. Show no generosity of thought, word, or deed; keep tight hold of your possessions, whether material or not, so that there is no chance of having to share them; venture nothing in the hopes of a return, since there will be no return. (The drink and the whore were beyond my scope at that point.) Why these commands? Because the world is a terrible place, nasty, mean, brutish, etc. You must act in this reprehensible (to me, at any rate) manner in order to be an agent in the world rather than its victim, and—this is the crucial point—the wickedness of everyone else on the planet furnishes you permission for whatever you need to do.

If I grope around at this moment to understand why the worldview of "have more than thou showest" should have been so very threatening to me, I would say that it got bound up with my attempts to understand myself as existing in something I could recognize as a family. My examples in those early years weren't *Lear*—I was precocious but not *that* precocious, more like *Bonanza* and *My Three Sons*. It's curious that both of those shows, like *Lear*, operate on the premise of a dead mother (or, in the case of *Bonanza*, as I now learn from Wikipedia, three dead mothers—and I thought *my* family was weird). Whether television was involved or not, I can recall that there were some moments in grade school when I sought common ground among the other kids (which had already proved difficult on many levels) by saying proudly, "I'm the youngest. I have two older brothers."

Let's call that a *half*-truth. Or some more complicated fraction. I deployed this playground story about myself despite the many ways it reposed on troubled ground, both as to fact (not entirely the same parents, not close in age like the siblings of my schoolmates) and as to my own feelings of belonging within this smoothed-over family (as in the "Have more than thou showest" problem). After all, there were some people in the house for whom the world had indeed been a terrible place, a King Lear–in–the–Bronx whose strokes of ill fortune were more than enough to ground all that suspicion and self-protection that the Fool recommends. All the men in the family but me, in fact. No surprise that they looked upon the world with grave, unallayable suspicion, that they seemed to be conducting their lives with universal distrust and therefore plotting their own advantage even ahead of the time when their supposed adversaries had done anything worthy of distrust.

A vignette, far from *King Lear*. For a certain formative period in my middle teens I hung out after school at my father's drugstore. That's not quite true: I hung out in the *neighborhood* of my father's drugstore, which was in Greenwich Village. (I hope that makes me a little more cool.) Occasionally, I made deliveries for him or manned the cash register. One evening he asked me to do something a little different. I was to go to a far grander drugstore a few blocks away, and I was to say that my grandmother (I had no living grand-mother at this moment), whom I'll call Mrs. Teitelbaum, needed a copy of her prescription. What the cover story of this request was I can't remember; the real story was that my father must have been in a position to wrest all of Mrs. Teitelbaum's business away from his competitor if he could just fill that prescription. I can't recall with what proportions of dread and gusto I set about the few blocks' walk to the other pharmacy. After all, I did have a passion for theater, I liked playing roles, and I was definitely not above lying in my daily life. I can't have played this role very well, however, since I ended up being sent away empty-handed and told that Mrs. Teitelbaum would have to make the request in person. I returned to my father's store prepared to give him the news. But seconds after I entered, I realized that I had been followed by the competing pharmacist, who had guessed exactly what was going on, shadowed me à la *Dragnet*, and proceeded to stage a melodramatic performance of moral indignation in my face and at my father in front of all his customers.

Now, the moral of the story. My father was not angry at me for failing in the deception; after all, I was just a kid. He was not even particularly annoyed at losing Mrs. Teitelbaum's business—you win some, you lose some was appar-ently his philosophy. He was angry at me because of the way I felt inconsolably shamed by being exposed as a liar; the world being what it is (nasty, mean, etc.), I would get no sympathy on that score.

Why is it that I can remember no moment in my life, however early in childhood, when this point of view wasn't repugnant to me? I don't recall my mother, for her part, feeding me alternative messages of peace, love, and sunshine as regards the world; she, after all, had a complicated past of her own.

I'd like to be able to say that I earned the right to the life I lead—which is, as much as possible in this stinking sewer of a world, characterized by idealism, unguarded love, Mozart, Michelangelo, etc.—simply by believing in all those nobler callings already by age three. But that would be a grave error and an insult to those among whom I grew up. The real lie, the erasure that my playground mantra "I'm the youngest. I have two older brothers" perpetrates, is how incommensurably different my life was from theirs. I don't just mean all the sorrows and absences that the other men in the family had lived through and kept—so they thought—secret. I mean the fact that I was treated so differently. Back to Cain and Abel.

In this case, it wasn't God, it was my mother. *Their* mother was a mental patient; mine was an ambition machine. There is another cache of mysteriously preserved photographs, not Ben and Pauline in the 1920s but me solo in the 1940s and a little beyond. They're not for the most part homemade snapshots but professionally produced, and that is the first sign of difference. They are evidence of something I had (conveniently?) forgotten: I was being groomed for a career as a child model. There were in fact other groomings. Some as pathetically doomed as the modeling career: I recall protracted rehearsal under my mother's stern guidance of a skit in which I impersonated Liberace at the piano; I eventually delivered it—God help me—at some seedy agent's office in the West Fifties. And dance classes, a skill for which my talents were so abysmally lacking that *all* parents were banished from the final performance simply so that my mother wouldn't be able to witness how utterly she had wasted her money on sending me there.

Other grooming was not so doomed: I never attended a single day of public school in my life. At the age of five I was sent for special testing, which proved (scientifically—we are, after all, in the 1950s) that I ought to begin school in the third, not the first, grade. When that occasion arose, it was so catastrophic—children are not simply IQs, after all—that I was bumped down to second grade before the day was out. Things started looking up, slowly, after that, leading eventually to what must have been for my parents a painfully expensive private school of stellar reputation, where I learned Latin and moviemaking, etc., etc. At those respective ages, my half brothers were groping their way through New York City public schools and seeing their mother, if at all, in a state hospital. Yes, I was obediently grateful, and I acted upon that by (mostly) fulfilling the promise that my parents were paying for, under whatever mixture of duress and mimetic desire. But what does all this say about my idealism and my rejection of the Fool's mantra? Easy enough for me to maintain Mozart and Michelangelo in a classroom full of kids grooming themselves for the Ivy League.

My half brothers need have only looked at me, whether in those modeling snapshots or in real life climbing on the school bus that would whisk me away to bosky Riverdale, to have every bit of cynicism confirmed. For all that I tax them with as regards this jaundiced worldview, I should say that I cannot remember a single instance where they made me feel guilty for my privileges. Which made things even worse.

Am I Cordelia, then? "Although the last, not least. . . ." "I loved her most. . . ." The favored youngest child of fairy tales. Have I unraveled the reason why she cannot play the game that Lear designs for her? Was it because she had reached the limit of her ability to tolerate being the all-favored child? I don't know whether Shakespeare expects us to look at Cordelia's position as burdensome. I do know that, whether in childhood or adulthood, gifts always obligate. The child who is blessed by fortune—in this case, being spared the horror show of the schizophrenic mother—and then in addition being blessed by a shower of attentions and gifts, fancy private schooling, "a third more opulent than your sisters," is a child whose indebtedness can never be paid off. To respond by being the best little girl or boy in the world is fearfully hard work, and what it gets you is further redoubled reward, which in turn has to be repaid with more demonstrations of best girl or best boy.

What happens if I dare to take this experience as data, as legitimate critical material for understanding Shakespeare's play, if I break the rule of distance in the face of a poetic fiction? What has Lear's preference for Cordelia looked like in the play's prehistory? More jewels, more frocks, a shinier sports car when she turned sixteen? And what do we do with the fact that Cordelia is a good person, while the other two—Cinderella alert here—are *not* good people? What kind of circle, vicious or otherwise, has been operating in the past between the good girl's good fortune and the bad girls' not-so-good fortune? Whatever the signs have been in the past of Lear's partiality to Cordelia, and I have every reason to believe he didn't hide it (it wasn't very well hidden in my house), he has now arrived at payback time. This is, after all, a late-life moment of summing up, not only the reckoning of dividing British land into three parts but also the reckoning of family credits and debits. In other words, this is the moment when Cordelia is being expected to repay everything she received, material and immaterial, throughout a lifetime of receiving preferential love. Such a repayment is impossible. The only answer when you're asked for infinity is to respond with zero.

In my sophomore year of high school, I was assigned some reading by the great American zoologist Marston Bates, and—for what reason I don't recall—I mentioned it to my mother, who was at the time (just to give the flavor of the old world) at her sewing machine. She let out a whoop of laughter, which completely mystified me, and said, "They're teaching masturbation at Horace Mann?!?!" I'd never heard the word. (I knew the thing, just didn't know it had a name.) I asked her what it meant. It was clearly something very funny, since she couldn't stop laughing, but she refused to define it. I was ordered to look it up in Webster's, which I proceeded to do. Having learned the meaning, I faced a dilemma. To me, it felt beyond the unspoken house rules, regarding both education and sexuality, that I could either report back with a full account on the subject or simply wander off to another part of the house as though nothing had happened. I was saved by the fact that I loved the dictionary (does that surprise anyone reading this?) and therefore had done my assigned research of the terminology quite thoroughly. I returned to my mother at the sewing machine and reported, "No luck. All it said was *onanism*, so I looked up *onanism*, and all it said was *masturbation*." At least I was getting the hang of the house rules, indeed (as I now think of it) playing them against themselves.

Shakespeare knows all about sex jokes—and not only in the plays about romantic love. *King Lear*, however, is the place where sex is not a joke. The guy talk at the beginning, including Gloucester's casual revelation and Kent's "I cannot conceive you," points, as I've suggested, in the direction of comedy, but the laughter stops there. Obviously, Gloucester's adultery will have consequences of the deepest abjection—desire entered through the eyes, so the eyes must be plucked out. But adultery, having been amusingly established at the play's opening, becomes a kind of phantom explanation in the workings of the main plot. When Lear responds to Goneril's first serious attack on his presence, with the fool and the hundred knights, etc., by saying, "Are you our daughter?" (1.4.210), it's not just a vague gesture of rejection; it is an announcement of the uncertainty of his fatherhood. And in case it seems muted at that point, there can be no mistake when, in the following act, he is beginning to suspect that the daughters will present a united front against him. Regan says formulaically, "I am glad to see your highness," and Lear responds,

> Regan, I think you are; I know what reason
> I have to think so: if thou shouldst not be glad,
> I would divorce me from thy mother's tomb,
> Sepulchring an adultress.

> (2.4.130–33)

There is a complicated myth at work here, going back to the instance of genuine adultery. Edmund has already traced his own character—in his view clever, quick, enterprising, in our view mendacious and homicidal—to his origins as the product of adultery. And, conversely, he has ascribed what he sees as the namby-pamby character of Edgar to origins that are legitimate. We can call this philosophy "good sex makes bad babies, bad sex makes good babies." Others, like Lear, who don't subscribe to that causality and who have a high opinion of their own worth, expect their offspring to be mirrors of themselves. When they are *not*—and three of the five children in *King Lear* fail to be the proper loving replica of their fathers—the explanation has to be sexual. If Regan at this point turns out bad (we know she will, and Lear is beginning to suspect it), Lear's deceased queen must have been a serial adulteress.

However children may behave in the play, biological parentage—specifically fatherhood, since there are no mothers, which itself excludes the nurturing aspect of procreation and leaves us only with the sex act and the uncertainties of fatherhood—is a set of shackles. When a child betrays or seems to betray the father (and that covers, at one time or another, all five of the play's offspring), either they are the product of adultery, which is bad, or they are betrayers of the ties of blood, which is worse. Hence Gloucester to Lear in the presence of Poor Tom, "Our flesh and blood is grown so vile, my lord, | That it doth hate what gets it" (3.4.131–32). And the same goes for the absurdity, a few moments later, of Gloucester's "I had a son, | Now outlawed from my blood" (3.4.151–52), as though Law could actually sever the blood tie of a father and son bound by the sexual act of procreation so insisted upon at the play's opening. Thus the design of the play is to give us in the subplot a case of real adultery, with its clear mix of good sex and bad baby, while in the main plot we have phantom adultery, invoked as an inadequate explanation of how some particular babies turn bad.

This set of mechanisms in the play helps explain why the rock-bottom point of Lear's madness has him raving on the subject of adultery:

When I do stare, see how the subject quakes.
I pardon that man's life. What was thy cause? Adultery?
Thou shalt not die: die for adultery! No:
The wren goes to 't, and the small gilded fly
Does lecher in my sight.
Let copulation thrive; for Gloucester's bastard son
Was kinder to his father than my daughters
Got 'tween the lawful sheets.
To 't, luxury, pell-mell! for I lack soldiers.
Behold yond simpering dame,
Whose face between her forks presages snow;
That minces virtue, and does shake the head

> To hear of pleasure's name;
> The fitchew, nor the soiled horse, goes to 't
> With a more riotous appetite.

(4.6.106–19)

Lear is being tortured, and Shakespeare is torturing us, with the indissoluble bond between sexuality and procreation. For a culture like Shakespeare's—and many more recent cultures including, doubtless for some people, our own—this amounts to a terrible contradiction. Lust is bad, making children is good—and coming up with rules issuing orders that subdivide anything as uncontainable as sexual desire is bound to produce even more torment.

There was a period in my professorial life when I used to say quite often, and rather extravagantly, "In the years after my father died, I could not bring myself to teach *King Lear*." Reflecting on it now, it looks like a rather grand piece of self-dramatization. Was it even true? In those days, I was the Shakespeare-teaching workhorse of my department (nice work if you can get it), and I'm not sure it would have even been permissible for me to leave his greatest play off the syllabus. And—perhaps a more interesting question—was I really engaging with the texts in so intimate a manner that I would worry about risking painful personal exposure by merely delivering lectures on this play? That would have been the very thing that my pedagogical method—*everyone's* pedagogical method—was designed to obliterate or at least downplay. And, even allowing that I might have experienced a few more frissons from this play than from, say, *Two Gentlemen of Verona*, what were the things in the text of *Lear* that might be responsible for them?

Of *his* father I know nothing. His mother (per *my* mother) was something of a brute; his elder brother, whom he idolized, died in the flu epidemic of 1918; his beloved younger sister—they were the two babies of the large family—succumbed to cancer in early middle age. He attains what must have been the lowest rung of the upward-leading ladder for an immigrant Jewish boy who had no family business to enter but had fared pretty well in school: hence his profession of pharmacist. He married, let us say, a little bit *up*; perhaps that explains the costuming, both the wish to appear so photographable in public and the means to carry it out, if not quite the style to bring it off. His young wife . . . but here the path becomes uncertain. There is every reason to believe that she may have been hospitalized before the stay during which she died. By some accounts, the younger child was brought up largely without a mother and by incompetent or indifferent household help, which would place Pauline in some kind of institution as many as seven or eight years earlier.

Perhaps it was at this previous stay that the medical advice to have her conceive a second child was offered. No wonder the photographic trail runs cold.

What I have in its place is, to begin with, a tissue of imaginings. The young husband spent his whole professional life (that is, until my mother whipped him into viable commercial shape) as a mere salaried employee working long hours in a series of drugstores where the boss got the daytime schedule and all the profits. When the going was rough at home, with a child to raise, he had to play father, mother, perhaps psychiatric practical nurse, all of it solo. Of Pauline's stays at Dover (or wherever else), I am thrown back on my imagination. There exist some extraordinary photographic essays of the Harlem Valley facility in its dilapidated current state. If I stare at them long enough, repaint the walls, reassemble the furniture, replace the shattered glass panes in the windows, I still see monstrous dehumanizing surroundings. Unimaginably long unvaried corridors with strings of identical cubicles barely larger than the beds in which the inmates are confined. Repose in these spaces is dire, the treatments worse. Ben is walking these halls in search of his wife, his son back in the city meanwhile, cared for by hired help.

If I look at these pictures and think of *him*—not the horror-movie hospital or the young woman declining into madness or the abandoned six-year-old back in the Bronx—I have an intuition not so much of sorrow as of emptiness. It's not, in other words, tears that come to my eyes but a perception of . . . nothing. But a Nothing so palpable that it is somehow a Something. Of course, it may be I think of it that way because I have read *King Lear* and because at some moment in the last century I unearthed seventy-two *nothing*s in the play.

It's also possible, though, that I think of it that way because I knew my father. Or didn't. I recall a moment when a much-loved cousin, at the end of a wine-besotted family weekend, watched my father leave the room and whispered in my ear, "Who *is* he? There's nothing there." I have precious little with which to fill up that nothing. *Pater semper incertus est*: Roman lawgivers, you didn't know the half of it. I harbored no doubts that he had begotten me, though it was canonical in my family that I was the spittin' image of my mother—she herself being the keeper of that canon. In fact, one morning, near the beginning of what could be called my old age, as I was washing my face, I looked in the mirror and, myopically, received a reflection that was suddenly in every feature my father, already by that time long deceased. As I jokingly said to myself, "who is that?" I remembered what my cousin had said and realized that that was the question I might have asked when I looked not at the mirror in old age but at my father when I was a child. "Who *was* he?" Near the beginning of his travails, at the early signs of his mistreatment, Lear says, very feelingly, "Who is it that can tell me who I am" (1.4.222). When the king expresses his agony in this way, we are likely to think in terms of status: Do any of the others onstage recognize that this suffering individual is the king? But when the individual is a mere mortal—a pharmacist, for instance—it seems more appropriate to say to him, "How come, after all these years, you don't know who you are?" Of course, a king is a mere mortal as well.

The oblivion, the silences are part of the story; perhaps they *are* the story. When I now try to fill in the blanks—the vast, gaping blanks—in the life of my father, from the young bourgeois gent with the right togs for every occasion, to the husband who had to travel two hours each way visiting his schizophrenic wife in a state hospital, to the null set as diagnosed by my cousin, to the man who received those messages of my unhappiness but returned no sign to me, I realize that it's all a story about silence and silencing. For me in my childhood and for my father in his middle age and beyond, the most important thing about the family secret was the fact that it was so deeply and effectively buried a secret.

It was also a secret of many layers. Both my parents had in fact been married before: Under certain rare circumstances, this might be alluded to, but only among those who already knew it. My mother had been divorced: That might even have a certain cachet as a local throwback to the Roaring Twenties, casting a bit of glamour on my plump middle-aged mom. That we three brothers were not 100 percent brothers was risky territory, particularly when it began to be clear that I might have some advantages, whether by genetics or fate, over the other two, a subject that yet even in these pages I can barely broach. Then we arrive at the impossibles. My brothers' mother died insane: For me that came with a kind of anesthesia owing to the fact that it was too large to grasp, but what did it mean to *them*? The rule of silence was doubtless meant to ease the torment, but such fixes never work. Then there was the deepest-buried secret of all, passed down from my great-grandmother to my mother to me. The absurdity is that quite possibly it's a piece of ignorant, old-country lore. Pauline's madness was the result of syphilis. This secret my mother never shared with my father, though they had known each other almost all their lives and though Pauline and my mother had lived together precisely at the moment when Pauline married him. The only person she ever seems to have shared it with was me; I was thirteen years old at the time. From that moment on, I was blessed with the understanding that my father's greatest suffering was that he didn't know why he was suffering.

"Sons at perfect age and fathers declining, his father should be as ward to the son, and the son manage the revenue" (1.2.71–73): Who makes this proposal in *King Lear*? In truth, nobody. It's a piece of quoted speech, only it was never really spoken. It's one of Edmund's fabrications, here offering his father a fictitious account of Edgar's supposed incitement to a revolution that would end up dividing the earldom of Gloucester evenly between the two brothers. Under those conditions, Edmund would "live the beloved" of his legitimate, and elder, sibling (another fabrication, suggesting a somewhat surprising wish-fulfillment fantasy on Edmund's part; is the motive behind all his crimes disappointed fraternal desire?). Only minutes earlier in the play, a real division among siblings—different siblings—has taken place, not the strategic lie of a Machiavellian manipulator but a freely chosen ruling laid down by the father himself—a father whose words, true or false, wise or foolish, have the weight of law, at least for the moment.

The parallels of the Lear and Gloucester plots are all too clear and will remain so at many points in the play. But I am not so interested in the questions of power and property as in the image that Edmund conjures up of, as he puts it, a "father declining." When Edmund deals that particular card near the beginning of the play, it hasn't gathered much weight: It's a mere hypothesis attached to a lie, and neither of the two real fathers has yet declined very much. Things move fast, however. At the very beginning of his travails, when Lear is encountering a lack of respect under the supposed protection of Goneril and Albany, he poses the most fundamental question about the self in relation to the surrounding world: "Who am I?" The Delphic Oracle enjoins us to answer that question, yet it's not the Delphic Oracle that Lear is addressing here but Goneril's personal hatchet man, Oswald, who replies confidently, "My lady's father."

Many scenes later, near the end of his travails, when Lear has been rescued, Kent has resumed his own identity, and Cordelia is about to receive her father, she asks one question about his condition: "Is he arrayed?" (4.7.18). In other words, is he clothed or naked? The answer is (reassuringly for all of us) yes, but the question reverberates not only with the play's own imagery of "unaccommodated man" and "off, off, you lendings," as intoned by Lear at an earlier stage of his own collapse, but also with a biblical primal scene when Noah, drunk with wine, is glimpsed (and perhaps something more intimate than glimpsed) in his full nakedness by his offspring (Genesis 9:20–27; it actually turns into part of the vile biblical grounding for racial prejudice), a circumstance we are to understand as the ultimate mortification.

These early and late stages in Lear's undoing point to a particular vision of what it means for an individual to be taken from the heights to the depths. It's not so much the inexorable turnings of the wheel of fortune that move a man

from exaltation to ruin, though Kent will mouth some clichés on that subject. It's children; once again the fatal consequences of a father's sexuality,
whether blessed like Lear's or unblessed like Gloucester's. Lear's degrada-
tion, embodied in that title of "my lady's father," is a shocking diminution of
his power in the world, but the terms of this insult are not so much dynastic
as familial. The collapse of Lear's value is tied directly to and identified with
his status as a father. At the other end of the story, the child as witness—to the
possibility of nakedness—is the marker of the horror that we are to understand
as the complete stripping away of humanity.

Between these two points *King Lear* is a pageant of paternal humiliations, dealt
out to the father and either administered or witnessed or signaled by the
offspring: Lear's retinue subjected to arithmetical reduction from a hundred
to zero in some kind of ugly mirror held up against the love auction of the
opening scene; the still-sighted Gloucester being led by Poor Tom, whom he
does not recognize as Edgar, then the blinded Gloucester being led over a cliff
by his son in a different guise; the double dance of abjection when one father,
who is blinded and either has or hasn't fallen from Dover Cliffs, meets another
father, whose sanity has been gravely compromised.
     But it's the running commentary on this action that locates the force of the
drama on the act, and the consequences, of procreation. The Fool accuses Lear
of having turned his daughters into his mothers, then giving them the rod and
pulling his own pants down; spanking isn't the only thing that comes to mind.
Gloucester tells Lear, "Our flesh and blood is grown so vile, my lord, | That it
doth hate what gets it" (3.4.131–32). And Lear himself sees his daughters not
just as his flesh and blood but rather a disease in his flesh, "a boil | A plague-
sore, and embossed carbuncle" in his blood. When he looks at Poor Tom, he
declares mistakenly but, under the circumstances, understandably, "Nothing
could have subdued nature | To such a lowness but his unkind daughters." Not
to mention unkind *sons*: In the context of fathers undone by their offspring,
Edgar's manufactured catharsis of leading Gloucester up a little hillock, then
persuading him that he has fallen from Dover Cliffs and been rescued by some
sort of demonic miracle worker places us beyond an ability to distinguish for
certain between great love and great cruelty.

Speaking, admittedly, as a son who has never been a father, I find myself a bit
resentful at the way this deck has been stacked. In the setup of *King Lear*, there
seem to be only two options as regards the father: either Cordelia's chillingly
contractual

> You have begot me, bred me, loved me: I
> Return those duties back as are right fit,
> Obey you, love you, and most honour you.

(1.1.87–89)

Or else the fantastic hyperboles of the evil daughters, which—forgive the exaggeration, but it's in keeping with the speeches themselves—only a father on the verge of senility would receive as truth.

I'm recalling what must have been the summer before my tenth birthday. My mother and I were in the country, where each weekend began with the ritual of picking my father up at the train, after which the three of us would have dinner at an Italian place nearby. When he appeared on this weekend, however, it was in the company of a gentleman with a doctor's bag. My father was a bit pale and disoriented; we were told to take him straight to the local hospital. As I now reconstruct, he'd had some kind of cardiac episode, or something that resembled a cardiac episode. It was determined that he was well enough to complete his journey so long as he could be taken to the hospital.

I can't reconstruct much of the medical story. It must not have been a heart attack, since his stay at the hospital was brief, and, among the various health woes of advancing age, cardiac problems were not featured in the succeeding twenty or so years of his life. What I do remember was that a few days later I received a talking to. It was very formally framed in a manner completely alien to the habits of the household: It was announced that it would take place at a certain hour, that I should be ready for it, that dinner would be delayed on account of it, and that I must prepare to pay attention to it in a superior way to what was deemed my usual level of attention. I'm afraid that's most of what I remember—more the prep than the talk itself. At least from the parental side; from my own side, what I remember is an understanding that I had to find ways to be a better little boy than I had previously been. From the perspective of a literary life many decades later, I find it rather intriguing. It's like a nifty premise for a novel, perhaps a *Bildungsroman*, in which our young hero embarks upon a lifetime of introspection owing to the demand laid upon him at age ten to assess himself and improve what he sees. Does he, in fact, improve?

In real life, I wasn't ready for that introspection at the time, and I recall entering into some kind of guilt search—now I keep thinking of Catholics, and confession, and St. Augustine, all thankfully unavailable to me in 1954—without much guidance as to the appropriate paths of good and evil for a very sheltered pre-teen. I'm sure that if I'd known *Lear* at the time, I would have consented readily to never forcing my half-naked parent out into a storm, like Regan, and to making every effort not to be mistakenly believed to have sought to kill him, like Edgar, or to plan the murder for real, like Edmund. I suppose it's part of the ancient cry against literature (Plato and so forth) that it's so much better at offering bad examples than good ones, but I would like to know more about the thread that connects the bad daughters' fulsome claims in act 1 to their unspeakable atrocities in the subsequent acts. I didn't have the goods on *Lear* at age ten, but if I had, I'm pretty sure I would have wondered how to proceed, safely, in the Cordelia direction. *Much* later—like now—I note with some gratification that the perfect (too perfect?) child Cordelia, having said, perhaps in a tone of uncharacteristic frustration, "Sure, I shall never marry like my sisters, | To love my father all" (1.1.94–95), turns out—via Shakespeare's manipulation of the plot—never to have to prove this; the author disposes of the king of France, her husband, with a vague reference to "something left imperfect in the state," and she is left to be a full-time daughter after all. I'm also struck by the fact that her great line of paternal allegiance, "O dear father, | It is thy business that I go about" (4.4.24–25), is pinched from a moment in the New Testament (Luke 2:49) when Jesus is rejecting his earthly parents in favor of God the Father. Is Shakespeare covertly resisting the obligation to portray Cordelia as perfect? The fact is that Cordelia wouldn't have been of much help to me. After all, if I had concluded the discussion at that delayed dinner hour, after listening to the injunctions to be a better little boy, by saying, "You have begot me, bred me, loved me . . . ," etc., it would have probably meant no dinner at all that night, not even a late one.

Something happens toward the end of *Lear* that feels very different from the equivalent phases of the other heroic tragedies that Shakespeare was writing around this time. Let's call it whimper versus bang. The duel scene in *Hamlet* dispatches everyone with a single onstage mechanism. *Othello*, very different and written in the key of erotic passion, places the couple before our eyes in a scene of concentrated desire and violence. In *Macbeth*, the spectacle of resolution is, fittingly, military, along with an outcome presided over, albeit in absentia, by the seemingly omnipotent, or at least omniscient, witches.

In *Lear*, the humiliated father, whom we've already met, turns into the humiliated tragic hero. Blindness and madness obliterate the fundamental qualities that make even a deeply flawed hero great: the ability to perceive the world in all its pain and the ability to gain the kind of insight that elevates the experience of that pain from melodrama to tragedy. But it gets worse—or more extreme. In the closing minutes of *Lear*, it's almost as though Shakespeare himself gives up on the project of a hero whose final life experiences can be commensurate with the map of his suffering.

The truth is that, from the point of the reunion between Lear and Cordelia late in act 4—forgive me, bardolaters, of whom I am one—to the end, the play is a bit of a mess. The reunion itself is, of course, material for a happy ending, say, as one finds in *Pericles* or *The Winter's Tale*, but it can't have a happy ending here. The real problem is that the drama has from the start put a broad set of narratives in play. It's not just that we have a bona fide subplot with the stories of three different family members to tell but also that the main plot has by this time experienced a kind of multiplication. This tragedy will not resolve itself, like *Hamlet*, with a single instrument that punishes and judges everybody, nor will it be sufficient, as in *Macbeth* or *Othello*, to resolve the stories of a closely connected pair or trio of characters, whose death will tie up pretty much all the loose ends.

In place of those relatively neat packages, we have, first, the military defeat of Cordelia and Lear, which is settled with almost absurd speed, and then the resolution of Edgar/Edmund, on the one hand, and of Edmund/Regan/Goneril, on the other, both of which are settled with rather less speed than one might wish for. But I'm not so interested in these narratological mechanics as in their consequence for the figure—now I would say figures—at the center, Lear and Cordelia. By the final scene of the play, the drama gets so wound up in the lives of the two sets of offspring that Lear suffers a humiliation on the level of narrative and dramaturgy that belongs at the same annihilating level as the madness itself. After all, it's only the return of Kent—no kin to any of these people—that results in a reminder to the survivors and the audience that Lear has been left perilously unattended while subplots have monopolized the stage. "Great thing of us forgot," says Albany, one of the few (like Kent) whose hands are clean. No other Shakespearean tragic hero gets "forgot" at such a crucial moment.

Shakespeare is doing some forgetting or some ostentatious narrative sleight of hand on his own here. Edgar delivers his beautiful speech about the final meeting with his father, ending with Gloucester's heart "too weak the conflict to support—| Twixt two extremes of passion. Joy and grief | Burst smilingly (5.3.194–96). Edmund's response may surprise us:

> This speech of yours hath moved me,
> And shall perchance do good. But speak you on—
> You look as you had something more to say.

> (5.3.196–98)

It's certainly a surprise that Edmund is experiencing a conversion, brought on by his brother's account of their father's death. But it's even more a surprise, and of a different kind, that Edmund, having intended to do good—which we know consists of calling off the murder of Lear and Cordelia—interrupts himself with a rather casual "do tell me more." The result is the tying up of yet another loose end in the plot, the fate of Kent, or, rather, the narration of Kent's meeting with Gloucester. Edmund's opportunity to "perchance do good" is thus suspended for some twenty-five lines and then interrupted by the news of the stabbing/poisoning of Lear's evil daughters. Only after that does Kent appear in the flesh and precipitate the fatal "Great thing of us forgot," which, as of course we know, comes too late to save Cordelia. In effect, the narratives of these ancillary and, in most cases, evil characters have been delivered to us at the price of Cordelia's life. It's a kind of conspiracy whereby the truly tragic characters get sidelined—and lose their lives in the process.

Even our experience of the death is deprived of the kind of dignity that comes with clarity. About five minutes before the play's final curtain, Lear comes on stage carrying Cordelia. He declares her to be "dead as earth," but in the same instant he requests a mirror, which is to be placed in front of her face; if she is still alive, any sign of breath will mist the mirror. The text gives no evidence that this experiment is tried; no one, in other words, responds to the king's command (so what else is new?). Lear then says, "The feather stirs. She lives," which tells us that he has, silently, undertaken a different test to determine Cordelia's condition; it seems he has found a feather somewhere and has concluded from it that Cordelia is alive. No one else onstage seems to share this conclusion, though, and he asserts with seeming finality, "Now she's gone forever," though he immediately proceeds either to hallucinate or pretend that he is in conversation with her ("What is 't thou sayst?").

Shakespeare is toying with us, withholding the catharsis of finality. The balance as regards Cordelia's condition tilts heavily toward dead, since only the mad Lear believes otherwise—and even that intermittently. The matter appears more or less settled when Lear declares, "And my poor fool is hang'd! No, no, no life! | Why should a dog, a horse, a rat, have life, | And thou no breath at all?" (5.3.300–2). Except, of course, for that strange reference to "fool," which, while presumably equating to Cordelia (but why exactly call her a fool?), yet with a notable surplus left over to divert our attention toward *the* Fool, who is associated with Cordelia and who made his final exit in the third act, without explanation or mention thereafter. The uncertainty isn't over yet, at least not in the Folio. In both texts, Lear makes one more request, "Pray you, undo | This button," though it's not clear to whom he makes the request or (more interestingly) whether it's his own or Cordelia's button that he wishes undone.

Quarto Lear, after an "O, O, O, O!," dies (though in both texts, just to add confusion, Edgar's immediate response is, in fact, "He faints"). Folio Lear says, "Look on her, look, her lips, | Look there, look there," and he dies. From which we must conclude that, under whatever state of delusion, he believes Cordelia to be alive. It's as though there is a kind of antitragic impulse at the end of this tragedy, a sense that the dead do not quite deserve the glory with which tragedy invests them.

If I read the end of *King Lear* with a sort of *ressentiment,* a sense of grievance that Shakespeare failed to respect the tragic worth of his own tragic characters— an absurd proposition, I know—it's in part because of my own experience in my father's hospital room, not back at the time of the faux cardiac event but much later. After all the things I've said about him, oscillating between tyranny and nonentity, I feel I have something more to reckon with, something that I've learned from *King Lear*, or perhaps I should say from a lacuna in *King Lear*, and something I want to put back there.

There's no definition of tragedy—certainly not the professional one, which insists that it's not just a whole lot of suffering but rather "a serious drama typically describing a conflict between the protagonist and a superior force (such as destiny) and having a sorrowful or disastrous conclusion that elicits pity or terror" (*Merriam-Webster*)—that could properly fit the scene of my father in his tiny private room at Beth Israel Hospital. It was a drab little space with a window looking out upon the minutest courtyard I'd ever seen, even in New York. The TV droned on continuously with the Watergate hearings (this was the summer of '73). I stumbled in, fresh from San Diego, courtesy of a long-delayed red-eye flight.

Under the circumstances, he may have been more alert than I. We had an unmemorable but thoroughly lucid conversation, after which I retreated to my mother's apartment to catch up on sleep. I returned to the hospital room the next morning, ready for more meaningful chat, only to discover what seemed like a different person, his mind radically wandering. There was one monologue about my dog Sasha when she was a puppy (pretty recent history) and another, in either Polish or Yiddish, in which he seemed to be identifying imaginary passersby still residing in the Old Country (not such recent history). He was actually starting to sound a little bit like King Lear—a thought that I promise by all that's holy I did *not* have at that moment. I was, of course, curious about the change in his mental state: Was it a sign of his illness, or of the drugs given him in response to the illness, or of something else?

Desperate, as one always is in that situation, for something to do, I located one of the residents and asked her what to make of this alteration in my father's mental state. She obligingly came into the room and administered what I took to be the boilerplate rationality interrogation. She fixed him in the eye and asked peremptorily, "What is today's date?" He muttered something that might or might not be the name of a month and a number below thirty-one. Then, even more sternly, "*What day of the week is it?*" He gazed into the middle distance, apparently not quite recognizing that he had been asked a question. Finally, she arrived at what must be the Hail Mary test, the question that even a dazed, long-term hospital patient should be able to answer. "*Who is the president of the United States?*" Suddenly, his eye contact with her was unerring, and without pause he shot back, "*A mise meshunah soll im einnemen.*" (Roughly: He should only drop dead in excruciating pain.) I burst out laughing, which brought him a little back to reality; he laughed, too, and added, this time in English, "They should impeach the bastard." He was smiling, even if his eyes told me he didn't know exactly what's funny.

I recognize that I have been complaining about *King Lear*—surely, one of the greatest literary works of all time—because I resent the fact that Shakespeare denies his hero a certain kind of grandeur at the end, even the grandeur of erroneous certainty, like Othello, or of single-minded violence, like Macbeth. Of course, it's more reasonable to say—since it's Shakespeare—that he did exactly what he wanted to do. He is in the process of bidding farewell to heroic tragedy, either altering what sort of thing the hero is a hero *of* or else abandoning it altogether in favor of tragicomedy. Perhaps those ringing pronouncements of formerly glorious persons with one foot in the grave—things like "I kissed thee ere I killed thee. No way but this | Killing myself, to die upon a kiss," or "Lay on, Macduff | And damn'd be him that first cries, 'Hold, enough!'"—no longer seem as true to life experience. For me, remembering the summer of 1973, I'm quite satisfied with "*A mise meshunah soll im einnemen.*"

2

Athens Scrambled

As Leonard Barkan brilliantly suggests . . .

—PETER HOLLAND, ED., *THE OXFORD SHAKESPEARE*
"A MIDSUMMER NIGHT'S DREAM"

By a reasonably careful count, I have taught A *Midsummer Night's Dream* between fifty and sixty times in the course of my academic career—to kids fresh out of high school and to PhD students, to English majors and engineers (on one occasion enrollment reached 450; on other occasions I could barely scrape up the six souls necessary so that the class wouldn't be canceled), to adults striving for an associates' degree in the evening, to well-heeled and well-traveled senior alumni of an Ivy League university, to younger colleagues from institutions with heavy teaching loads spending their summer in an effort to recharge the intellectual energies that had brought them to an academic profession. I have staged scenes from the play in dozens of classes, sometimes using the students themselves, at other times bringing in ringers. The play has figured, in a major or minor way, in five of my books (not counting this one), and it functioned as the pièce de résistance in the most substantial article I've ever published, back in 1980. So much for the study and the classroom; then there's theater. In the early '70s, I saw Peter Brook's production of the play, in London, in New York, and in Los Angeles, a total of seven times, becoming just short of a groupie; the adjective widely used for this experience (in which I concur) has been "life-changing." A few years later—from the sublime to at least a few steps in the direction of the ridiculous—I acted the role of Bottom in a production of the play at a theater on Chicago's Northside.

This record of my engagement with the play no more tells the full story than a reading of my curriculum vitae would lay bare my soul. I can't recall my first encounter with the play: a circumstance I consider not merely a failure of memory but a sign that there is no retrievable moment so early in my life that the *Dream* (in my head, this work is simply *The Dream*, no need for qualifier) wasn't already foundational. I happened to encounter Bruno Bettelheim's *The Uses of Enchantment* at an early age, though not so early that I was one of the children whose consciousnesses he so brilliantly explores. In that extraordinary book, Bettelheim argues that fairy tales, with all their irreality, their darkness, and their violence, are not, as might be imagined, threats to a child's innocence; rather, they count as a kind of reassurance that the darknesses that have already been implanted in the child's psyche, from whatever source (and there are plenty), do not belong to him or her alone, uniquely.

I'm simplifying a very subtle argument; it probably remains frozen in the language that I first used to understand it most of a lifetime ago. What I know for certain is that, almost as far back as I can remember, A *Midsummer Night's Dream* was my enchantment. The previous chapter of this book will have already introduced the reader to some of the disenchantment that circled about me when I was quite young. The brunt of it, as I have made clear, happened to other people; still, those people lived very close to where I lived. I wasn't an unhappy child, I wasn't a child who suffered hunger or pain or grave indifference from those around him, but I had plenty of uses for enchantment.

It's also likely that I saw Max Reinhardt's amazing film of the *Dream*: So it was later reported to me, and when I saw it again as an adult, some of it looked familiar—rather as though it were itself a dream that I partially recollected. All I know for certain is that the magic of the play, and all the forces of darkness that the magic first makes worse and then makes better, somehow got installed as proof that darknesses could encounter light, that threatened tragedy could encounter true laughter, that rhyme and music and dance and silly impersonations existed at the readily accessed margins of the ever-threatening world, and that Shakespeare had invented a fable that told the truth—*my* truth—about everything.

For once, I'll start not with the opening of a play but with something well along in the action, a throwaway line of Hippolyta's from an easily forgotten moment in the fourth act:

I was with Hercules and Cadmus once. . . .

(4.1.111)

What does it take to be able to say this? What does it presuppose? Needless to say, neither Hercules nor Cadmus plays any role in the drama. Hippolyta herself is barely necessary at this point. The dramatic purpose of the scene is to mark the transition that will bring the young lovers back to Athens, properly paired off and given the seal of approval that they lacked three acts earlier. Hippolyta's flashy reminiscence is not only incidental to the action; it's not even an accurate piece of mythography, at least in regard to Cadmus, who has a vivid Ovidian pedigree but no connection with Hippolyta or the Amazons. (Not to mention the fact that in at least one version of the story, Hercules kills Hippolyta.) Shakespeare's Hippolyta is, in short, name-dropping; Shakespeare is name-dropping. And with all the problems of entitlement and nonentitlement that the concept of name-dropping implies, except that this text lays them out for us with no shame. The sign of true mastery as regards a tradition—in this case, the classical tradition—is the ability to treat it, in almost the literal sense, with abandon.

Take the question of this mastery and entitlement back to a past slightly less remote than the Athens of Theseus or the London of Shakespeare—say, my own professional education during the mid-1960s. I knew I wanted to study in an English department because . . . well, that was my native language, and I knew enough of a couple of other languages to understand how disadvantaged I would feel if I hung out my shingle in French or German. The trouble was, English departments were so *English*. Not just English, but Anglican. And not just Anglican, but High Anglican.

I can't deny that this aspect of my chosen path had its attractions, and I've written elsewhere about the encounter between Ivy League intellectual Episcopalianism and the formation of a secular Jew whose parents were born in places where life was structured between shtetl and pogrom. I lodge no complaints about being tracked through this alien territory: At the time, I was all too complacently willing to assimilate (even *pass*), and in the long retrospect that I now enjoy it's clear that I owe a great deal to both the frictions and the embraces of the twin streams in which I swam. It may seem ironic, if not perverse, to frame the discussion of a play that so explicitly advertises the Renaissance principle of *discordia concors*—"How," asks Theseus in act 5, "shall we find the concord of this discord?"—in the context of unresolvable opposites. And yet perhaps it is the very casualness with which the play (Bottom-like) weaves opposites together that exposes one's own life as a decidedly inferior piece of textile.

My own cautious step in graduate school was to place some distance between myself and the Anglo-Anglicans and to cultivate an individual who was (horrors!) merely a *visiting* professor. Rosalie Colie was a little bit French, a little bit Dutch, and 100 percent mesmeric. In one of our many conversations—for a period of time she asked me to be her driver; when I told her I didn't have a license, Manhattan-born boy that I am, she said that was no problem, she would do the driving but just needed someone to talk to—I must have signaled my general sense of disaffection, the more urgent since she was herself leaving that university, not perhaps exactly by her choice. Amid various other responses and reassurances, she said, "Have you ever heard of a book called *Pagan Mysteries in the Renaissance*? I hadn't, but I went straight to the library, grabbed it off the shelf, and scarcely exited my carrel until I was halfway through Edgar Wind's nigh-maniacal itinerary among the Three Graces, Orpheus, Botticelli's *Primavera*, and the rest.

I doubt that Miss Colie—forgive the old-fashioned way that we referred to her, at least until we dared to call her by her nickname, Posy—was handing me Edgar Wind as some sort of specific gloss on *A Midsummer Night's Dream*. Shakespeare's play would have been too conventional a school text for someone whose tastes ran to Spinoza's *Tractatus Theologico-Politicus* and Robert Burton's *Anatomy of Melancholy*. Nonetheless, whether Shakespeare was involved or not, Wind's book became the entry drug leading me in a number of much broader directions, the two most obvious being the discipline of art history and the multidisciplinary world that traces itself back to Aby Warburg and his many brilliant followers. The art history part of my experience I discuss elsewhere in these pages, but *A Midsummer Night's Dream* seems like a good place to talk about the Warburgians.

Wind's premise is that there existed in antiquity—especially late Greek or Alexandrian antiquity—a vibrant subculture of mystic deities surrounded by cults of initiation and that, via the most arcane strands of (mostly) Neoplatonism, these developed a new life in the Renaissance, always and intentionally covered in mysteries, lest they be profaned by the unworthy. Of course, the whole operation may hinge upon a sort of hermeneutical Catch-22: If the meanings that I derive out of these various cultural expressions seem far-fetched and the lines of influence among them unprovable, that only goes to demonstrate how successfully I have penetrated the esoteric qualities of the system and how secret the practitioners were in their communication with one another.

This is in some ways a frivolous objection, and I wasn't demanding scientific verifiability in my pursuit of the humanities (nor am I now, as these pages attest). In fact, I was hooked by Wind's opening sentence:

Any attempt to penetrate the pagan mysteries of the Renaissance should perhaps begin with the admission that the term "mysteries" has several meanings, and that these already tended to become blurred in antiquity, to the great enrichment and confusion of the subject.

He had me at "enrichment and confusion." Doubtless I am being unfair to all those Episcopalians—may their spirits in Anglican heaven forgive me—but I don't recall ever hearing from them that "enrichment and confusion" of meanings was a good thing, something to be proudly asserted on page one of their books.

Wind's page one isn't the whole story, of course. As I progressed to Warburg and Panofsky, Gombrich and Saxl, it wasn't just the prospect of hermeneutic free-for-all that inspired me. Their slice of the past was so full of unexpected beauty, the documents on which they performed their analyses were chosen with such freedom, and they were so liberated from the tyranny of calendars, maps, and provability. And, after all, if I chose to follow their itineraries, I'd be residing, figuratively or literally, in Venice and Florence rather than Warwickshire and East Anglia. If that seems intellectually scandalous, it gets worse. In particular with Wind as one's guide—less in the case of Panofsky and Gombrich, who cling to notions of science—the world of the pagan gods and the transhistorical aesthetic that they inspired take on some of the qualities that a system of faith, even a religion, must possess for those who embrace it. There was a divinity existing before time and it was called beauty; its followers across the ages are linked together by that belief; and our theology is called aesthetics, our worship is called desire, our history is called the History of All the Arts, and it is gloriously intertwined.

With that theology in mind, it's no wonder that I keep taking potshots at those Episcopalians. I was a Jew who had worked effectively and contentedly to become inculcated in the world of Dante and Milton. Good job, but there would always be a sense of distance. Now I was being initiated into a densely layered culture, both sacred and profane, with an enormous intellectual question-and-answer game behind it, but one that didn't hang upon the otherwise ubiquitous sphere of the Father, Son, and Holy Ghost. If I was going to invent cultural sources for myself, if I was going to experience Freud's family romance (I'll get back to that) and make up my own origins, Christianity was somehow too alien and too omnipresent at the same time, and the narrow piety of my devout ancestors made too many demands with too little return. So, as a secular Jew, I was going to become a congregation member of the once-and-forever classical antiquity. There is, in short, something more than chance in the demography of the Warburg discipleship.

There is a dissonance in all this, however, a discord in the midst of concord that is perhaps unavoidable. It's really very simple, but one might say that it bedeviled the whole discipline of iconography as that animated the study of Renaissance art and literature over several decades and occasionally does still. The late antique worldview whose documents form the substratum—literally, as in the footnotes—of a study like Edgar Wind's come from a world of (for want of a better word) mysticism. That's part of the reason they were so lovable, as I've already suggested. But the exercise of remapping them onto Renaissance art and literature begins to look more like mathematics and geometry than mysticism. When Wind identifies the exact genealogy and therefore the meaning of each figure in Botticelli's *Primavera*, suddenly the pagan mysteries aren't mysteries anymore; they turn into Renaissance allegories. And several generations of scholars, especially in art history, followed in this direction by making iconography into a discipline of puzzles solved. There is much to be said—for instance, pedagogically—for delivering works from the remote past into the present by (let's call it) *unpacking* them, but something of the life of the garments is lost if I can see them only when they are neatly folded on the bed.

This is where Shakespeare comes to the rescue. There are, to be sure, certain respects in which the *Dream* qualifies perfectly in this tradition. Notably, it brandishes a pedigree leading directly back to Apuleius's *Golden Ass*, which I consider something like the smoking gun for the presence of a mystic and secret life brought down to us in the mainstream literature of later antiquity. A lovable but in some ways dunderheaded man is transformed into a jackass and spends a year of animalistic travail, at the end of which he experiences an initiation that gives him the privilege of intimate membership in the mystic rites of the Egyptian goddess Isis. A lively, and quite free, translation into English was published in 1566 and popular enough to go through several editions.

The relation between Apuleius's romance and Shakespeare's play, in other words, reaches that sweet spot of source study, where the later text actually seems to advertise the relationship—at least to those in the know. And, of course, being "in the know" is fundamental to the circulation of pagan mysteries, even if in this case it required only some familiarity with a popular recent book. Yet despite this pagan mystery heritage Shakespeare introduces the classical material with gloriously perverse nonchalance. Hippolyta, as we've already seen, name-drops Hercules and Cadmus. The city of Pericles and the Acropolis also contains a cohort of clods, and that cohort takes merciless possession of a tragic Ovidian love myth. A pair of supernaturals concocted out of incompatible myth strands is having a domestic spat that turns into a dirty joke. A buffoon who, one hopes, is better at weaving than he is at acting (but isn't acting itself weaving?) has an experience of ecstasy in which he ventriloquizes Plato and St. Paul. An ancient Athens is fantasized in which it is traditional wedding night practice that groups of proletarian amateurs vie for the privilege of incompetently performing mythological dramas whose stated purpose is "abridging" the painful waiting period between dinner and sex.

Occupying a special category of classical name-dropping ad absurdum on the margins of ancient civilization is the deliciously preposterous menu of theatrical entertainments that are presented to Theseus and the court but rejected in favor of "Pyramus and Thisbe": "The battle with the Centaurs, to be sung | By an Athenian eunuch to the harp"; "The riot of the tipsy Bacchanals | Tearing the Thracian singer in their rage"; and "The thrice three Muses, mourning for the death | Of learning, late deceased in beggary" (5.1.44–53). It amounts to the theatricalization of a rhetorical device with many names— *occupatio, praeteritio, apophasis, paralepsis* (one wonders why it needs so many names)—that is, bringing up a subject so as to say that one is *not* bringing up that subject. Normally, it is a way of delivering a quick slur against someone or something without having to be held accountable for the accuracy of the claims; in this case, it seems like a joke on the sheer density of tedious and depressing materials that classical civilization might visit upon us if we're not lucky. Tonight, however, we're lucky.

A *Midsummer Night's Dream* is triumphant precisely because its Renaissance rediscovery of antiquity is so cock-eyed, so jagged, so approximate, more antic than antique. In fact, it is best described with a phrase from the work of another Warburgian, not always given his due. Fritz Saxl describes Titian's *Bacchanale of the Andrians* as a "Humanist Dreamland": That may be the final word on Shakespeare's comedy as an invocation of antiquity. Such improvisatory freedom in the face of authority, in this case that of ancient mysteries, remains the model for *my* Renaissance humanism. Not fidelity to some reimagined pagan theology—if you want fidelity, go study Dante and Milton—but a set of cultural resources that affords both rich material and the freedom to recollect it with all the condensation, displacement, and sheer folly (thank you, Erasmus; you, too, deserve credit) of a dream.

As Hippolyta's bit of heroic reminiscence suggests, classical myth is loaded with prestige even when it emerges as a non sequitur or when the details are garbled. Indeed, part of that prestige is the supposition that these figures possess the kind of orthodox authenticity—like, say, St. Paul or Julius Caesar—that makes garbling possible. But Shakespeare takes care to muddy these waters in the *Dream* by expanding and hybridizing his particular pantheon. Theseus and Hippolyta, however authentic their membership in classical mythology may be, are mortals. Oberon and Titania, on the other hand, are to be understood for the purposes of the play as divine; their heritages, however, are distinctly sub-Olympian. Oberon was the name given in many literary expressions, both

French and English, to the king of the fairies. He is thus cast quite logically in the role he plays here, but his realm of divinity is as a sort of miniature forest sprite (three feet tall, as is sometimes said), which is rather a comedown from the quasi-Jupiter Pluvius role that Shakespeare assigns to him. Titania's origins are also mixed. There is no such figure in the Celtic world that Oberon inhabits, nor is there anyone of that name in Greco-Roman mythology. The closest one comes is the fact that Ovid uses that name for any female divinity who is the daughter of a Titan. One such figure is Diana, and that folds in nicely with the play's various emphases on chastity (pro and con) and the embodiment of that virtue in the moon.

We have, then, on the one hand, a pair of ancient heroic mortals with unimpeachable classical bloodlines and, on the other hand, a pair of dress-up divinities, who are locally quite powerful, it seems, but whose ancient credentials don't bear too much scrutiny. All of which is to say that Shakespeare loves the idea of divinity and antiquity but at the same time wants to be free to scramble it. The operation of the two fairy-gods owes a great deal to the squabbles of Jupiter and Juno in the *Metamorphoses*, and Shakespeare bestows on them a framework of Ovidian-style divine discord, suggesting cross-liaisons with Theseus and Hippolyta fleshed out with accusations of adultery. Fittingly, during this marital spat Oberon's alleged inamorata is given a pastoral name ("amorous Phillida") whereas the catalogue of Titania's supposed liaisons is all classical (Aegles, Ariadne, Antiopa; she seems to be starting at the beginning of the alphabet). All of this, though, is mere décor in comparison to the real provocation of their warfare, and here Shakespeare has moved into territory entirely his own.

I should make it clear at once that there is almost nothing in A *Midsummer Night's Dream* that I find more magnetic, more inscrutable, more irresistible than the Changeling Child. I don't claim to be very original in this judgment, as witness a symposium on the subject that included the observations of no lesser personages than Stephen Greenblatt and Maurice Sendak—not to mention the latter's enchanting and frightening *Outside over There*, which clearly owes something to the tradition. That a figure who never appears in the play (or never speaks, at any rate; directors occasionally bring him on stage) and who is mentioned in only two scenes should be at the very center of the narrative is already intriguing.

But there is a lot more. To begin with, this changeling child fails to fit the definition of the term as it was widely diffused in the sixteenth century. And it was quite widely diffused, since one of the symptoms of the religious anxiety in England at the turn of the sixteenth century was an explosion of interest, generally of a prurient or sensationalist nature, in witches, goblins, and spirits, in short the non-Christian (or at least non-Protestant) supernatural. Within this menacing slice of alternative reality, there was a well-established use of the term "changeling child," referring to a demon creature whom the witches leave as a substitute when they steal an especially beautiful infant whom they covet for their own perverse world. The central conceit of this operation is that the demon stand-in is a perfect double of the child that has been sto-len away, with the result that the parents are unaware of the switch until such a time—bound to come sooner or later—when the ersatz child's demonic nature asserts itself.

This is in itself so irresistible a plot that it's a wonder Shakespeare *didn't* use it: Parents raising their seemingly angelic offspring who without warning or explanation turn into Rosemary's baby. Or—in a more narrowly domestic scene—another angelic child turns against its parents (as they are prone to do), who now have grounds for disowning their progeny because it has proven to be the spawn of witches rather than the adorable Sheila or Sheldon they thought they were rearing. Or even—stretching things a little further—it gets woven into the infidelity plot: Once again, *pater semper incertus est*; the child is not mine, says the father, but emerges somehow from the operations of demons.

The Changeling Child of the *Dream* is none of the above. Not that the imagery of this story, trailing all of its grave insecurities, isn't highly relevant to the concerns of the play. It's all too obvious to rehearse the Ovidian—that is, metamorphic—aspects of the play, or the memorable "Bottom, thou art *changed*," with which the newly transformed weaver is greeted once Puck has worked him over. Change, let us say, is in the air. The matter is given a specifically genetic turn right at the start of the play when Theseus lays down the law of patriarchy to Hermia:

> To you your father should be as a god;
> One that composed your beauties, yea, and one
> To whom you are but as a form in wax
> By him imprinted and within his power
> To leave the figure or disfigure it.

(1.1.47–51)

The subject is approached even more directly at the very end of the play, just before Puck's dreamy epilogue, when Titania and Oberon bring up something much less dreamy. As they bestow their blessings upon the future offspring of the newly married couples, their focus is on the prevention of deformity, then presumably even more than now a fundamental anxiety of those on the way to becoming parents. That melancholy circumstance, too, might be laid at the door of the fairies and their sinister infant-changing activities.

All of this hovers over the Changeling Child, but it is not the story that Shakespeare chooses to tell us about him. The *changeling* in traditional usage is always the defective substitute left among the mortals, not the lovely infant that they abducted; to call a child (or a grown-up, as in Middleton's play of this name) a "changeling" is never a compliment but instead an accusation of something demonic. So, even before we get to the specific heritages that are assigned to the child in this play, we are presented with a piece of revisionism: In the bosom of the mortal family, with which we're all familiar, a changeling— that is, a child gifted by fairies—is demonic; who is to say that in the bosom of the fairy family, to which the play gives us special access, the stolen child might not also raise demonic possibilities?

But we get ahead of ourselves. In fact, the first thing we learn about the child appears to conform quite closely to the traditional story. Puck is explaining the squabble of his master and mistress:

> Oberon is passing fell and wrath,
> Because that she as her attendant hath
> A lovely boy, stolen from an Indian king;
> She never had so sweet a changeling.

$$(2.1.20–23)$$

A "lovely," "sweet," and royal infant would make a perfect target for the familiar kidnapping narrative. But we soon move further from the traditional story, even contradicting it. Titania adores the child, we're told ("crowns him with flowers and makes him all her joy"—not the last time we'll hear about such activities from the Fairy Queen). A few minutes later, we hear about the child in Titania's own voice: "His mother was a votaress of my order," she explains, and she recounts how the votaress, when pregnant with the child, would "sail upon the land, | To fetch me trifles. . . . | But she, being mortal, of that boy did die" (2.1.133–35). At which point we're presented with an origin story that is almost impossible to correlate with Oberon's story, and along the way the whole changeling myth is wrenched a bit out of its frame. A fairy did not steal this child; rather, Titania maintained a loving friendship with the mother, who (like many mothers in 1600) died in childbirth. And that is the crucial common term between this changeling story and the traditional one: Humans, however lovely, suffer from mortality.

I don't think it's merely the gender sensitivity of the twenty-first century that leads me to feel—at least as of the opening of the second act, when we first hear all this—that Titania's claim on the child is the more powerful. Oberon "would have the child | Knight of his train, to trace the forests wild" (2.1.24–25). Big deal. Titania, on the other hand, is engaged in an act of mourning and, so far as possible, of recompense as regards the one thing she cannot bestow on her dear departed friend: immortality.

These clear waters will get very muddy very soon, however. Whatever the technicalities of the term *changeling* may be, the real question is: Why does Shakespeare design one of the central conflicts of his play—the only conflict that isn't in the predictable realm of boy-meets-girl, boy-and-girl-get-together-by-sometime-in-act-4-or-5—around the struggle over some sort of proprietorship (itself, as we'll see, vaguely unsettling), over a child who never appears onstage? Furthermore, if, as I believe, the Titania-Oberon-Puck triangle is some sort of replay of Juno-Jupiter-Cupid, then the erotic is being grafted somewhat uncomfortably onto the parental/familial. To the extent that we can make sense out of this tale, it will have to do with the details of the war that the two combatants wage. If we limit our question to the prize over which the war was being fought—the boy—then there is no question that Oberon wins. The question becomes how we got there and what other strands of the play are either raveled or unraveled along the way.

Oberon determines to steal the boy away from Titania. His tactic has a certain logic. When I was seven or so, I was playing with a cousin of mine who was about two years younger. Whatever toy I picked up, Tony would grab out of my hands. I appealed to our two mothers, who bestowed on me (in a whisper) exactly the right tactic: "Leonard, dear, why don't you pick up some toy that you don't really care about? Tony will take it away, and you can go off and play with the toy you really want to play with." (Tony is now emeritus from the faculty of the Scripps Institute of Oceanography; we are no longer interested in the same toys.) Was I being instructed in my first ever piece of devious behavior? Probably not the first; probably I didn't need instruction in deviousness. Anyway, it was effective.

The situation in the play is a little more complicated. Oberon has a two-pronged strategy (and there will be a third prong once it is executed by Puck, but we'll leave that out for the moment). The basic plan is, of course, that he will find a different toy for Titania, one that she will vastly prefer to the votaress's son. This will, of course, add yet another definition to "changeling," as both objects of Titania's attention will find themselves in a relationship of exchange. (More on Bottom later.) The other prong has to do with the means by which

Titania will be induced to *change* her object; it seems that she will require more than my cousin Tony did. Fortunately, Oberon has at his disposal a drug suited to the purpose:

> The juice of it on sleeping eye-lids laid
> Will make or man or woman madly dote
> Upon the next live creature that it sees.
>
> (2.1.170–72)

In such a magical world as that of the *Dream*, Shakespeare doesn't really need to render his special effects scientifically explicable, but in this case he chooses to do so, providing a background story that renders the force of the drug completely logical. Once upon a time, he tells Puck, Oberon witnessed something extraordinary; he saw

> Flying between the cold moon and the earth,
> Cupid all arm'd: a certain aim he took
> At a fair vestal throned by the west,
> And loosed his love-shaft smartly from his bow,
> As it should pierce a hundred thousand hearts;
> But I might see young Cupid's fiery shaft
> Quench'd in the chaste beams of the watery moon,
> And the imperial votaress passed on,
> In maiden meditation, fancy-free.
> Yet mark'd I where the bolt of Cupid fell:
> It fell upon a little western flower,
> Before milk-white, now purple with love's wound.
>
> (2.1.156–67)

Translation: Once upon a time, Cupid aimed his arrow at Queen Elizabeth. The erotic force of this missile's payload was so concentrated that it would have been sufficient dosage for one hundred thousand ordinary people to fall in love. Cupid knew what he was doing: That must have been the quantity required to awaken the Virgin Queen's all too dormant sex drive. Unfortunately, Cupid's aim was imperfect, as a result of which the arrow passed through the rays of the moon—notorious for their desire-chilling capacities. In this case, however, they didn't completely nullify Cupid's powers; when the arrow finally landed, it still had some of its powers left, let's say, sufficient for fifty thousand hearts. Still high concentration; hence the extraordinary powers of "love-in-idleness."

It's a remarkable conceit. The whole story of Queen Elizabeth's virginity, a source of her cultic status but by the time Shakespeare wrote this play equally a disturbing reminder of her childlessness, is grafted onto the fantastical instance of fairy love in a wood near Athens. In place of an heir to the throne, we have the love-crazed world of A *Midsummer Night's Dream*—which will, of course, end with fertility, though not the kind that assures England's future.

But we are clearly in a literary conception that is much wilder and more unstable than political allegory. The play binds the boy in a circle of eros. Titania has possession of the boy; Oberon wants the boy. Both sets of stated motives are insufficient, and in a play where everything seems bathed in the passion of love-in-idleness, it becomes easy to see through them. The moment of truth—and I think the exquisitely decorative qualities of the play tend to obscure just how radical it is—comes when Oberon decides to win the game by substituting a sexual object for a maternal object. Not, in other words, just giving Titania an alternative toy but by bestowing upon her a gift that she will wish to bind to herself via a radically different realm of human impulses. Oberon wins, in short, by introducing into the equation violent excesses of sexual desire. The idea that either of the two of them desires the boy sexually is, in a sense, forbidden and unspeakable, whether we call it homosexuality or pederasty or both. But that is the way of dreams, which both expose and disguise forbidden desires. This is the most disturbing change at the heart of the changeling story.

It should be no surprise when we come to the phase of the play where reality is superseding dream, that the resolution of the forbidden love triangle is anticlimactic. Indeed, it is shunted offstage and relegated to a brief bit of narration by Oberon. Titania has shifted her affections in a direction one small step less perverse than an underage boy, and she gives up the Changeling Child without a fight, shipping him back to Oberon's fairy bower.

It's difficult, at least for me, to be altogether satisfied by this resolution. It is, after all, the special technique of this play to expose some very real terrors—for instance, the love-of-all-against-all that tortures the four young people in the middle of the play—and then to offer (dare I say?) somewhat facile reassurances, notably that it was all a dream. Anyone who finds that reassuring has never had a bad dream or had a dream professionally analyzed. The Changeling Child, on the other hand, counts for me as undigested matter. Partly it's because he never appears or gets to speak for himself, rendering his symbolisms so labile, and partly because he gets so summarily disposed of. But partly I have my own reasons.

My immediate family, as has already been recounted in this volume, harbored some quite disturbing secrets, and a considerable proportion of family life was devoted to building multiple rounds of protective gear against their exposure, even within subgroups of persons well acquainted with their contents. Yet there was one piece of intimate information—concerning me, sort of—that was merrily narrated with ever more decorative embellishment in any and every social situation and at the slightest provocation. To wit: I was born at the beginning of October; my mother learned that she was pregnant at the end of July. Do the math: She went through more than six months of pregnancy in a state of oblivion.

God, or in this case comedy, is in the details. My mother was in her forties and had never had a child. Her menstrual periods had always been irregular—even this was part of the customary narration, like I needed to hear about that in my early teens while grown-ups laughed themselves silly—and it was not unreasonable to suppose that she might be entering upon menopause. She did notice that she had been sick to her stomach with some regularity, but she ascribed this to the fact that at the beginning of this phase she had on a memorable occasion greedily eaten an entire can of tomato herring, *right out of the can!* (I'm quoting here.) And, yes, she was having the disturbing experience of weight gain, but this had been reversed by regular attendance at a "reducing studio," where she spent hours being pummeled by something called the Slendo Massager (or it might have been Kellogg's Fat Roller): A number of 1940s newsreel-style videos accessible on the internet illustrate what violence was being done to her—or, should I say, us.

Obviously, this was all played for laughs, and I would be lying if I said I didn't enjoy the attention. After all, it was difficult to turn this story into one of those festering wounds that can be such valuable currency in family life; better to be the center of laughter than to be ignored. But there was a lot more at stake for me in this narrative beside the jokes, in ways that I couldn't have quite formulated then and not so easily now. Perhaps the most general way to describe it is to say that the story about my mother's—what shall I call it?—heedless pregnancy produced a wholesale bringing to light of everything about "where-do-babies-come-from?" and, more pressing, "where-do-*I*-come-from?" that is probably, for the sake of a young child, best left in the dark as long as possible. Sexual intercourse, planned and unplanned children, the roles of parental DNA: I'm intentionally using terms that were completely unavailable to me. In place of answers to these questions, never mind a scientific formulation of them, I experienced a cloud of unknowing. I already had an unresponsive father with his own complicated past; now—I'm trying to formulate this at a vast distance of time, and I have no hope of rendering it accurately in the terms of a child—I had a mother who was somehow separate from me just when our relation ought to have been most absolute. Was she perhaps not exactly my mother? Was I a changeling child?

But that leaps too far too soon into the world of *A Midsummer Night's Dream.* A proper transition requires another authority of, I would say, comparable talent to Shakespeare's in mapping the human condition, though in this case I am drawing on one of his very briefest works, almost a pamphlet. The authority is Freud, and the work is "Family Romances," as it is titled in the English Standard Edition, though its original title would be something like "The Family Romance of Neurotics." (It would be interesting to know why James Strachey et al. made this change, which seems to have the effect of rendering the phenomenon both more universal and less . . . well, neurotic.)

The family romance is the habit common to children of inventing fantasy parents who are preferable to their real parents. That formulation is a good deal more straightforward than Freud's, thus leaving a lot out. For one thing, Freud introduces the subject with a strikingly paradoxical claim about this phenomenon, which he doesn't quite seem to recognize as a paradox. "The liberation of an individual . . . from the authority of his parents is one of the most necessary though one of the most painful results brought about by the course of his development": I hear in this one of the most lovable (for me) of Freud's voices, the voice that recognizes sympathetically the inevitable pain that accompanies the stages of human development, stages that he recognizes as nevertheless inexorable. Freud cites this instance of that phenomenon by introducing a class of persons for whom this act of individuation is simply *too* painful. They fail to separate themselves from the previous generation and thus enter the circle of the neurotics.

The paradox is that Freud is on his way to declaring that the invention of fictional parents is not—as you or I might imagine—a sign of distancing or dissatisfaction with the real parents but, quite the contrary, an *overattachment* to them. Hence the "neurotics" of the title. He takes the argument through the territories of class consciousness, sexuality, the Oedipus complex, sibling rivalry, and so on. He arrives finally at the claim that the substitution of fantasy parents, whom he characterizes particularly as of superior social standing, is *not* a rejection of the real father and mother but an attempt to build them up so that they regain the glorious aura that they enjoyed back in the early days of the child's life. The argument eventually, and uncharacteristically, turns into a set of reassurances to the parents of such children: "If any one is inclined to turn away in horror from this depravity of the childish heart . . . he should observe that these works of fiction, which seem so full of hostility, are none of them really so badly intended, and that they still preserve, under a slight disguise, the child's original affection for his parents." The reassurance, of course, comes along with Freud's diagnosis of such children as neurotics, so it's a kind of good-news-bad-news situation.

The truth is, I'm not interested in reassurances or neurosis, and I'm in-different to the role of sexuality in the process. What interests me is the fact that I consider myself a champion perpetrator of the family romance. I have made up stories about my origins and rewritten my parents for as long as I can remember; indeed, a wary reader might even suspect that I am engag-ing in some such neurotically tinged enterprise in these pages, though I hereby deny it. I take special pride in Freud's designating of these falsehoods as "works of fiction." Actually, he uses an even loftier term in German— *Dichtungen*—a not easily translatable designation for imaginative literature of all kinds. So be it. Perhaps the family romance is the originating impulse of all fictions.

As a child, I had an Aunt Dorothy who visited me whenever I was being punished and who confirmed the injustice of my punishment. I had no Aunt Dorothy, of course, but I could have told you what her apartment looked like (it was beyond a Manhattan child's imagination to locate such a person in an enchanted forest) and what goodies she laid out on her immaculately napped kitchen table to coax me into a better mood.

But that was kid stuff. I've written in two other books about my long sequences of pretending not to be a Jew, *q.v.*, so I won't rehearse it here (except to say that Aunt Dorothy herself has a definite aura of the *goyish* about her). But I can offer something a little more—what?—whimsical. I'm in my mid-teens, looking at a particularly attractive Saks Fifth Avenue window display; I have no recollection of what it contained. A lady of a certain age also stops to notice it, and she makes some bit of stranger-to-stranger small talk as we gaze side by side at the display. I respond in a British accent, and out rolls a narrative, completely impromptu, according to which I am the child of a British diplomat posted in New York, my father went to Harrow and Cambridge, we were previously posted in Marseille (I couldn't make it Paris?), so I speak perfect French. "Your mother must have beautiful gowns," said the lady (we were, after all, in front of Saks), so I obliged by describing three or four of them and the occasions when she left our flat (!) wearing them. Just a few years later, I remember telling a college classmate—and this would be much riskier than fabrications offered to an utter stranger I'd never see again—that my father was about to retire (that part was probably true) and my parents were moving to Vienna. Why Vienna? I have no idea.

"Romance at short notice": This is what the great short story writer Saki calls it in his classic tale "The Open Window," which turns on the fiction-making propensities of a very young girl; she manages to drive a recovering mental patient back into insanity with a deviously clever fabrication. I hope I have never used my practice in the service of evil. The most I've done, and as an adult, is to weave the theory of the family romance into a theory of history, though that is rather too lofty a term. My scholarly work has long been focused on the way in which the Renaissance began to emerge out of the Late Middle Ages. I've characterized Petrarch and others of his transitional moment as individuals whose "real" parent was medieval Christianity but who invented for themselves a much loftier set of (fictitious) progenitors: classical antiquity. The Renaissance thus becomes nothing more or less than a family romance. It's the sort of thing one may say offhandedly in a graduate seminar; I hesitate to publish it, except here.

The Changeling Child of A *Midsummer Night's Dream* is vitally important but utterly absent from the actual cast of characters. A considerable part of the action orbits around him—indeed, depends absolutely on his desirability. After all, the plot of the play is so designed that no less a pair of personages than the King and Queen of Faerie are engaged in a battle royal (literally) to acquire him, to elevate him to majesty from his humdrum status as the orphaned child of a single mother, now deceased, who was in service. Of course, he doesn't appear on stage; he is in point of fact the dreamer who has dreamed the midsummer night's dream. The play we have before us *is* the Changeling Child's family romance. Everything orbits around him.

Needless to say, the Changeling Child is not the only dreamer in the play. Hermia has a terrible dream, which is in a symbolic sort of way prophetic; the four lovers are (in my view, unpersuasively) told that their whole experience in the woods was a dream; and at the end Puck tries to make the entire audience believe that they have dreamed what they watched. But there is only one character who makes a persuasive case that what we saw with our own eyes on stage was the enactment of a dream, and he has plans to take that dream on the road.

How is it that I ended up on the stage of the Chicago Theater Building in the spring of 1979 wearing an ass's head? If your answer is that the director of the production felt he needed some Shakespearean scholarly talent as a ringer among the young hopefuls of that cast, you've guessed wrong. James O'Reilly—may his memory be a blessing—was (as he is quoted in an admiring obituary published in the *Tribune*) "the personification of the grizzled old Chicago theater veteran." As Irish as his name suggests, father of fourteen children (with one wife!), hard drinking, hard smoking (dead, alas, at sixty-three), there was nothing about Jim that would admit to any form of awe in the presence of someone with a PhD from Yale and a tenured position in the Northwestern English department. Nor did I want any of his awe. It was an honor to follow his instructions and bliss when I received a compliment.

But that still doesn't explain how I got there. There is a longer-range answer and a shorter-range answer; we'll take them in that order. I was stagestruck from an early age, but even in the very small ponds of grade school and junior high I never became a big fish, indeed often didn't get to swim at all. I have a decisive memory—parental trauma would be too strong a term, but I can't think of a better one—of having told my mother that I was cast in the leading role in a fifth-grade play. It wasn't true, and in order to protect this lie I had to add another lie, that parents weren't allowed to come see the production. The story may veer off into the surreal when I add that the role in question was Aida. (All boys' school; don't ask.) When my mother next saw my teacher, she expressed sorrow that she'd not been allowed to come see her "little Aida." Perplexed, Miss Pringle replied, "Leonard didn't play Aida. He was . . . [I'm guessing here] . . . third slave in the tomb." To her great credit, my mother understood that I needed support more than I needed chastisement.

There remained always this thread of—what shall I call it?—settled mediocrity in my theater efforts, and I can't even say that there was a steadily continuing improvement. But occasionally I would get the right character part, for instance in high school, when I performed a showy nonleading role in Maxwell Anderson's *High Tor* (very creaky even in 1960), and about two minutes after I came onstage, I heard a loud whisper from the audience in a surprised tone: "He's *good!*" (And it wasn't my mother.) Or I would write a play good enough so that people wanted to stage it. Or—and this proved to be the real paydirt, such as there ever was—I discovered that I had some ability as a stage director. I talked my way into getting directing jobs when I was in graduate school, did a couple of quite successful productions, along with a couple of stinkers, rubbed shoulders with some very famous names at the Yale Drama School. Make no mistake, though: I was on the margins.

It's at this point that the short-run story kicks in, and it's mostly not about theater. When I say that I talked my way into directing jobs while in graduate school, I am confessing to academic heresy. To anyone who has been in a PhD program that had nothing to do with theater (and academic literary study in those days had *nothing* to do with theater), the idea of putting in the kind of time and energy that directing a play requires—for the record, I did ten major shows in the same years when I was getting my doctorate—would be inconceivable, not to say suicidal.

Why did I do it? It's easy to explain the beginning of it. Doing five nights a week from six to midnight in a rehearsal hall is certainly no help to earning one's doctorate. On the other hand, earning a doctorate can be really punishing: too old to be lectured at, too young to lecture; job prospects uncertain; emotional satisfactions few and far between; and that's not even counting the draft and the Vietnam War. I'm sure that show business added a year or two to my time in graduate school, but I had a fellowship, I made more friendships— more passionate friendships, anyway—in the rehearsal hall than in the seminar room, and at the end of it I actually got a directing job. (Which, however, brought me back to my typical scorecard with a couple of striking successes and—just as an example—a show with a cast of thirty-five, a theater seating 650, and exactly eleven occupied seats at the final performance, not counting my own.)

So I didn't stick it out in theater. I got academic job offers and found myself ensconced on the professorial ladder. Or not. I have already spoken about my disaffection in graduate school and the rescue via Rosalie Colie and Edgar Wind. Four or five years later, I was discovering the grown-up joys of teaching students about literature, and I was launching myself in the direction of scholarship and publication, which, for good or ill, was and remains the road to elite status in the academy. And yet I was about to become a theatrical recidivist.

History and geography have something to do with it. We're still in the time of the Vietnam War and other sorts of social upheaval. I'm in a very conservative Southern California city but among colleagues who are very radical; weeks before I got there, a student had immolated himself in protest on the central plaza of the campus. I then move to a more appealing place, with a university more to my liking and a city much more to my liking. But throughout this time, no matter where I am, there is an intellectual revolution in the study of literature, and the humanities in general, for which I am fundamentally unprepared. My colleagues in the first university tend to be on the extreme front of the battle lines in this revolution; my colleagues in the second university tend to be moving in the direction of what I'll call neurotic overcompensation, clinging to extremely conservative positions or else acting out exaggerated forms of the avant-garde. I am suited to none of it. A book project that I have been nourishing for five, six, eight, ten, twelve years begins to look fatally out of date and in any event unfinishable.

For nearly a decade, first in San Diego and then in Chicago, I despair. And despair sends me back to the theater. Both cities offered real opportunities. In California I played a leading role at the Old Globe Theater and became the mainstay performer/director at a suburban music theater. (Overheard by a colleague of mine in the audience when I made my grand stage entrance as the Lord High Executioner in the *Mikado*: "That's my Shakespeare professor. He worked his way through Yale singing and dancing in bars." Inaccurate on every count, but delightful to fantasize.) In Chicago, I directed workshops; I spent a couple of hours with John Malkovich, who was seeing whether I might fit in to Steppenwolf. And then I auditioned for Jim O'Reilly and got to play Bottom. It's not exactly a happy ending. I was living a kind of lie as a professor: There must have been three or four years during which I scarcely touched my book manuscript. I had no callbacks after the *Midsummer Night's Dream* production (none from John Malkovich, none from James O'Reilly). And, whether it was sour grapes I'm not certain, but I grew weary of the theater world, at least that to which I had access. Everyone seemed either too young or too jaded or (most often) both. Then in some off moment during one of the summers I managed to give that long-suffering book some appealing shape, a friend suggested a snappy title for it, I found a good publisher, it was awarded one of the most prestigious prizes in the academy, and the intellectual life of the scholarly humanities began to look more welcoming. Except for occasional experiments in the classroom, theater simply evaporated in the mix of my life. But I could always look back on having starred as Bottom in a Chicago *Midsummer Night's Dream*.

I want to pose the same sort of question about Bottom and the players as I did about Hippolyta's reference to Hercules and Cadmus. What does it presuppose about your contract with the audience that you devote, say, 25 percent of your stage time to the rehearsal and production of a patently dreadful piece of theater, whereas the other 75 percent is presumably the best theater you can manage to produce? The answer is a little bit like the answer on the subject of Hippolyta but a lot more democratic. Hippolyta's outing with Hercules and Cadmus, so casually dropped in the midst of other matters, speaks to a long-established imagined community—indeed, a very prestigious one: classical anitquity—the membership in which the Amazon queen can take for granted. We, however, cannot; at best, we look at it enviously from the sidelines. There is, however, another community, not quite so long established but also imagined, in which we *do* take part. In fact, we're taking part in it at this very moment. We're watching a play. And although it may not require quite as much learned study as it would if we were plunked down in the middle of Ovid's *Metamorphoses*, it requires something at least as sophisticated.

What it requires is not just that we know the difference between reality and re-presented reality but that we can maintain multiple levels of engagement and belief. A famous classical love tragedy is being played out before us but with abundant cues such that we know it's not real. At the same time, we understand the individuals performing it as real because of a different set of cues. Shakespeare's audience is being both educated in reading levels of reality and flattered by the assumption that they already know how to do this reading. We are enabled to juggle, or perhaps bracket, the powerful emotions of a classical love tragedy, the class-based comic ineptitudes of those performing the story, and the very real discomfiture, sometimes suffering, of those same performers, which is clearly distinguishable from the fictional suffering of the classical lovers but also from the sensation of superiority that characterizes the audience's awareness of incompetent performance—whether we mean the real or the fictional audience.

Shakespeare doesn't leave any of these complicated operations to chance, which is to say that he doesn't take it for granted that his real audience will be completely up to speed in these discriminations. And that's where Bottom comes in. He is there, like Blake's idiot questioner or like the youngest child at the seder, to lead us all to wisdom. During the first sixty seconds of our acquaintance with him, he reveals himself to be overbearing and underinformed, a deadly combination. He usurps, or attempts to usurp, Peter Quince's managerial role (there's no sign that Quince needs help), but he doesn't even know who Pyramus is ("What is Pyramus? A lover, or a tyrant"). In fact, Bottom might not be the only person in the theater who doesn't know who Pyramus is, so his confusion will help with the clarification, if need be, of *ours*. Which puts some of us, at least, in Bottom's camp.

Not me, however. I've omitted to mention that the book I was allowing to languish until it would become a festering sore and that was itself driving me into the rehearsal hall was in fact all about the place of Ovid's *Metamorphoses* in the artistic culture of the Renaissance. It isn't just that I knew who Pyramus and Thisbe are, it's that every gesture in Shakespeare's play was something I had labored over and, in effect, laid aside in frustration. I had nothing in common with Bottom's ignorance as to the identity of Pyramus. On the other hand, I was able to embrace a more exciting aspect of the character: It doesn't matter whether Pyramus is a lover or a tyrant because Bottom is prepared to play them both. As a lover, he can make the audience cry; as a tyrant (which he prefers), he can noisily "make all split." Why stop there? He can perform every role in their drama. He has the high voice for Thisbe and the roaring voice for the Lion. From the point of view of literary analysis, I would say (and did say in *The Gods Made Flesh*) that Bottom's preposterous boast raises all the most thrilling and disturbing questions about the roles we play. What is personhood? What is actorly personhood? How can an actor be one person at one moment and another at another moment? Is there any form of identity that *isn't* acting? For me (things I didn't say in *The Gods Made Flesh*), the performance of this colossal self-congratulatory ignorance, covering exactly the same ground where I was erudite, counted as a step toward liberation. It's also a way to get a lot of laughs, and there is plenty of liberation in that.

Bottom, alongside his double Shakespeare, gets more technical once the play is actually in rehearsal. Peter Quince seems to have all but ceded control of the whole project to his lead actor (been there, suffered that). Bottom, it turns out, has a punch list of problems that he insists on bringing up before any rehearsal begins; in fact, his first agenda item lets loose a cascade of issues that becomes a bit of a free-for-all. Bottom's problem is that Pyramus "must draw a sword to kill himself, which the ladies cannot abide." Once that is addressed, Snout raises the related problem of the lion, also too terrible for an audience to contemplate. Finally Quince gets into the act with a somewhat different kind of worry, quite appropriate to a director, who oversees all the play's necessities: The story requires both moonlight and a wall, both of which may need to be provided for.

It's easy enough to see the drift of these worries on the part of the acting troupe. Even quite small children, we are told by many modern cognitive psychologists, develop a sense that there is a category called "stories" that has its own special brand of reality, true and untrue at the same time. Every one of this troupe's concerns speaks to some radical ignorance on this subject. An audience would not tolerate witnessing an actual suicide or being in the presence of an uncaged lion; therefore they must be protected from such terrors in the theater. A fiction that depends on meeting by moonlight and being separated by a wall would not be credible unless authentic versions of those plot necessities were securely in place.

Part of the joke, of course, is that we can already guess, even without hearing a single speech of Quince's play, that its capture of verisimilitude is likely to be so catastrophically unsuccessful that these problems of belief are the last thing the troupe should be worrying about, perhaps the only thing they *needn't* worry about. But the joke on that joke is that *every* form of mimetic undertaking, including the most perfect—yea, even unto this play called *A Midsummer Night's Dream* (indeed, *especially* this play)—demands that its audience make enormous leaps of credulity and, generally, succeeds in that demand.

Then we get to the solutions. The Moon and the Wall enact a kind of theatrical in-joke. The logic of the plot requires that there be something that approximates a nighttime effect and something that constitutes a partition between the lovers' houses. The search for a solution to these problems in both cases begins with the real: opening the actual window of the great hall, bringing in a suitably shaped piece of wood. Neither of these expedients is opted for, however. The eventual solution to the two problems is identical: An actor must play the role of what is essentially an inanimate object. Peter Quince and his troupe in effect choose the unreal over the real, and the fact that the unreal in both cases takes the form of appropriately costumed persons who will discourse to us about their identity suggests that the players have less faith in the real than in their own scripted creations. Big mistake.

There are larger difficulties to be overcome than the absence of the right set piece. The unbearable pain for audience members of coming to terms with the death of Pyramus will be assuaged, according to Bottom, by the expedient of his identifying himself, his profession, and the fact that he isn't dead. It would seem that he had this answer already prepared when he raised the objection at the opening of the scene; perhaps the objection was no more than a ploy to perform this little act of self-advertising. Pyramus is dead, and Bottom lives: After all, who really counts in this entertainment you've been watching?

Bottom's other solution is more complicated. For his own role, he wishes to assert the actor's supremacy; freed from his ego-investment, however, he recognizes for Snug-as-Lion that there is some sort of reciprocity between actor and role:

> Nay, you must name his name, and half his face must be seen through the lion's neck: and he himself must speak through, saying thus, or to the same defect . . . not to fear, not to tremble: my life for yours. If you think I come hither as a lion, it were pity of my life: no I am no such thing; I am a man as other men are.
>
> (3.1.33–40)

Apart from his dream soliloquy, this last statement is as eloquent as Bottom gets (and that's pretty eloquent). This is the human cry of all those figures across the world of Greco-Roman culture who have been metamorphosed by the will of the gods. Notably, it follows in the heritage of Ovid's Actaeon, who has been punished for (accidentally) beholding Diana in her nakedness and who has earned the punishment of transformation into a stag whom his own dogs will hunt to the death. Though Bottom offers it as a speech for Snug, it is clearly beyond the capacities of an "actor" who worries about memorizing lines that consist of nothing but roaring. If it's beyond the capacities of Snug, it's also beyond those of Peter Quince; only Bottom could enunciate this credo. And, of course, only Bottom will find himself in the metamorphosed position where such an assertion—"I am a man as other men are"—is appropriate.

There was an education for me lurking in these rehearsal scenes, and the fact that it was an education in the medium of Shakespeare and Ovid is one of those accidents in life that may lead one to suspect there are no accidents in life. When we first meet the players, all that is at stake is mimesis, the representation of reality, understood in quite straightforward terms: How can each of these lowly laborers persuasively imitate someone else? How can a weaver or a tinker, an Elizabethan fictional character or a twentieth-century scholar be stretched far enough to inhabit the world of Ovid's *Metamorphoses*? The mechanicals enact the problem of stretch: Most of them cannot extend themselves into their assigned roles; Bottom, though no more successful (for the moment, anyway), lays claim to unlimited reach, which is at least as much of a problem. When we next encounter the group, persons and roles have been paired up, for better or worse, but the act of mimesis itself is proving to be something more complicated than a simple equation.

What I was learning, though I didn't really know it at the time—apologies for exposing myself as professor of comparative literature—is the stretch from Erich Auerbach's epochal work *Mimesis*, published in 1946, to the kind of intellectual project, as influential as Auerbach's, that would soon be embodied in the scholarly journal *Representations*, which first appeared in 1983. When Auerbach subtitles his monumental work "The Representation of Reality in Western Literature," he is composing a paean of praise to the capacity of literature to render real experience in all its fullness and authenticity on the page; he is also demonstrating, via his polymathic scholarship, that these mimetic undertakings vary in both substance and style as one moves among different times and different European cultures. Mimesis thus proves to be as supple an activity as individual instances of reality require.

Decades later, the world has grown more skeptical, and literary analysis has taken on the multiple hues of linguistics, philosophy, political theory, and the efforts to uncover and undo past oppression. The consequence, or one of the consequences, is that mimesis needs to be seen not just as varying from one country to another or one century to another but rather as a set of propositions about equivalence that need to be called into question at the same time as they are being entertained. (At the same time as *we* are being entertained.) When singular *Mimesis* becomes plural *Representations*, what we're being told is to keep an eye on the process of equation itself. Shakespeare has the knack of turning all questions into questions about performance; in this case, the problem of mimesis is the problem of the actor. The consummate actor, of course, is Bottom. More specifically, he is the consummate *bad* actor. The bad actor is the hero of the drama of representation, inspiring all those complex and sometimes creaky acrobatics of audience response that, as I suggested earlier, occupy 25 percent of the *Dream*.

Pyramus is not the only role that Bottom is called upon to play, and keeping in mind this designation as "bad actor," it's worth following him a little further into the story. Which takes me back to Chicago. Our production may stand as monumental in my autobiography, but the truth is that we would have to designate it, generously, as "semiprofessional." The cast consisted of eager, and in some cases gifted, young adults with some college or community theater experience; for many, this was the first time they were being paid to perform on stage ($50 per week, as I recall). There was an exception, and she played Puck; when I say she pretty much stole the show, I don't have a smile on my face. Forgetting the *All about Eve* dimensions of the experience, though, she taught me practically everything I know about Puck; what follows is the fruit of that learning experience.

If we look upon Puck as largely an instrument of his (I use the masculine pronoun with apologies to my fellow-performer of 1979) master Oberon, we're missing some quite crucial moves in the action. I've already discussed the backstory of the love juice and made the claim that Oberon uses it so as to transform a maternal subject into one that is violently sexual. All true, but what we must also notice are the ways in which Oberon's purposes go awry when Puck carries them out. The first occasion, producing much of the play's hilarity, is the mistaken choice of Lysander rather than Demetrius for the inoculation. This errand is itself supplementary to Oberon's real purpose of tormenting Titania; he has seen Demetrius rejecting Helena's love, and, since he already has some of the magic herb on hand, he thinks he can right that wrong chemically. In pursuit of this goal, Puck makes what is in part a perfectly innocent mistake, as he will later protest to his master. Puck is to recognize his victim by the "weeds of Athens" that he is wearing; Lysander is indeed so attired (as was, of course, Demetrius).

Appropriate costuming is, however, not the only piece of evidence Puck uses in selecting his victim. Lysander and Hermia, it will be recalled, have escaped from the city but now find themselves (following a great tradition) lost in the woods. It's nightfall, and the sensible thing is to go to sleep until the sun comes up and helps them find their way. Under these propitious circumstances Lysander is eagerly prepared to—gasp!—sleep close to Hermia, but he is very properly rebuffed and told to "lie further off"; "such separation," she adds, "becomes a virtuous bachelor and a maid." Enter Puck, whose worldview, it seems, does not comprehend virtuous bachelors and maids in that way, or perhaps at all. When he sees the distance between them, he has no doubt that this must be the young man Oberon told him about, the one who was rejecting the girl's love pleas. Such behavior deserves swift punishment, and Puck has the perfect instrument for fulfilling Oberon's orders and rendering the circle of love unbroken. Hilarity ensues, all as a result of Puck's (significant) misreading.

This is all merely the prelude to the play's principal inoculation; once again, there is a swerve, but it is of a more complicated nature. Oberon's instructions to Puck regarding the creature he envisages as future object of Titania's instant desire—"lion, bear, or wolf, or bull, | . . . meddling monkey, or . . . busy ape" (2.1.180–81)—would appear to allow for a certain amount of flexibility, but for the most part they speak to what are conventionally understood as the terrors of the woods, that is, the very wild beasts that have rendered the escape from the city so ominous. (And which, of course, are notably absent from Shakespeare's woods, peopled as they are with different terrors.) What Oberon does *not* say to Puck is to make up a monster of his own.

This is as important a shift as that which set the whole process in motion, transforming a maternal subject into an erotic one. What, after all, was supposed to happen between Titania and "lion, bear, or wolf, or bull" under the influence of the love juice? Not a pretty picture. One thing we can say, then, about Puck's swerve in fulfilling his instructions is that they saved Titania's life. We're not really encouraged to think that way, admittedly; it's the actual nature of Puck's deviation, his original contribution to the plot, as it were, that commands our attention. It all takes place at the rehearsal of Pyramus and Thisbe, and what led me to this line of thinking was my colleague's extraordinarily powerful reading of Puck's aside when coming upon the players:

> What hempen home-spuns have we swaggering here,
> So near the cradle of the fairy queen?

> (3.1.72–73)

Our Puck was enraged: How *dare* these clumsy incompetents pollute the space of the Queen of the Fairies, even if it's currently my job to embarrass her? Whereupon Puck finds a love object more exquisitely embarrassing than "lion, bear, or wolf," etc. He finds a bad actor. And in case that doesn't produce quite enough embarrassment, he reaches into his bag of metamorphic tricks and selects a beast that was often understood as some sort of parodic or surrogate human. (Apuleius, once again, is never far from the picture, but so are various practices of more modern witchcraft.) Later he will boast to Oberon that "my mistress with a monster is in love" (3.2.6), but he will also continue to focus on acting, especially bad acting (he refers to Bottom as "my mimic"), as the crime for which he has designed the appropriate punishment.

The actual encounter of Titania and Bottom—we see them upon their first meeting when Bottom is newly metamorphosed and then a couple of scenes later when they're exchanging pillow talk—will never for me recover from Peter Brook, and I mean this in the most positive way. When Brook brought down the curtain on the first half of his production with a sudden and deafening rendition of Mendelssohn's "Wedding March" as the fairies carried Titania and Bottom aloft, with one of the fairies shooting a stiff arm upward in phallic formation between Bottom's legs, Brook accomplished in my view the (nearly) impossible: He improved on Shakespeare. Brook recognizes that this episode is, among other things, a dirty joke. It is also, with full recognition of everything that Edgar Wind had in mind, a pagan mystery in the Renaissance, an enactment of some sort of initiation wherein a mortal—the lowest of mortals, as his name suggests—comes face to face with divinity, as is clear when Titania responds to Bottom's little ditty about the finch, the sparrow, and the lark:

> I pray thee, gentle mortal, sing again:
> Mine ear is much enamour'd of thy note;
> So is mine eye enthralled to thy shape;
> And thy fair virtue's force perforce doth move me
> On the first view to say, to swear, I love thee.
>
> (3.1.130–34)

In effect, she is pronouncing the blessings of the Platonic ladder upon him, climbing from the physical senses up to heavenly virtue. Yet Bottom never ceases to be the mortal that he is, remaining true to his own credo in the advice he imparts to Snug-the-Lion, to say while under the influence of performance/metamorphosis: "I am a man as other men are." If versatility is an important skill in performance, perhaps Bottom isn't such a bad actor after all.

All that having been said, it may still be the case that the meeting of Bottom and Titania is one of those life experiences that is even better in the recollecting than in the experiencing. I can't pretend—I've made this clear along the way—that I have spent my whole life as an actor, but I would wager that even if I had, there would be nothing to equal the privilege of being asleep on stage for ten or fifteen minutes while all the most important plot elements of the play are resolved, then, once the stage is completely cleared, being given the opportunity of slowly arising, yawning, stretching, staring out into the audience and saying:

> When my cue comes, call me, and I will answer: my next is, "Most fair
> Pyramus." Heigh-ho! Peter Quince! Flute, the bellows-mender! Snout,
> the tinker! Starveling! God's my life, stolen hence, and left me asleep!
> I have had a most rare vision. I have had a dream, past the wit of man
> to say what dream it was: man is but an ass, if he go about to expound
> this dream. Methought I was—there is no man can tell what.
> Methought I was—and methought I had—but man is but a patched
> fool, if he will offer to say what methought I had. The eye of man hath
> not heard, the ear of man hath not seen, man's hand is not able to
> taste, his tongue to conceive, nor his heart to report, what my dream
> was. I will get Peter Quince to write a ballad of this dream: it shall be

called Bottom's Dream, because it hath no bottom; and I will sing it in the latter end of a play, before the duke: peradventure, to make it the more gracious, I shall sing it at her death.

$$(4.1.198–215)$$

Time has dealt a great many cards to the other characters—cards in which their domestic lives and loves have all been happily resolved—but for Bottom, time has stood still.

Let us take advantage of that pause, holding Bottom and me in suspension for a short while, and pick up the story of the young lovers, which reaches its own crisis in the midst of Bottom's encounter with Titania. I had lots of time to think about this when I was playing Bottom because right after I was anointed with the ass's head and took my exit in amorous conjunction with Titania, there followed the long, *long* scene among the four lovers in which the misplacing of their desire—previously, both men loved Hermia, now they both love Helena, and Hermia is chopped liver—reaches its climax. It was a fact in our production, and it is a fact every time I have ever seen any production, that this is the funniest scene in the play, possibly the funniest scene in *any* play. Far be it from me to complain, but there I would sit in the stage-left wings, listening to the audience hilarity and asking myself what any actor would ask himself: Why is that getting more laughs than I am? The fact that this quandary was being explored by a scholarly individual wearing a fur and plastic donkey's head (it was too complicated to take it off and on again in time for my next entrance) may also bear on the question. If what follows is asinine wisdom, go tell it to Apuleius.

What's so funny? Two comedy fundamentals. First, we in the audience are in on the joke, courtesy of a detailed conversation between Oberon and Puck, but the characters aren't. Second, the world has turned around 180 degrees: Previously, both men loved Hermia; now both love Helena. From here it gets a little more complicated. How does it happen that she cannot even for an instant consider each young man's change of heart as (I hesitate to use the word) *real*; she cannot, in other words, indulge in a moment of belief and therefore of gratification that she is finally the universal object of desire (the Helena of Troy, as it were) rather than the universal object of loathing. What makes *that* funny is, first of all, that in place of this quite natural response she leaps instantly to the conclusion that she is being mocked, and then she elevates, or tries to elevate, the (mistaken) idea of being the object of ridicule into some sort of occasion for tragic pathos. She suffers more when they both love her than when they both didn't love her.

Just when the joke may have started to wear thin, Shakespeare introduces a new wrinkle that is exquisitely nonsensical. Suddenly Hermia understands everything: This tragic reversal in Demetrius's love (and presumably the equivalent toggle in Lysander's love, though she doesn't care so much about that) has taken place because Helena is *taller* than she is and has used this attribute to steal away Demetrius's love: "She hath urged her *height*, | And with her personage, her *tall* personage, | Her *height* forsooth. . . ." The irrelevancy of this can only be described as a work of genius in its own right. But just when we want to jettison height, it gets metamorphosed into other registers where its relevance is, though still absurd, clearer: Hermia can call Helena "a painted maypole," transposing height from a (supposedly) positive attribute to a (definitely) negative one. And should we get stuck on that, height does another shift when Helena, now proudly owning her newly bestowed maypole status, boasts that she can escape the scene more readily than her rival because, as she says, "my legs are longer . . . to run away." Finally, one crucial matter about the comedy, not hilarious in itself but offering permission for hilarity. From the very beginning of the scene, we know that there is a cure: Oberon is present and equipped with the antidote. Not only is help on the way; help has been there all along, and (like us) it's having a grand old time watching, probably texting LMAO all over Athens.

What, to begin with, does Bottom call his experience? He hovers between *dream* and *vision*. In fact, the play teases us with some promise of a fundamental distinction between the two terms, for example, Oberon: "When they next wake, all this derision | Shall seem a dream and fruitless vision" (3.2.370), or Puck, who urges us to think that we "have but slumbered here, while these visions did appear; | And this weak and idle theme, | No more yielding but a dream" (5.1.416). There is a ready-made distinction: Dreams are a normal part of the brain's nighttime experience, whereas visions are sent by supernatural forces. Notably, when Oberon releases the four lovers from their spell, he declares that they will "think no more of this night's accidents | But as the fierce vexation of a dream" (4.1.67), which may suggest that he is arranging their consciousness so as to minimize the otherworldly nature of the experience; they will be made to believe that it was all just something they dreamt, even though it wasn't. (And, as we've seen, this is pretty much where they do go with it.) Moments later, though, when it's Titania's turn to wake up, she declares of the union with Bottom, "what visions have I seen" (4.1.175). In this case, there is no demotion to "dream"; she goes on to say, "Methought I was enamoured of an ass," which seems to place it in a rather authentic realm of sense experience—albeit of a misguided kind.

So far as what Bottom talks about when he talks about his vision/dream, partly it is what he *doesn't* talk about. Bottom may not know that he is making use of aposiopesis, the rhetorical device of breaking off a speech, or omitting a climactic term, often for special emphasis (paradoxically) on the word that is missing. But it is essential to his complex rhetoric here. In the simplest sense, we are being told that his experience was more than can be captured in language. The vision/dream distinction is just a symptom of this impossibility. Where he breaks off—"methought I was . . ."; "methought I had . . ."—he is obviously unable or unwilling to say "jackass" and "donkey's ears," which, in a down-to-earth way, may signal his shame in the face of the most ridiculous or, indeed, most appropriate form of his metamorphosis. But that silence is also the injunction laid upon those who are initiated into mysteries, notably the case of his avatar Lucius Apuleius (who doesn't, of course, keep quiet about it; he wrote the book on it).

If that once again fulfills the terms of pagan mysteries in the Renaissance, it doesn't stay pagan very long. Bottom proceeds to deliver a garbled version of a widely quoted passage from 1 Corinthians 2:9–10, here in the Bishops' Bible version:

> But as it is written: The eye hath not seen, & the eare hath not heard, neither haue entred into the heart of man, the thynges which God hath prepared for them that loue hym.
>
> But God hath reuealed them vnto vs by his spirite: For the spirite searcheth all thinges, yea the deepe thinges of God.

Paul's letter is in many respects an angry piece of preaching. The community of believers in Corinth is fractious and a little prouder of its own theology than Paul (or his boss) would like. The letter is in part an expression of his frustration with the challenges of spreading the gospel. Hence, his remarkably frank and cogent expression of the difficulties he is having in attempting to bring diverse belief systems together:

> For the Jews demand signs and the Greeks demand wisdom, but we proclaim Christ crucified, a stumbling block to Jews and foolishness to Gentiles.
>
> (1 CORINTHIANS 1:22)

It's one of my favorite passages in the whole of the New Testament because it renders the two great civilizations so succinctly in their difference and so hopelessly from the point of view of a new faith that wished to provide shelter to both. The context, then, for the line that Bottom mangles is an exhortation to look away from the intellectual particularities of theology and to something more mystical and spiritual: revelation, in other words, rather than reasoning. Though the action of Shakespeare's play could hardly be less theological, it certainly urges the authority of revelation over reason. And the Corinthians passage in particular maps itself onto this moment in the *Dream* because Paul declares that "None of the rulers of this age" has understood this truth; rather, it is revealed by God. In the Geneva Bible, in fact, the truth is character-ized as "the bottom of God's secrets." And if Bottom performs the move of synaesthesia ("eye hath not seen," "ear hath not heard," etc.) in common with his theatrical colleagues in the *Dream*, we can take it as a sign that pagan mysteries are leaving their mark on Christian mysteries.

Finally, it seems that Bottom has his own evangelical project to send his dream out into the world, despite the fact, or on account of the fact, that "it hath no Bottom"—that is, it lacks foundation, or because it is unfathomably deep, or because it can live independently of the individual who dreamed it, this last being common to messianic religions. As further signs—and, again, ambiguous ones—of the future life of his revelation, we have the brief scene that follows. It begins with the rest of the acting troupe heartbro-ken that they have lost their star, whereupon to great jubilation he suddenly appears to them—as one might say, resurrected. His message is, to say the least, ambiguous:

> Masters, I am to discourse wonders; but ask me not what. For if I tell you, I am no true Athenian. I will tell you everything right as it fell out.

> (4.2.26–27)

Which are the wonders? Will he recount them or won't he? Is the "true Athenian" the person who is initiated into the Delphic Oracle and sworn to secrecy? These wonders are never directly picked up again; instead we follow the happy news that these players' theatrical offering is among the finalists for the wedding entertainment.

Switching to another register, let me tell you something I learned as an actor from the experience of performing Bottom's big speech. At this moment, more than Hamlet about to say "to be or not to be," more than Lear about to outface the storm, Bottom *owns* the stage. The audience is looking at someone who— if he played his cards right—made them laugh every time he opened his mouth. We have just seen him in an interlude as bizarre as it is sexy, as mysterious as it is farcical. Now he is about to go one on one with the audience, and they're not going to miss a syllable; they are going to listen. We can tell Shakespeare was aware of that because he has written into the speech a series of open spaces. Bottom's silences, in short, are as important as his speech. No need to rush through the waking up. He can take his time, between sleep and waking, as he looks for his companions one by one. Naturally, he starts with Peter Quince. No answer. What does that mean? Where am I? OK, maybe Flute will respond: That's his Thisbe; she should be close at hand because—again—his experience at this moment is that zero time has elapsed since he was plucked from his rehearsal. He can go faster looking for the rest of them, since he's starting to realize that they have all abandoned him.

It's no easy transition, though, from my-mates-have-abandoned-me to I've had a vision, I've had a dream. Then we get to the heart of the speech. Bottom has to use his words to capture something that words cannot capture. Until he gets to Peter Quince and the idea of the "ballad," Bottom is holding in his head something so all-encompassing and so ineffable that the actor has to be sending out visions that are completely independent of the words he uses. Where would I get them from? Of course, I could picture in my head the actual scene I had played with Titania, but, as I've already said, that meeting doesn't really rise to the level of the play's idea about it. Which may be exactly Shakespeare's plan: It's not going to be Bottom's onstage meeting with the Queen of the Fairies that we take away as divine; it's going to be this moment, the recollection that Bottom delivers, which in turn has to outstrip the actual words he uses.

I started to think about things in my own life that I could locate in that realm where my own words would fail them. I might be acting in a comedy, but these focal points for my imagination didn't need to be frivolous or light-hearted. What exactly did I have in 1979? I had Dante's *mezzo del cammin di nostra vita*: I was exactly thirty-five years old. I was, as already noted, in a professional quandary, fearful of turning a corner from promising to he-used-to-be-promising. I was living a particularly loveless moment—devoid even of (what should I call them?) harmful objects of desire. I lived in a great Chicago apartment, which I shared with someone who could have become a harmful object of desire but had no conceivable inclination that way; the square footage was so lavish that weeks could go by without laying eyes on each other. Every Wednesday night I would have dinner with a colleague and his wife, who lived in a handsomely appointed flat down the block; I'd bring a first course, they produced main and dessert. Not much material for visionary experience there.

All this makes it sound as though I had no idea where to turn for transcendent sensations, but that's not really true. The problem was that they were transcendently sad. The period of rehearsals and performances of the *Dream* coincided precisely with the decline and death by euthanasia of my beloved German shepherd Sasha. I had acquired her more than a decade earlier when she was six weeks old; she lived with me in half a dozen different residences on one coast, then the other, now in the middle. For much of that time she suffered from epilepsy, which was at this point becoming notably worse; I administered medication wrapped in her beloved chunky peanut butter, but it proved effective in preventing seizures only at dosage levels that turned her into a sleeping zombie. In the classic manner of shepherds, she was now developing hip problems. I was regularly having to carry her up and down the three flights of stairs to my great Chicago apartment.

I'm pulling your heartstrings with my boy-loves-dog, boy-loses-dog story, but that's really not quite honest. What I should say is not only that I was losing Sasha but that I believed I had not for a long time, perhaps ever, been a worthy keeper of Sasha. I never took her on great runs in great parks; she was fed well, but on my schedule, not hers; I yelled at her fiercely when she misbehaved. I never seemed to stay home for her sake—after all, at the very moment when I was having these feelings, I was off all evening in a rehearsal on Belmont Avenue rather than at home with Sasha on Oakdale.

"*Use it!*" they say in (mostly fictional) accounts of the actor's process, but what kind of path could I carve out between the love and guilt that bound me to Sasha, on the one hand, and Bottom's dream on the other? Of course, the play is all about the permeable border between persons and beasts, so I seemed to be on the right track. On the other hand, the play, for all its terrors, is joyous, and, in regard to Sasha, joy was very hard to recapture at that moment. The speech, as I've said, is full of breaks, of ellipses, of failures to get the right word out. That might be useful, considering how little I had been able to articulate my feelings about Sasha. Could I use them to recollect not the sadness but the joy of our time together? I fixated on our first meeting. I had gone to see a litter of shepherd puppies, certain that I would pick out a male dog, since I'd grown up with a male shepherd. In the barn a little girl from the family of the breeders was playing with the adorable litter of six-week-old pups. For fun, I asked her which I should choose. She darted immediately to one of them—they all looked identical to me, but evidently not to her—picked that one up, and said, "This one's the *squirmest.*" That did it: I converted on the spot to bitches, and from that point Sasha remained, until those recent days, the very embodiment of *squirm.* The joy, the sadness, the little girl, the joke: They all helped me with Bottom's dream.

The play's final scene opens, and I, as reader, as exegete, enter a realm of radical uncertainty. It's evident that the four young people have recounted their "dreams" a few moments earlier—dreams about whose status we have every reason to be uncertain: mental activity while asleep? real events but of a fantastical nature? visions in the transcendent sense of the term? Whatever it may have been, we were ourselves eyewitnesses. Theseus, on the other hand, though he witnessed the awakening of the lovers in the previous act, has only just now heard it all narrated (offstage). Here I must intervene with recollection of our production's Theseus-Oberon (that familiar and very effective doubling made famous by Peter Brook). Our actor was a young, tall African American man with a knack for teasing the truth out of every syllable and leaving one helpless to question anything he said.

Which only added to my lifelong problem with Theseus's big act 5 speech. Hippolyta has called the lovers' story "strange," which is a cautious and noncommittal judgment. Theseus shuts down those uncertainties with "more strange than true." He continues authoritatively:

> I never may believe
> These antique fables, nor these fairy toys.
> Lovers and madmen have such seething brains,
> Such shaping fantasies, that apprehend
> More than cool reason ever comprehends.
> The lunatic, the lover and the poet
> Are of imagination all compact:
> One sees more devils than vast hell can hold,
> That is, the madman: the lover, all as frantic,
> Sees Helen's beauty in a brow of Egypt:
> The poet's eye, in fine frenzy rolling,
> Doth glance from heaven to earth, from earth to heaven;
> And as imagination bodies forth
> The forms of things unknown, the poet's pen
> Turns them to shapes and gives to airy nothing
> A local habitation and a name.
> Such tricks hath strong imagination,
> That if it would but apprehend some joy,
> It comprehends some bringer of that joy;
> Or in the night, imagining some fear,
> How easy is a bush supposed a bear!

(5.1.2–22)

As performed by my actor colleague in Chicago, I would buy *any* used car from that man; I'd probably even repurchase my 1960 Citroën with nipples in place of pedals, which died at the tollbooth as I was driving it home from shelling out $700 for it in Queens. It's no surprise—even for those who didn't have my good fortune in hearing this actor perform it many times—that the speech has been extracted from the particulars of the play as some sort of universal truth, forever sentencing lunatics, lovers, and poets to a shared, and none too elevated, status. (Personally, I've known members of all three groups and find them quite distinct.)

In a nutshell, per Theseus, they're all liars at worst and victims of hallucination at best. Lunatics see things as worse than they really are, lovers see them as better, and poets undersign both these sets of delusions by gracing them with language. Now, it's not just that I don't buy it as a life truth; I don't buy it as an account of what I've been witnessing in the last couple of hours. Of course, it's well within Shakespeare's bag of tricks to introduce characters who offer misguided accounts of the action that we've witnessed, but they're usually stupid, like Polonius, or evil, like Iago, and so we recognize the error. Theseus's speech, on the other hand, is mightily persuasive, as exquisitely rational as a mathematical equation. There is in fact some evidence that Shakespeare did a lot of rewriting in this speech, elaborating on the neat triad of lunatics, lovers, and poets, which may suggest that he wanted to take the rationality angle and lay it on thick.

That's the best I can do to convince myself that I understand the author's design. He is offering us a free choice: We can enter into the world of dream, or we can enter into the world of syllogistic argumentation. Or we can move from one world to the other, a shift that is equivalent to the passage from adolescence to adulthood. I recoil from this equivalence, however, since I don't like to think of myself as perpetually adolescent. Besides, there seems to be a soft-spoken alternative in the air, which appears not in the voice of Theseus but of Hippolyta. First of all,

HIPPOLYTA
'Tis strange, my Theseus, that these lovers speak of.
THESEUS
More strange than true.

(5.1.1)

Well, no. From *my* experience, Theseus's claim, or implication at least, that it wasn't true—in other words, it never happened—is patently mistaken, since it's clear that I witnessed everything that the lovers have presumably been narrating. Then, a more serious challenge from Hippolyta in direct reply to Theseus's lecture:

HIPPOLYTA
But all the story of the night told over,
And all their minds transfigured so together,
More witnesseth than fancy's images

And grows to something of great constancy;
But, howsoever, strange and admirable.

$$(5.1.23–27)$$

Hippolyta, it seems to me, has won this point handily, and even on the play's own (as one might say) conservative grounds: The story of the lovers is authoritative because it was a *shared* story. "Fancy's images" (roughly equivalent to Theseus's lunatics, lovers, and poets) are solipsistic; the lovers' story was "transfigured so *together*." (That phrase is masterful: *Transfigured* is the visionary part, parallel to Christ's appearance to the Disciples; *together* is the social, or shared, part.) Hippolyta's angle of defense is in itself a brilliant joke, since in the midst of their dark night of the four souls, the experience was anything but shared. We are left, in short, with a richly presented quandary: Shall we understand the experience of the play from Theseus's perspective or from Hippolyta's? Lucky for us that the instrument offered to lead us through this uncertainty is the production of "Pyramus and Thisbe."

What can I say by way of analyzing "Pyramus and Thisbe" that doesn't sound more absurd than the text I am analyzing? All the prefatory material—the mispunctuated prologue and the ponderous self-explanations by Wall, Moon, and Lion—return us to some of the play's insistently articulated paradoxes about belief, imagination, and the special sort of contract that we enter upon with fiction, and particularly performed fiction. The efforts of Snout, Snug, and Starveling to convince us that they *are* the nonhuman objects they are playing have precisely the contrary effect, that is, of exposing the mechanics of creating verisimilitude, and we're thrown back not on Wall, Moonshine, and Lion as operators in the narrative but on the hapless, overburdened "real" people struggling with their theatrical tasks.

The joke on the two "human" characters is somewhat different. There are, of course, the malapropisms, the silly rhymes, and the antiquated verse patterns, in general the hopeless inadequacy of the play's language to rise to the level of life and death that the plot requires. All of this having been said, it is really very difficult to explain why "Pyramus and Thisbe" is so *very* funny. Part of it (and this is true in all comedy) is that we as audience members enjoy defining ourselves as a sophisticated and collective body. We know what *good* plays sound like, and finding "Pyramus and Thisbe" ridiculous confirms that. But not every audience member is a theater critic. The thing we've all been asked to do for the previous couple of hours is, in Coleridge's famous formulation, to suspend disbelief. Unless we are very fiction-phobic—and there are such persons, notably in Shakespeare's time, when they wrote treatises attacking the theater—we enter into that contract willingly, even enthusiastically. (If we cannot, we just stay home and watch the news. Ugh.) It is nevertheless the case that this suspension of disbelief can be back-breaking labor on at least two counts. The first is contained in Coleridge's term: We have to work hard to overlook the preposterous combination of fantasy and coincidence that constitutes, in this case, the plot of the play. The second is that we experience very real emotional pain when fictions turn dark, even if it's a comedy and we know they'll get better: This, too, is hard work. (Admittedly, I speak for myself here, as someone who suspends disbelief so utterly that he can scarcely bear to watch any movie in which something bad happens, however provisionally, and even if it's totally clear that Meg Ryan and Tom Hanks will get together at the end.)

Thus when we come to Pyramus's 5× "die" (5.1.300) or Thisbe's 3× "adieu" (5.1.341), we are almost literally dying to laugh, to enter into the communal recognition that none of this—not Pyramus and Thisbe, not Egeus's tyranny over his daughter, not Hermia's snake dream, not Helena's sense of victimization—was real. Admittedly, this is a sort of big-picture explanation that doesn't quite do credit to the minuscule hilarities provided by the language in which the tragic lovers express themselves. For a glimpse at this, the best I can do is to refer back to my own experience on stage. As a performer of Pyramus's lines I was, of course, forbidden to show any sign of amusement myself, and since there were a couple of passages where keeping a straight face was just short of impossible, no matter how many dozens of times I spoke them, I can try to unpack the underlying joke that required me to exercise such self-control. The two passages cover similar territory:

> O grim-looked night, O night with hue so black,
> O night which ever art when day is not.
>
> > (5.1.168; N.B.: I cannot even type this last
> > line with a straight face)

and

> Sweet moon, I thank thee for thy sunny beams.
>
> > (5.1.266)

The (fictional) author of these verses seems to have understood, in a dim sort of way, that the job of poetic language is to provide some kind of supplement to mere denotative meaning; in other words, that such language isn't merely decorative but provides information along with ornament. But what should that supplement be, especially given that *night* and *moon* are so familiar that there is nothing much new you can say about them? The pitiable results of this search are to be seen in these quotations. About night we are given by our poet precisely zero information; about the moon we are given information that is precisely the opposite of true. In the one case tautology, in the other case self-contradiction. I am conscious that I am here in the terrible realm of trying to explain a joke, and indeed a joke that perhaps only I find quite so funny, but I can claim at least the authority to say that on each occasion when I had to speak these words in front of an audience it was necessary for me to invoke some imagined personal catastrophe, at the least a parking ticket, at the worst—well, probably Sasha, alone in my apartment, would come to mind.

As with any theatrical event, a real analysis of the experience doesn't confine itself to the performed text but embraces its reception as well, and on this matter we are given extensive data in the course of the actual staging. Though it's difficult to take our eyes off the train wreck that is the Mechanicals' performance, we are nevertheless provided with a powerful set of impressions as regards the onstage audience's reaction. It is a mixed bag: Hermia and Helena do not open their mouths. The young husbands score lame wisecracks off the beleaguered performers, coming off very badly, to the point that Starveling as the Moon ends up dropping his character and marching offstage.

Theseus and Hippolyta—no surprise—are sources of more interesting reactions. From the moment when Philostrate tries to discourage the choice that Theseus has made among the entertainments, Theseus takes what we might call the *de haut en bas* or *noblesse oblige* line. The monarch is subjected to many such ghastly proletarian performances, and he exhibits the loftiness of his condescension by respecting the intentions of the poor performers, with special awareness of the loyalty they are showing by going to all this trouble. For instance,

> Where I have come, great clerks have purposed
> To greet me with premeditated welcomes;
> Where I have seen them shiver and look pale,
> Make periods in the midst of sentences,
> Throttle their practised accent in their fears
> And in conclusion dumbly have broke off,
> Not paying me a welcome. Trust me, sweet,
> Out of this silence yet I pick'd a welcome;
> And in the modesty of fearful duty
> I read as much as from the rattling tongue
> Of saucy and audacious eloquence.
> Love, therefore, and tongue-tied simplicity
> In least speak most, to my capacity.

(5.1.93–105)

Later, when Hippolyta has delivered a more direct opinion—"This is the silliest stuff that ever I heard"—without any gesture toward the political utilities of the enterprise, Theseus finds slightly different grounds for his positive, if highly condescending, approach to the play, basically declaring that he and the rest of his aristocratic audience will turn a bad play into a good one by the exercise of their imaginations, presumably as distinct from the imaginations of those who made the play. These reactions (minus Hippolyta's "silliest stuff" comment) come to the same thing: The play may be garbage, but the experience is positive, as a result of the work that the audience performs upon it, whether that is the recognition of their subjects' fealty or something more aesthetic, the replacement of the actual performance with some higher-class Pyramus and Thisbe of the mind not available to the Mechanicals.

I have always found this a very troubling point of arrival for what is possibly the greatest dramatic comedy ever written. Theseus disdains his subjects, Shakespeare disdains his dramatic predecessors, the theater audience consists of snobs and fools, and I ask myself what exactly am I laughing about, or, as Bottom, what agenda am I following when I succeed in looking as ridiculous as possible. There seems to be one moment that rises above this, however. We've already seen that Hippolyta, however much I would place her on the right side of the argument about the imagination, fails to defend this particular act of the imagination; she also appears to be uninterested in the loyalty of Theseus's subjects. The best that can be said for her is that she is direct, rather than strategic, in her reactions. One piece of this directness strikes me as different from everything else that the onstage audience produces. When Bottom dies—no surprise that I am especially conscious of this moment—Hippolyta says, "Beshrew my heart, I pity the man" (5.1.283). I even invented (with neither encouragement nor discouragement from the director) a piercing look of gratitude and love from my agonized eyes to Hippolyta's as I lay laboriously dying. The question is: Which man did she pity? Both the character and the actor deserved it, and to bring them together, wasn't Shakespeare writing into the script some kind of rave review for Bottom's performance?

Yes, but one can only make so much of "I pity the man" and the way it seems to confirm that Bottom's performance has made Pyramus come alive for Hippolyta. Thinking along these lines—and it's well nigh irresistible—signifies an attempt to make the performance of Pyramus and Thisbe and the onstage audience's reaction to it into the play's model for the kind of transaction that Shakespeare understands the theater to be. And I spent years, including during the time that I was performing in the play, handing that line to students. As of the present moment and the writing of this text, however, I've come to see the matter quite differently. A *Midsummer Night's Dream*, not "Pyramus and

Thisbe," is the model for the transaction of theater: The writing is better, the performances are better, and we as audience—here's the payoff—are being called upon to do a better job of responding. We should not be whispering bits of snide cleverness; we should not imagine that *we* rather than the actors really make the play. We should not, as Theseus does, tell the performers that "if he that writ it had played Pyramus and hanged himself in Thisbe's garter, it would have been a fine tragedy." If we *do* behave ourselves, as the onstage audience does *not*, then and only then will we experience the blessings that Titania, Oberon, and Puck distribute in the closing moments of the play: the benediction upon our offspring and the knowledge that we have all shared in a dream.

3

Mothers and Sons

It will become clear, if it isn't already, that I have something of a fixation on the openings of Shakespeare's plays, that I relish the state of uncertainty that can be hypothesized in those early minutes, that I may even go so far as to deplore the fact that for many of the plays the cultural noise—as I've called it—surrounding some of the world's most famous literary works renders it impossible to replicate the experience that Shakespeare expected his audience to be having. Of course, I know that no such replicating is possible. What I am really fixated upon is the idea of the innocent reader, or the innocent theatergoer. I want, at least by way of something like a thought experiment, to hypothesize readers/viewers who bring to this encounter with a fiction nothing but their own nonfictional experience. It's quite impossible, I know. Unless one is a small child, or perhaps neurologically compromised, the encounter with fictional stories is itself a familiar category of experience with its own rules of engagement that distance and distinguish it from all the nonfiction that comprises ordinary life. Be that as it may, I entertain the fantasy that somehow in the opening minutes of receiving a fiction, we are not yet fully conditioned into the grown-up ways of detaching it from ourselves. And it seems appropriate, since I am about to talk about two plays that are somewhat less universally familiar than those discussed in the previous chapters, to take special note of what Shakespeare lays down for us during these magic moments.

In particular, I want to call attention to a pair of early utterances (in one case the very opening words of the play, in the other case some three minutes into it) that have the potential to stop me in my tracks; both of them, as it happens, concern mothers. I should add that in beginning the present chapter by paying close attention to this pair of sentences, I'm veering away from what must be an almost inevitable opening gesture when addressing this topic: the assertion that mothers are shockingly neglected in Shakespeare's oeuvre. (I make that point myself elsewhere in these pages.) Well, yes and no. Of course, women of whatever life stage are bound to be as neglected in fictions as they are in real life, during whatever period of history, including our own. Historically speaking, there is a certain amount of rescue that comes via the sentimental literature of the eighteenth century and the growth of the novel in the nineteenth. Shakespeare's genres, however, are not very woman-centered. The world of history—despite the obvious fact of a female on the throne of England for much of his career—foregrounds kings, battles, and male-dominated statecraft; tragedy is in many ways a subset of history (or vice versa); and as for romantic comedy, the focus, beyond the obligatory adolescents of both sexes, is on a father and rarely on a mother. Not to mention the fact that if I were in the business of delivering scripts to a theater company where female roles were all assumed by prepubescent boys, I might shy away from inventing plots resembling those of *To the Lighthouse* or *The Golden Girls*.

But back to those early moments featuring mother. Does *All's Well That Ends Well* begin well? Well you may ask. If anything is possible in this initial instant, when we see a small group of grand personages, including a stately lady and a young man, everyone clad in mourning, what door is opened when the Lady says, "In delivering my son from me, I bury a second husband" (1.1.1)? Read that line over, slowly, pausing on *deliver* and *bury* and then on *son* and *husband*. The data, upon reflection, will become clear enough: The husband in question has recently died, and, as the speech implies and the young man will immediately confirm, the son in question is leaving on a journey. But there is more going on here than the transfer of plot information. Death and birth are melded, to begin with, but it's the entanglement of son and husband that may offer an even more distinctive signpost for this play. As has often been pointed out, *All's Well* is the only play of Shakespeare's that opens with a female speaker (leaving aside *Macbeth*, which is opened by a witch, not exactly a human female), and it's logical in the gender world of 1600 that she would immediately establish herself via the cardinal points of the two crucial males in her life. But Shakespeare chooses to deliver this commonplace material with a mashup of death-and-birth, son-and-father that inaugurates a presentation of Mother that is as unsettlingly ambiguous as is possible to offer in a mere twelve words. What does it mean for a mother to say that her son is her "second husband"? And what does this proposition have to do with death—that is, with the mother's widowhood? Is the son who is going out into the world dead to her, or is she dead once her son goes out into the world? Are we ever going to be comfortable with the equation between son and husband, in particular when the death of the (real) husband renders the mother eligible to marry again? And if you're thinking about a much more famous play that Shakespeare was writing at exactly the same time, one including a mother, a son, and a second husband, you may well be on to something. (And I'll get on to it later.) Suffice it to say that there will be quite a lot to resolve in this play, whose title, after all, suggests the text's self-satisfaction with its capacity to resolve things.

If the role of Mother undergoes certain disturbing vibrations at the opening of *All's Well*, it is subjected to a veritable earthquake in the course of *Coriolanus*, and this gets announced at the outset as well. The play opens with Rome in a state of incipient rebellion. The crowd of starving plebeians led by the First Citizen is already prepared to slaughter our title character under the supposition that he is their chief enemy. Only the Second Citizen attempts to restrain the angry throng, reminding them of the services that Coriolanus has done for his country. It is in a nutshell a problem that the whole play will explore, but the hero's past support of Rome cuts very little ice at this point. The First Citizen discounts these services on the grounds that "he pays himself with being proud" (1.1.30–31); in other words, he did it not for Rome but for his own glory. When the less hot-headed Second Citizen dismisses this as malice, the First Citizen adds an additional motive:

> Though soft-conscienced men can be content to say it was for his
> country, he did it to please his mother and to be partly proud, which
> he is even to the altitude of his virtue.
>
> (1.1.36–39)

In part, it's a familiar question in the face of a figure like Coriolanus: When heroic action is traced to the motive of overweening pride (as it often can be—certainly in tragedies, possibly in real life), is the heroism therefore contaminated, no matter what positive results it may bring about? It is an interesting problem and certainly one that the play explores. But the heart of the drama follows the First Citizen's other line of attack: *He did it to please his mother.*

Pretend (if such is necessary) that you don't know anything about Coriolanus—again, I'm asking for a naïve audience here—and you hear this assertion in the first five minutes of a tragedy bearing that hero's name. Isn't there something preposterous here? Whatever might animate the heroes of republican Rome or imperial Rome, who collectively built a civilization of law and power, language and culture, stretching from Spain to the Baltic, from Hadrian's Wall to the Nile, while subduing barbarians and nonbarbarians for something like a thousand years: *They did it to please their mother?* Did Julius Caesar cross the Rubicon *to please his mother?* Did Brutus and Cassius assassinate Julius Caesar *to please their mothers*? Did Mark Antony extend Roman sway to Egypt and have sex with Cleopatra *to please his mother*?

I hope the point emerges: Given a sense, shared in Shakespeare's time and in our own (to the extent that we think of such things at all), that ancient Rome is the very defining space of heroic masculinity, it's scarcely possible to imagine a more deflationary fact to put at the center of a Roman drama than the idea of the hero who is motivated by the desire to impress his mother. One feels this deflation instinctually—at least *I* do—but it takes a bit of probing, and in some rather delicate territory, to nail down the reasons for that slightly queasy reaction. The most straightforward, most sanitized way to explain it would be to say that pleasing one's mother is the activity of a child, that once you are able, for instance, in single combat to save Rome from its encircling enemies, you're probably old enough to be interested in pleasing someone other than, or at least in addition to, your mother. The other pathways (intertwined, as it happens, with each other) bear simple proper names, and to cite them is essentially to make the point: Oedipus, Freud. No matter how you scan these cultural data, from Sophocles to *The Interpretation of Dreams*, there is something questionable about a man who has the wrong kind of attachment to his mother. By which, of course, we mean an overly *close* attachment.

Previously, by way of suggesting the play's possible shock values, I postulated a viewer/reader who comes upon the First Citizen's claim about the hero and his mother as a surprise. The fact is, though, that in the literature that the early moderns read obsessively as they patterned their own political world along the lines of ancient Rome, Coriolanus was famous precisely for this trait; it was, in fact, the cornerstone of his fame. Indeed, Plutarch, Shakespeare's source for the play, unless he is exhibiting a *very* dry sense of humor, may be quite immune to the ironies so apparent to me in the First Citizen's character sketch of the hero: "But whereas other men found in glory the chief end of valour, he found the chief end of glory in his mother's gladness." The terms that Plutarch uses—*arete* versus *euphrosyne*—are red-letter cultural markers for very different, even opposite, values: the pursuit of glory versus the attainment of (roughly) mirth. The phrasing is actually a bit more critical than that: *Euphrosyne*, says Plutarch, *was* Coriolanus's *arete*, and not even his own *euphrosyne*, but his mother's. In other words, within the grab bag of storytelling from antiquity, Coriolanus *means* mother's boy. That's what Shakespeare was looking for when he pulled Plutarch off the shelf.

When I think about early childhood—of the sentient kind, from which one has coherent recollection—I land upon a little summer house that my parents bought just before I was six and that they kept until I was in junior high school.

It was about an hour from New York, so we could go there on the weekends, but the focus of my memory is the summers. When school was out, we moved there as a family, except that my father still worked in the city. So my mother and I spent most of the summer alone together, my father arriving on the weekends: a classic situation for middle-class New Yorkers, though we must have counted as occupying the lowest rung of the ladder privileged to enjoy that set of arrangements.

So, speaking arithmetically, my memories of this time are about two-sevenths of a three-person family and five-sevenths of a two-person family. I divide things up in this way because I want to recount one of each kind of memory, and the numbers are significant, if only by accident, because the two-sevenths memory is of a single occasion, whereas the five-sevenths memory is of an entire habitude.

I'll start with the latter. My mother and I, alone during the week, had a fixed ritual, and like all the best such rituals it was self-invented, and, again, like the best of them, its exact origins are forgotten. My parents were card-playing people, like many of their generation, and our ethnic identity being what it was, there was very little bridge but quite a lot of pinochle. I never really became a card-playing person, not having much of a head for the rules of the game—*any* game, as we'll see—but there were long summer evenings with just my mother and me, and, with television still not having penetrated our Putnam County hamlet, we gravitated to the card table. Poker—at least the rules, though not the strategy—was deemed easy enough for me, so we must have tried it, but it lacked excitement, presumably because it was so rare that either of us, let alone both of us, had much of a bettable hand.

Thus there was invented Poker with a Pinochle Deck. Pinochle, as you may or may not know, gets rid of all those puny twos, threes, fours, and so on through the eights: Those cards do not exist in the pack. As for nines, tens, aces, and face cards, there are twice as many of them! Under these conditions poker starts to get interesting, at least to a nine-year-old. Second innovation. You have to play poker for money, but real money couldn't very well be moving about between my mother and me on all those summer evenings. So she took an old and rather beautiful silk change purse and filled it with pennies. We each started with exactly half the pennies, they moved in the course of the evening back and forth with the fortunes of the game, there was eventually some kind of reckoning (did we play until one of us went "bankrupt"? That seems a little too cutthroat), probably when it was time for me to go to bed, at which point the pennies all went back into the silk purse, and we lived to play another day.

The excitement was nonstop. With double the number of kings, queens, etc., and the complete expulsion of those plebeian deuces, treys, and their ilk, practically every hand was worth bidding up to the skies. Did I hold three jacks? My mother had four tens! Did she go the limit of her pennies with a full house, queens high? I had a straight flush! (Lots of plumbing jokes there, my mother's wit being what it was.) I started to get good at it. I discovered that if I was cautious, I was liable to become penniless, but if I risked big, I would win big. (Is this true in real poker? I have no idea.) Poker with a pinochle deck taught me the thrill of victory alongside the prudence of magnanimity, all the ups and downs protected by a sense of security that at the end of the playtime every single penny would go back in the beautiful little purse. I've never had much interest in games of chance as an adult, probably because nothing could equal the kind of excitement coupled with the kind of security that I found in Poker with a Pinochle Deck. Eat your heart out, Las Vegas.

The two-sevenths, as I've said, happened only once. On one of his weekends, my father brought back from the city a child's bowling set, everything suitably miniaturized (my parents were bowling people as well as pinochle people, my mother particularly avid), and on Saturday morning he proudly erected it on the long straight concrete walkway that led from the road to our house. The play among the three of us began with a little crisis the details of which I cannot remember, but the upshot was that I was relieved of the burden of actual bowling, per se, and transferred to the job of scoring. (This exclusion should probably be the point of the story, but let's just say that my lifelong ineptitude with balls, bats, clubs, rackets, shuttlecocks, pool cues, etc., must have exhibited itself embarrassingly.) No matter: My mother handed me the specially prepared printed forms for scoring, gave me a few instructions, and assured me that mine was really the important job at a bowling alley; I attempted to fulfill her expectations by carefully writing down numbers inside each of the boxes.

The play between my parents started to become a bit aggressive. There was a dispute. My mother, in order to prove that she was in the right, seized the score sheet. Alas, she recognized at once that I had not done my job well at all. I'd counted how many pins fell down each time and put little numbers in the boxes. I knew I was supposed to do something about the littler boxes inside the little boxes, but I wasn't quite clear on that. My mother was furious; after all, she had explained it all to me, and now I had ruined her game— deprived her of the right to claim victory. She started to resume her throwing stance, but halfway to releasing the ball she turned around and ripped the score sheet out of my hand. I did what any self-respecting child would do: I ran howling into my bedroom and slammed the door.

What happened to that nice lady with the pennies? It was very simple. Even a person of single-digit age could work it out. A mother was one kind of grown-up; a wife was another. That they should be the same person was very, very confusing.

Coriolanus, then, is one long disambiguation, one long series of weeknights with no Daddy, which in some ways simplifies the problem. Clearly, there is in the world a customary genealogy of the hero, which follows the male line, and it is violated by the utter absence of a husband/father in the case of Coriolanus. The closest we get here is in the form of a hypothetical; the speaker is the mother in question, Volumnia, who is attempting to infuse some of her own stalwart qualities into her daughter-in-law:

> If my son were my husband, I should freelier rejoice in that absence
> wherein he won honor than in the embracements of his bed where he
> would show most love.
>
> (1.3.2–5)

Is it possible to imagine anything more perverse? Not only is Volumnia declaring that she prefers a warrior who is absent (and in mortal danger on the battlefield) to a husband who is present in her bed—this much could be chalked up to Roman heroic virtue—but the whole assertion rests on the premise of herself as her son's husband. And this, let's not forget, spoken to the individual who actually *does* share "his bed where he would show most love." It renders by comparison rather colorless the son-husband comparison with which *All's Well* begins. With the fate of Rome hanging in the balance, the husbandless mother of the hero/savior edges toward absurdity, as when Menenius, trying vainly to stage manage the hero's role in making peace with the plebeians, is forced to say to him, "is this the promise you made your mother?" (3.3.87), which sounds to me like a laugh line delivered on the playground or something I heard in my head at a prepubescent age, not an exhortation to decisive political action in the Roman forum.

But Shakespeare has woven, ominously (or so it appears to me), another thread into the fabric of Coriolanus's Rome. With the ferocious mother-father-lover rolled into one at the center of this particular Roman world, it seems as though perversity is on the loose everywhere. Nothing in the rulebook of epic heroism accords with Coriolanus's rapturous reception of his ally Cominius,

> O, let me clip ye
> In arms as sound as when I wooed, in heart
> As merry as when our nuptial day was done. . . .
>
> (1.7.29–31)

And this in turn pales in comparison to the brutal antagonist Aufidius's erotic reception of his erstwhile enemy Coriolanus:

> Know thou first,
> I loved the maid I married; never man
> Sigh'd truer breath; but that I see thee here,
> Thou noble thing, more dances my rapt heart
> Than when I first my wedded mistress saw
> Bestride my threshold.

(4.5.114–19)

This is a world, then, in which the point of comparison for masculine heroic action in regard either to comrade or adversary is the taking of one's bride's virginity—part love, part violence, in other words. Such contamination of the heroic with the erotic does not escape the notice even of Aufidius's servingmen, contemptuous of the way their master dotes on Coriolanus: "Our general himself makes a mistress of him, sanctifies himself with's hand, and turns up the white o' th' eye to his discourse" (4.5.199–201).

The comic relief for this thread of perversity—at least I think it's comic—is the transformation of Coriolanus's ally and father-figure Menenius from the chatty sage who attempts to pacify the plebeians with the fable of the belly into the giddy recipient of a letter from the hero, fresh from his victory in Corioli. Volumnia reports to Menenius that she has had a letter from her son. "The state hath had another," she goes on to say, "his wife another, and I think there's one at home for you" (2.1.105–7). Menenius overlooks his lowly place in this hierarchy of letter recipients and elatedly declares, "A letter for me? [I read this as *pour moi?!*] It gives me an estate of seven years health"—in other words, I'm feeling young again. And Menenius will try to take this to the bank later in the play when he seeks to meet with Coriolanus, now encamped with Aufidius and the Volscians, by saying to the sentry, "Thy general is my lover" (5.2.15).

A pause to ask what exactly Menenius means by this. In R. B. Parker's excellent Oxford edition of the play, *lover* is glossed here as "dear friend," a reading that gets bolstered by reference to Coriolanus's own speech a few minutes later in which he says to Menenius, "I loved thee," and then to Aufidius, "This man . . . | Was my beloved in Rome" (5.3.87, 91). I'm not certain, however, that we can equate "love" and "beloved" as spoken by Coriolanus with "my lover" spoken by Menenius. Across all Shakespeare's works, the term "lover" is almost always erotic; only rarely does it refer to nonsexual friendship. In those instances, it tends to concern itself with classical heroes like those of *Troilus and Cressida* or *Julius Caesar*. It also gets used in reference to the relationship of Antonio and Bassanio in *Merchant of Venice*, which is clearly of an ambiguous nature. Suffice it to say that Shakespeare is fully capable of exploiting the ambiguities of the term, and in the charged erotic atmosphere of *Coriolanus* we have every reason to be left with an amplified sense of what we should be hearing when Menenius says, "Thy general is my lover."

Am I, then, a messenger bearing the rather distasteful news from Shakespeare that a husbandless, gender-bending mother releases sexual perversity in the world? Not so fast. As I've presented it, and as I think the play does in its earlier phases, the mother-son relationship verges upon the perverse or even the comical: She is the masculine figure (her son jokes at one point that if she had married Hercules she would have undertaken six of the hero's labors herself and saved him half his trouble), and he is the passive respondent who achieved his macho triumphs in order to please her. But the narrative will reshape the terms of this relationship. By the beginning of the fifth act, every Roman man has, in one way or another, failed Rome. Coriolanus has gone over to the enemy; the patricians and the plebeians have bickered their way into an angry stalemate; and Menenius, the self-proclaimed "lover" of Coriolanus, has been repulsed while attempting to bring him back from the Volscians. Only Volumnia, with her little band of women plus one child, can rescue Rome. Now is the time for her to release her power and her persuasiveness. No surprise that she is able to let loose her fearsome rhetoric upon the son who has been inflamed with her war cries throughout his life. The surprise, however, is that she proclaims peace:

> For either thou
> Must, as a foreign recreant, be led
> With manacles thorough our streets, or else
> Triumphantly tread on thy country's ruin,
> And bear the palm for having bravely shed
> Thy wife and children's blood. . . .
> If I cannot persuade thee
> Rather to show a noble grace to both parts
> Than seek the end of one, thou shalt no sooner
> March to assault thy country than to tread—
> Trust to't, thou shalt not—on thy mother's womb,
> That brought thee to this world.

(5.3.114–26)

If he fails to make peace at this moment, he is trampling on her womb: What more can a mother say? It is a visionary solution that she proposes, potentially redeeming her exercise of power and reversing all that lurid battlefield worship that has animated her rhetoric previously.

We are, however, in a tragedy, and Volumnia's oration on behalf of peace has been rendered obsolete by circumstances around her that, for all her martial intensity, she cannot control. Her son, in the very act of fulfilling what have become her pacifistic biddings, recognizes the consequence:

> Behold, the heavens do ope,
> The gods look down, and this unnatural scene
> They laugh at. O my mother, mother, O!
> You have won a happy victory to Rome;
> But, for your son, believe it, O believe it,
> Most dangerously you have with him prevailed,
> If not most mortal to him.
>
> (5.3.184–90)

A few pages back, I offered my own rather casual claim that "there is something questionable about a man who has the wrong kind of attachment to his mother." Now, nearing the end of the tragedy, it's not just questionable anymore; it's *unnatural*, as Shakespeare contrives here to make this circumstance into the hero's death sentence. The mother's intervention to rescue the son will spell his doom. What was instantly apparent to the son was invisible to the mother: that saving Rome will be a death sentence for Coriolanus, now subject to the wrath and military might of his former enemy Aufidius, who, as we already know, is itching to rid himself of Coriolanus even as an ally. In the larger sense, and with Volumnia at the center of our attention, which she surely is, this is the great tragic mother moment in Shakespeare. The heroic female figure who, for all her heroism, has looked more like a monster of ferocity than a figure of love, arrives at a turn of events where her ferocity can generate an act of love whose benefits will transcend even the mother-son relationship; that act of love inescapably brings about the death of the child she so fiercely loves. Granted, her failure at this moment can be read as the inevitable exclusion of women from power; given my upbringing, however, it strikes me as the condition whereby a woman—a mother—can be elevated to the status of tragic hero.

There's no husband in *All's Well* either, as that coffin onstage at the opening makes clear, but there is also no Volumnia; with no Volumnia and no Coriolanus, the play exhibits a kind of hollow core where the maternal force should lie. We've already observed the opening moments, in which mother, son, and husband get entangled with one another and with death. After about three minutes of stage time at the outset, the mother and son will not appear together until the final scene of the play. The notion of mother is hardly forgotten, however; in fact, it is soon subjected to a rather rigorous close reading that begins with the Countess, mother to the play's principal male character (I avoid the term *hero*, considering that he will reveal himself in the course of the play to be every possible form of obnoxious and undeserving), saying to her protégée and the play's heroine, "You know, Helen, | I am a mother to you" (1.3.132–33). It's not literally true, of course, and the play is unsparing in the presentation of social structures that ought to place the lowly Helena out of the running as any kind of daughter to the Countess. But for that very reason this casual gesture on the Countess's part is all the more admirable, or so it would seem. That's not the way it plays out here, however. "Mine honorable *mistress*," responds Helena, correcting the Countess, who replies insistently,

> Nay, a mother
> Why not a mother? When I said "a mother,"
> Methought you saw a serpent. What's in "mother"
> That you start at it? . . .
> God's mercy, maiden! Does it curd thy blood
> To say I am thy mother?

(1.3.139–50)

It's a wonderful instance of something I like to call Shakespeare's "words in quotation marks"—occasions when characters use words to mean, essentially, the instance of uttering that word, when a word operates more as an example of a speech act than as a means of signification. (Philosophers refer to this as the distinction between *use* and *mention*.) Often, as in this case, it becomes a kind of ping-pong rally between characters, the word itself seemingly turning into an independent object that forces us to stop and focus our attention on its adequacy or inadequacy as a concept and the way in which the same word means different things to different people.

For anyone who has, or has ever had, a mother, the idea summoned up by the Countess that the word itself might be the equivalent of encountering a serpent or having one's blood curdled is, at the very least, startling. We learn very soon, or have guessed already, that the repulsiveness of the designation as Helena experiences it is all about the incest taboo. She doesn't hate mothers per se; rather, she finds herself in the awkward position where the Countess's loving gesture comes up against the fact that Helena is in love with the Countess's son, a circumstance she is cautiously revealing to the Countess in this very conversation. Shakespeare is enabled to accomplish this little bait-and-switch because in the language of his time, unlike our own, relations by marriage could be freely designated with or without the "-in-law" suffix. (See King Lear railing against his "son" Cornwall.) Still, whatever the technicalities of the case may be, a plot that will conclude, after many vicissitudes, with the

Countess as "mother" (in the "in-law" sense) to Helena begins with the designation of this relationship in memorably strong negative language.

All of which is preparing us for the perverse way that this particular mother-wife-son-husband cluster will get played out in *All's Well*. Helena will reveal, in the course of this same conversation, that she is in love with Bertram, but the process is laborious, almost to the point where we think the Countess must be either a bit dim or else unwilling to comprehend the possibility of Helena as her possible daughter-in-law. Once that possibility is made clear via a long, eloquent plea for the honorable quality of her passion for Bertram, the Countess changes the subject and moves the discussion toward the royal court in Paris, the king's ailment, and the possibility that Helena will travel there so as to put her father's medical skills at the king's service. As she well knows, Bertram is at the court. The closest the Countess gets to exploiting the ironies of the situation, the possibility of multiple motives for Helena's travel plans, is to ask— perhaps with an indulgent twinkle in her eye, perhaps not—"This [attempting to cure the king] was your motive for Paris, was it?" (1.3.231). Take special note— fellow irony hunters—of that ". . . *was it?*"

So what kind of mother/mother-in-law is the Countess? For me, this certainly counts as a problem in this Problem Play. The widowed mother does not seek a new husband—we'll get to that exactly contemporary play in a moment— but she also does not (like Volumnia) focus her energies upon her son, who as I stated earlier, does not occupy the same stage space again until the final scene. It's not an accident that Bertram and his mother appear together only at the beginning and the end of the play: Shakespeare has elided the all-important transfer of the Countess's allegiance from mother to mother-in-law *as* mother. In act 1 she could hardly comprehend what Helena had in mind as regards Bertram; by act 3, without mother and son being face to face, she expresses herself to Helena unambiguously: "He was my son, | But I do wash his name out of my blood | And thou art all my child" (3.2.67–69). (Later, she'll say of Helena, "If she had partaken of my flesh and cost me the dearest groans of a mother I could not have owed her a more rooted love" [4.5.10–12].)

It turns out that the principles of family love that underlie the loss of distinction between "daughter" and "daughter-in-law," that is, the welcome reception of one's child's spouse as one's own child, operate imperfectly in this world: The fable is so constructed that the Countess can extend her love either to her son or to her daughter(-in-law) but not both. By all sorts of measures, the Countess will be a very bad mother to Bertram and a very good "mother" to Helena. A mother, it seems, may only be as good a mother as the child she is mothering. Where the offspring is unworthy, can *mother* be transferable? The evidence of *All's Well* is not persuasive. If *Coriolanus* is the Tragedy of the Mother, *All's Well* counts as the Problem Play of the Mother. That hollow core of the maternal in *All's Well* defines the central subject as the mother function in search of an object.

Before we leave this strange play behind . . .

Just so that everyone understands how "all's well that ends well" is not primarily an expression of pure joy, as is sometimes casually assumed, here's a brief selection of times focusing on a decade or so in my younger life when I've had occasion to heave a great sigh of relief and say, "All's well that ends well":

Attaining a level of schooling at which Phys. Ed. was no longer compulsory (1962)

Walking out on a camp counselor job when I'd been hired to do theater but learned when I got there that I was to be the trampoline instructor (1964)

Turning the last page of Robert Burton's *Anatomy of Melancholy*, having read all three volumes from cover to cover to cover to . . . , etc. (1966)

Bidding farewell to Ronald and Nancy Reagan, having spent a full week in their company, some of it alone with them, bickering (1967) (Don't ask.)

Receiving my 1Y deferment from the New Haven draft board (1970)

Success, after several failed attempts, in getting through to my friend DeeDee as to why she shouldn't keep trying to set me up with her sister (1973)

Nixon's resignation (1974)

Nailing down the floating signifier in my case (or attempting to), it seems only fair to expand a little on that portrait of my mother as Volumnia with a kiddie bowling ball. Frumme Katz, as she is named in the earliest document that I can trace, was a passenger on the SS *Samland* ("Steam triple expansion engines, twin screw. Service speed 13 knots . . . Red Star Line, British Flag") departing from Antwerp on the 6th of March 1909 and arriving in New York Harbor twelve days later. She appears on the manifest along with her mother and her older sister and brother. She is listed as age three (plus an illegible fraction). This is the first but certainly not the last piece of unreliable truth in her story. Nor was it the last lie that was told about her age. We have reliable documentation that she was born on August 21 (or possibly 23), 1902, which means that, as she took her initial steps on the North American continent, the littlest Katz passenger was about 6½ years old but passing as three. It seems unwise to assign responsibility for this adjustment to the child herself (had her mother perhaps been told that children under four traveled free?); on the other hand, census records over the next few decades abound in surprises as regards her age, quite independent of this original prevarication and more likely traceable to her own initiative. In the 1920 census, for instance, her age is listed as seventeen, whereas in the 1925 census her age is listed as . . . seventeen. It's reassuring to note from that moment onward she remained perfectly consistent in subtracting four or five years from her real age.

The moral of the story is the moral that we all nowadays, with perhaps a little too much self-assurance, assign to pieces of historiography: Who knows what is true about the past? And in this case, does the intimacy of the son's relation to the mother—the womb thing; think of Volumnia saying that if Coriolanus doesn't make peace he'll be trampling on her womb—promise any sort of reliable authority? Take, for instance, two pieces of information about my mother vouchsafed to me by others. The first was delivered in 1955. A married couple of my parents' age had dropped in on us uninvited—and, I sensed, unwelcome. The lady declared herself to be my father's sister-in-law. I had a primitive, though serviceable, notion of what constituted that relationship but could not shoehorn her into it. I must have had an intuition that this had to do with family secrets, so I had already been made uncomfortable even before she took me aside while the other grown-ups were talking among themselves. "Did you know," she said, looking down at me with an odd smile, "that your mother was a *flapper*?" I was startled and a little disturbed, but completely uncomprehending. Various fish and birds ran through my befuddled consciousness, but absolutely nothing concerning bobbed hair or bathtub gin. The woman who called herself my father's sister-in-law soon abandoned me for the doubtless more responsive company of her fellow adults.

Some thirty years go by, and once again the irregularities of my family structure are in play. I am in the front seat of a car. My half brother, a couple decades senior to me, is taking me to spend a night on his houseboat; I haven't seen him in many years. My mother, who was not *his* mother, has recently died, and this has apparently stimulated in him a one-shot interest in pretending to act like a family. His tone is even more conspiratorial than that of the lady who declared my mother a flapper: "You know, back when I was a teenager, I had a big political argument with Frances. It was August of 1939, and Stalin had just signed the non-aggression pact with Hitler. Can you believe, *she was supporting Stalin?!*" I was only slightly better prepared on this topic than I had been on flappers when I was eleven, but I knew enough to be surprised that an American leftist, a *Jewish* American leftist, would be so orthodox—you should pardon the expression—as to be loyal to Uncle Joe when he seemed to be climbing into bed with the Führer.

What do these stories do to assist me in understanding my mother? It would be helpful, first of all, to know whether they were true. The self-proclaimed sister-in-law was considered in our house to be the very emblem of silliness, whether justly or not I still have no way of knowing. And so far as the half brother is concerned, on that very same automobile ride, he had proudly narrated episodes in which he was deliberately cruel to his dying mother (again, not *my* mother) by telling her that his grades in college were *lower* than they actually were. Let's grant these narrators perfect reliability: In what way do I "know" my mother from these pieces of "evidence"? My mother the flapper: jazz, automobiles, bootleg whiskey, the newly legislated women's right to vote. My mother the communist: the Spanish Civil War, the despotism of the Romanovs, the Triangle Shirtwaist Factory fire.

Does the portrait come into sharper focus if I splice together her own stories, perhaps with the same casual sense of history with which she delivered them to me?

My mother, probably in the immediate post–World War II years, designed, produced prototypes, and may have even gone into production on a bizarre apron/smock with three armholes. I recall her many years later sketching one on the back of an envelope for me: On a flat surface it looked like a work shirt for one and a half people, but, as she explained, if you knew how to don it properly—first arm in the first hole, second arm in the second hole, first arm (again) in the third hole—it provided, she asserted, fabulous coverage without the pesky business of having to tie a belt that forever comes undone.

At some point, circa 1933, on a whim, my mother (she told me) boarded the 20th Century Limited for Chicago in order to attend the Century of Progress World's Fair, for the sole purpose of seeing the fair's most famous attraction, Sally Rand's Fan Dance, in which the willowy lady cavorted about the stage (quite expertly, to judge from the extant films) seemingly in the nude, her body covered merely by huge ostrich feather fans, which she maneuvered tantalizingly front and back. My mother reported some disappointment at the spectacle, either because of the dance itself or because her attendance there didn't fall on one of the many days when the Chicago police came to arrest Ms. Rand and (temporarily) shut the place down. Having seen what she came to see, my mother reboarded the 20th Century Limited and chugged back to Grand Central Station.

Another narrative: My mother, in what may have been her first job, barely out of high school, worked as office help in the Standard Oil Building in Lower

Manhattan, operating a "Multigraph," which was some sort of cross between a typewriter and a printing machine (the 1920 census, in fact, lists her as "Multigraph Opr"). She attracted the attention of one of the very senior figures in the company (surely not John D. Rockefeller; she became shy about naming names), who referred to her as his "little printer's devil." This is exactly the moment of the Teapot Dome scandal, in which a member of President Harding's cabinet ended up going to jail for being bribed into passing federal oil leases to his friends. Until recent years, this was said to be the worst federal government scandal of all time. (A lot they knew!) Some very important and very secret and very criminal communications may have been, according to my mother, circulating in those very offices, possibly inscribed on the very papers that the little devil was printing.

My mother, fresh from divorcing her first husband—that part I knew was true—began to step out into the world beyond Manhattan and Brooklyn. Much of this exodus focused on coastal Florida, where she traveled frequently and stayed for months at a time; a small trove of quite enchanting photographs display her in stylish leisure costumes, in cocktail attire on land and sailor style on ship and shore. But she went north even more than she went south. At some point in the late 1930s she became a true believer in the enterprise of one Dr. Mahlon W. Locke, a wonder-working physician in a field roughly equivalent to what is now called reflexology, who operated out of his modest bungalow in the small town of Williamsburg, Ontario, to which (at the height of the craze) so many hundreds of patients bearing such a variety of ills flocked daily that Dr. Locke had to invent a kind of carousel wheel next to which he would sit stationary while the clients were rotated, one by one, in front of him so that he could do his magic wiggle of their toes, after which, from each patient, he would take a dollar bill and stuff it into his pocket. The craze abated after a few years, but my mother, recounting all this decades later, remained a true believer.

Only a few years earlier (my mother's stories were never consecutive), still New York based, my mother, who prided herself on her adoption of new technologies, became something called a comptometer operator (again, there's the evidence on census records where she is listed as such still in 1940), apparently a rapid sort of adding machine with something vaguely resembling a memory. She rose to the summit of this field, which was employment on the floor of the New York Stock Exchange, where she recorded and calculated transactions. She was on the job, in fact, on October 29, 1929, when sixteen million shares were traded in a single day; as she reported, she was still pressing buttons on her comptometer at 3:00 in the morning on the 30th.

Years later, my mother, as she reported to me, became zealously attached to the journalistic project of Ralph Ingersoll, a hero of the liberal (roughly, non-Communist) left, who founded a New York tabloid newspaper called *PM*, which signaled the purity of its politics by refusing to take advertising on the principle that advertisers, understood by definition as right-leaning Big Bosses, would always dictate editorial policy. With her by then considerable experience in the business world, my mother had high hopes of becoming something like *PM*'s voice of Wall Street. On some occasion of spring cleaning or house moving, I came upon yellowing copies of what must have been the eight or ten issues of *PM* to which she had contributed: The journalistic niche to which she was assigned, it turns out, was knitting. I instantly forgave her for neglecting to mention that.

It hardly needs to be said that between Volumnia and Frances Katz there is a special version of the yawning gap that characterizes all attempts to read Shakespeare and my life together. Volumnia was a widow; my mother was during these years briefly married, then divorced, in short, for most of the time, like her early Roman predecessor, an adult woman on her own. She was in her early forties when she remarried, and I was born a few years later. The comparison may be absurd, but it yields an interesting conclusion. The three-armed apron, the impromptu voyage to see the fan dancer, the instrumentality in a White House scandal, the supporting role in the greatest economic catastrophe the world had ever known: All of this is where a powerful, brilliant woman finds herself if she's not encumbered with a son. What she does when she *is* so encumbered we'll get to, but first, dear reader, you must read about some other Shakespearean mothers, a pair of queens.

Whether the comparison is more or less outlandish than that with Volumnia, I have to report that I can't read either *Macbeth* or *Hamlet* without thinking of my mother as much as I am thinking of Shakespeare. Or, to turn that around so that it looks a little more like legitimate literary criticism, there is nothing in these two extraordinarily capacious masterpieces that summons me as urgently as the subject of mothers and sons. What these monumental fictions point to is the deep mystery, the unknowability, to us as children, of the individual out of whom we have sprung. (It's worth repeating the obvious here: This is a deeply gendered matter. We are looking at the world through the eyes of a male author and, in the present instance, of a male reader of that author. Persons of all gender identities came into the world courtesy of biological females, and the story of this relationship, as well as this enigma of the mother, may be quite different when viewed from the perspective of a female offspring. Or, as I suspect, *not* so different, but that's for others to say.)

Lady Macbeth's motherhood is an ultimately undecipherable enigma. The mystery can be read from the start in her sexually charged self-presentation:

> Come, you spirits
> That tend on mortal thoughts, unsex me here,
> And fill me from the crown to the toe top-full
> Of direst cruelty. Make thick my blood;
> Stop up the access and passage to remorse,
> That no compunctious visitings of nature
> Shake my fell purpose, nor keep peace between
> Th'effect and it. Come to my woman's breasts
> And take my milk for gall, you murd'ring ministers,
> Wherever in your sightless substances
> You wait on nature's mischief!
>
> (1.5.39–49)

We should not overlook the fact that the sexuality she brandishes here is weighted toward the reproductive rather than the erotic. Her breasts are milk-bearing, and as for the "compunctious visitings of nature," I believe they refer to menstruation: Taking the rhetoric down a couple notches, what she is saying, I think, is that she hopes she won't have her period when it's time to murder Duncan. The paradox here, which is the entry point to a deeper maternal paradox, is that she is presenting these elements of her sexuality by declaring her determination that they be negated.

This is conceptual negation, but a couple of scenes later, and this time in the presence of her husband, she takes it a giant step toward something quite actual:

> I have given suck, and know
> How tender 'tis to love the babe that milks me;
> I would, when it was smiling in my face,
> Have plucked my nipple from his boneless gums
> And dashed the brains out, had I so sworn
> As you have to this.
>
> (1.7.55–60)

Perhaps not so actual. To review the data, or what passes for data in fictions: The play's most famous enigma, which has occupied detective story–minded readers since at least Goethe's time, is often expressed in the question, "How

Many Children Had Lady Macbeth?" Leaving aside the matter of quantity, the more pressing question becomes whether she had children at all. This early pronouncement is launched in the conditional mode: *If* I had made an oath as you (Macbeth) have, in your case, to murder Duncan, *then*. . . . But the fundamental fact, not subject to an *if* (remember Touchstone in *As You Like It*: "much virtue in if"; there sure is), is "I have given suck"; in other words, she is still speaking in the mode of female reproductive flow. *Has* she "given suck"? No little flesh-and-blood Macbeths are to be found anywhere. Late in the play, Macduff, à propos of the murder of his family under orders of Macbeth, will say to Malcolm, "He has no children," but it is impossible to be certain whether "he" in this sentence is Macbeth, who is capable of murdering children because he has none, or Malcolm, who is capable of far too casual a reportage of the grisly fact because he, childless as well, can't appreciate the horror of it.

For all the fame of this enigma, it seems to me that the mystery matter in Lady Macbeth's speech, interesting as it is, gets definitively upstaged by the framework in which she raises the subject of these hypothetical children. We're in the realm of analogy or metaphor, in which there is a "real" term to which an equation is being made; a hypothetical is being placed in parallel to an actual. If, says Lady Macbeth, I had made an oath to kill the king, nothing would stop me from fulfilling it, the implication being that some kind of moral rectitude governs the fulfillment of oaths, no matter what they are. (Heavy parallels here to a situation taking place due east of Scotland in Shakespeare's Denmark.) She is so upfront about the *no matter what* aspect that she proposes by way of parallelism a hypothetical oath that is among the few things that Shakespeare's audience can imagine as more horrible than killing a king. Monarchs, after all, have been murdered quite regularly both in real history and on the stage of Shakespeare's own theater; the particular act that Lady Macbeth proposes—a mother detaching an infant from her breast and dashing its brains out—not so much, one supposes.

The analogy, in short, virtually eclipses its "real" referent; killing Duncan has been temporarily upstaged as we find ourselves in the presence of a mother who, according to her own testimony, has had at least one child, whom she has breastfed, and she pronounces herself prepared to murder it. It's a child's nightmare. Elsewhere in these pages, I talked about the "changeling child" of *A Midsummer Night's Dream*, who never appears in the play but is the pivot point of all the action between Titania and Oberon; I even suggested half-facetiously that the changeling child is the author of the play, who has conceived of a narrative that revolves entirely around him. Here we have another phantom child, and I—once a child, myself, as it happens—am being presented with a monstrous act of infanticide that is wrapped up in the further monstrosity of radical uncertainty as to whether such a child existed or not. The question mark over the child's existence does nothing to diminish the horror of its violent death at the hands of its mother. In fact, since I for one gravitate immediately to any child in fiction, believing unconditionally that I am that child, the "how many children had Lady Macbeth" question points to my own nonexistence. Am I the child whose brains were dashed out, or am I the child who doesn't exist? The whole experience is a perfect nightmare for me because it is exactly in the form of a dream (a midwinter night's dream, complete with witches, etc.?), that is, something that feels very real in the moment but proves on reflection not to be real, *or* . . . ?

What Shakespeare has done by way of complicating—let's call it three-dimensionalizing—Lady Macbeth as mother/monster-mother/nonmother is to stuff the play with (more or less) *real* children. They are introduced, literally and on stage, in what may be larger numbers and with more prominence than any other Shakespearean play: Fleance and young Macduff, of course, but also the bloody child and crowned child of the pageant that the Witches stage for Macbeth in act 4. The final element in that pageant, a sequence of eight kings (plus Banquo), also contributes to this sense that, whereas Lady Macbeth may have no children, Scotland abounds in this vital dynastic resource. In fact, Holinshed's chronicles, the play's principal source, notes that nearly all the Stuart kings between the time of Banquo and that of James were underage when they acceded to the throne. This passage, joined with the dynastic history that Shakespeare closely followed, provides an intriguing perspective on the Scottish historical scene: All these child monarchs seem to suggest both the potential fragility of the royal institution and the fecundity of the royal family.

It's not just that a bevy of real children in the play renders the question mark of Lady Macbeth's motherhood more vivid; it's also the obvious fact that children are the inescapable currency of royal dominance. No member of the play's original audience (except, perhaps, those who were themselves children) would have forgotten what it had meant for decades of Elizabeth's rule to have no eligible child that would in orderly fashion grow up to assume the crown. And those with longer memories or knowledge of history would be well aware that this problem stretched far back into the time of Henry VIII or even to the moment a couple of centuries earlier when Edward III's eldest son predeceased him and left Richard II as a child monarch. (In fact, Shakespeare's own tetralogies of history plays, all written before *Macbeth*, cover exactly this period of problematic succession.)

Whether one reads the Shakespearean history or the "real" history of Henry VIII, one comes away with a quite clear sense that the job of a monarch was twofold: to rule the kingdom wisely and to provide an heir. It's not clear that anyone in England had accomplished that double feat for a couple of hundred years, or perhaps ever. No surprise, then, that Shakespeare creates the scene near the beginning of the play in which Macbeth and Banquo meet the Witches and receive a prophecy that Macbeth will *become* king, whereas Banquo ("lesser than Macbeth and greater") will *beget* kings. This is the dichotomy around which the play is built, the more pointedly so because audience members knew that their own present-day James I (James VI of Scotland) was descended from Banquo and Fleance. The issue becomes explicit when Macbeth reflects on the Witches' prophecies and bemoans the fact that

> Upon my head they placed a fruitless crown,
> And put a barren sceptre in my gripe,
> Thence to be wrench'd with an unlineal hand,
> No son of mine succeeding.

(3.1.60–63)

Once he proceeds from here to commission further murders in order to secure permanence, the matter of Lady Macbeth's phantom motherhood starts to edge toward being the absurd pivot around which the whole tragedy is built. Is Macbeth in the grip of a fantasy, ready to murder Banquo and, as he hopes, Fleance, so that some imaginary son of his can succeed him as king of Scotland? Is that "son of mine" the child whom Lady Macbeth had nursed— and bludgeoned? Or perhaps that is the child that, early in the play, is conceived in some offstage coitus after Macbeth has put aside his moral wavering and, as a result of his wife's encouragements, ecstatically regained his macho resolve to murder the king, declaring,

> Bring forth men-children only:
> For thy undaunted mettle should compose
> Nothing but males.

(1.7.73–75)

This is what he needed to get his engine going. When we look at Lady Macbeth–as-mother, we are left with a bloodstained question mark.

On to a mother who was definitely a mother but no less enigmatic for that reason. An obsessively articulate and manipulative son, a dominating husband who needs to suppress an explosive secret, and another husband whose return from the dead affords him what at least appear to be superhuman powers of truth-telling: Apart from sounding like the promo for a soap opera, all this doesn't leave Gertrude much room to speak for herself or, indeed, to reveal

herself. Question for a Shakespeare parlor game: Only once does Gertrude
challenge a man's wishes and succeed in getting her own way. When is that?
Answer:

GERTRUDE
The queen carouses to thy fortune, Hamlet.
HAMLET   Good madam.
CLAUDIUS   Gertrude, do not drink.
GERTRUDE
I will, my Lord. I pray you, pardon me. [She drinks.]
CLAUDIUS [aside]
It is the poisoned cup. It is too late.

(5.2.241–44)

It is indeed too late, but even more striking than her nearly five acts of deference
to male authority is the resistance (courtesy, of course, of her author) to revealing
her inner life. Lady Macbeth had an enigma; Gertrude *is* an enigma. And we,
or I'll be more modest and say *I*—are left to imagine the nature of the mother's
inner life, to "know" the mother—those scare quotes designed to remind us
that this "knowledge" is the theatrical equivalent of a legal fiction. It is, to be
sure, a necessary fiction in these pages because our premise is precisely to cross
between the real and the fictional as though there were no formalities at the
border. The undeniable fact is that Shakespeare is exceptionally stingy with
offering Gertrude's opportunities to present herself.

Sometimes numbers can help tell the story. Gertrude's part is remarkably
brief, even when the text of the play is presented in its composite form and
therefore becomes the longest of all Shakespeare's playtexts. Her part is less
than one-quarter the length of Cleopatra's, half the length of Volumnia's, and
only a little more than half the length of Lady Macbeth's; even Ophelia (and
this surprised me) speaks more than Gertrude. It's not just about the numbers,
of course, or about what she says. The fact is that Shakespeare fractures our
access to Gertrude, affording us sequences of disconnected glimpses, whether
from her own speeches (themselves few and often murky) or from the accounts
of her offered by the dominating trio of men who surround her.

Regarding Gertrude, and particularly the inner life of Gertrude, Shakespeare
doesn't give us a lot to go on. The very first time she is addressed, by Claudius—
"Our sometime sister, now our queen" (1.2.8)—the very basis of her identity is
ambiguous, and with a whiff of incest. That same whiff is repeated when the
Ghost's sexual accusations against Claudius ("that incestuous, that adulterate
beast . . ." [1.5.42]) encompass, obliquely at least, the possibility of Gertrude's

relations with Claudius before she became a widow. In the play-within-a-play episode, Shakespeare offers us Gertrude-surrogates by contradiction: Hecuba, profoundly faithful to a murdered husband, and the Player Queen, who equates second marriage with murder of the first husband. And in the report by Rosencrantz and Guildenstern of the queen's reaction to Hamlet's violent outburst at the play, her words—if they *are* her words ("Your [i.e., Hamlet's] behavior has struck her into amazement and admiration" [3.2.308]—are subject to completely opposite meanings, as Hamlet twists them when he receives the message. All of this is Gertrude, as we might say, in the passive voice.

Then there are those few occasions when Gertrude actually seems to make an assertion, for instance, in her first piece of advice to her son, "let thine eye look like a friend on Denmark" (1.2.69). But does she mean on the *country* of Denmark or, as would be quite common in Elizabethan usage, on the *king* of Denmark? Much depends on that distinction. She is quite silent during the long discussion between Claudius and Polonius about the possibility that Hamlet's madness can be traced to his disappointed love for Ophelia, a topic on which (unlike matters of state, perhaps) Gertrude might be called upon as an expert. Her verdict: "I doubt it is no other than the main, | His father's death and our o'er hasty marriage" (2.2.56–57), a conclusion that would seem absolutely definitive, except for the fact that it's completely impossible to know whether she is thereby taking some responsibility for this terrible alteration in her son's mental state. Her phrasing is maddeningly unrevealing; the information value is about as low as it is possible to be, reducing all the current perplexities of the Danish court to "the main," whatever that means. Then there is the invitation to Hamlet to sit next to her at the play, which he declines in favor of Ophelia (along with some sexual jesting in regard to the girl). Was the invitation a mere formality, or was Gertrude responding to the matter, so recently under discussion, of Hamlet's possible lovesickness in regard to Ophelia? We don't know, because Gertrude lets it go without comment.

Then, however, Gertrude delivers the most revealing utterance we have heard from her hitherto. In response to the Player Queen's protestations about marrying again, she says, "The Lady doth protest too much, methinks" (3.2.217). It has become such a cliché of English speech that we overlook the sheer oddity of this assertion, particularly given the fact that Gertrude so rarely offers an opinion on anything. The Player Queen has, as we've seen, made it clear that, should she be widowed, she will not under any circumstances marry again. Both of the player monarchs have made rather a big deal out of this, not only about the idea of widows marrying again but also about the sincerity of vows in general and the likelihood of individuals sticking to their promises, whatever those promises may be. (This always seems to me drawn from Hamlet's—and not Gertrude's—stream of consciousness, since he obsesses both about second marriages and about vows.)

Gertrude's own response to these pompous speeches is with a piece of proverbial wisdom ("Too much protesting makes the truth suspected"),* but it's a particular kind of wisdom that bears scrutiny, given the limited chances we have to observe Gertrude's interior processes. If this line has proven very durable in post-Shakespearean (in particular, post-Freudian) times, it's doubtless because we are accustomed to the idea not just that people don't always say what they mean but that their efforts to conceal their true meaning by proclaiming the opposite, when scrutinized knowledgeably, may turn out to expose the very truth they are attempting to conceal. If Gertrude is reading the Player Queen in this way, we have to grant her a consciousness quite different from, even opposite to, that of the passive and noncommittal bystander she has previously seemed to be. After all, both men in her life are definitely overprotesters—that is, they talk a lot, don't always mean what they say, sometimes lie. (It's of a piece with another of Gertrude's few interventions, when she cuts Polonius short with "More matter, with less art," when he has been overprotesting in his verbose windup to revealing, as he imagines, the cause of Hamlet's madness.) It is, of course, noteworthy that Gertrude reveals this hitherto hidden consciousness in response *not* to the two dominant "real" males who surround her but to her double inside the fictional "Murder of Gonzago," when that fictional character happens to be speaking on a subject with which Gertrude has some personal connection.

If the queen is opening up a bit here, that may be because we are on the way to an encounter that promises to blow the various sorts of cover under which she has been operating. That change is in the air is signaled before we ever get to the queen's chamber, when Hamlet, on his way to the meeting that his mother had requested, says,

> Let not ever
> The soul of Nero enter this firm bosom,
> Let me be cruel, not unnatural.
> I will speak daggers to her, but use none.

> (3.2.376–79)

---

*Proverb P614, in A *Dictionary of the Proverbs in England in the Sixteenth and Seventeenth Centuries*, ed. M. P. Tilley (Ann Arbor: University of Michigan Press, 1950).

Nero, of course, murdered his mother, and I can only read this speech of Hamlet's as announcing a giant leap into a wholly different modality of the play's actions and the relations among the principal characters. If we have been following Gertrude as an enigmatic player in the midst of a chess game with somewhat obscure rules, it appears that at this point the phase of enigma will be over, in favor of something more like crime and punishment. Such a change is also signaled by the fact that immediately before the closet scene Claudius comes out of his own closet and reveals, though only to us, both his guilt and his guilty conscience.

Even so, I am always astonished that Gertrude's possible complicity, which the play situates in a realm that I would call shadowy (adultery? incest? murder? none of the above?), is suddenly represented by Hamlet as punishable by death, via the Nero analogy. When Hamlet says, "You go not till I set you up a glass | Where you may see the inmost part of you" and Gertrude replies, "What wilt thou do? Thou wilt not murder me?" (3.4.20–23), the equation between unveiling the enigma of the mother—and there is always an enigma of the mother, a significance beyond the child's capacity to understand its origins, despite her role as the child's origin—and killing her becomes explicit for the characters and the audience both. The "inmost part" of Gertrude is exactly what the play has previously withheld from us; the question is whether Hamlet is a reliable informant on the subject and whether, having spent so much time offering up his moral consciousness to us, he is in any way a reliable guide to right and wrong, at least regarding his mother.

Debate all this as you will. But when Hamlet and Gertrude are finally one on one, it becomes very difficult, for me at least, to keep seeing a rosy glow around the hero. The conversation begins with that flexible use of terms for family relations that we've already observed in connection with Helena and the Countess, though the specific relation here is different:

GERTRUDE
Hamlet, thou hast thy father much offended.
HAMLET
Mother, you have my father much offended.

(3.4.10–11)

"Stepfather" was already in general usage, but, as was the case with "mother-in-law" in *All's Well*, the relations between the persons need to be understood as perilously labile, a purpose in which the language was complicit. Hamlet wants no part of this flexibility, however, and he begins his attack on his mother by nailing down her identity in no uncertain terms: "You are the Queen, your husband's brother's wife" (3.4.16), in effect laying the accusation of incest upon her (after all, Henry VIII's case for the annulment of his marriage to Catherine of Aragon, from which sprung the whole separation of the English church from Rome, was based on the idea that marriage to a deceased brother's wife was incestuous). Very soon, though, his account of her "inmost part" turns into a graver and more direct accusation. Hamlet has killed Polonius (in my view, with shocking casualness and nonchalance, comparable in certain ways to the later case of Rosencrantz and Guildenstern, of which more later), and when Gertrude quite rightly refers to that as "a bloody deed," Hamlet responds:

> A bloody deed. Almost as bad, good mother,
> As kill a king and marry with his brother.
>
> (3.4.29–30)

Gertrude is left dumbfounded to repeat, "As kill a king . . . ?" The accusation is so preposterous that it develops no traction. In answer to Gertrude's quite straightforward "What have I done?" Hamlet can only respond with extravagant nonspecifics:

>   Such an act
> That blurs the grace and blush of modesty,
> Calls virtue hypocrite, takes off the rose
> From the fair forehead of an innocent love
> And sets a blister there, makes marriage-vows
> As false as dicers' oaths—O, such a deed
> As from the body of contraction plucks
> The very soul, and sweet religion makes
> A rhapsody of words.
>
> (3.4.41–49)

A rhapsody of words, indeed. Gertrude's supposed crime is as nonspecific as her identity has remained throughout the play. Hamlet responds not by naming a specific act that she has committed but by shifting the evidence in this suddenly mounted trial from words to pictures—that is, adducing what we are to assume are the locket portraits of the two kings that he and she are wearing around their necks—as though the mere sight of Gertrude's two husbands as represented in portraits, to which Hamlet provides some heavily judgmental captions, will bring her to a confession of whatever crimes it may be that he wishes to lay at her door.

The surprising thing is that it works, at least up to a point:

>   O Hamlet, speak no more:
> Thou turn'st mine eyes into my very soul;

And there I see such black and grainèd spots
As will not leave their tinct. . . .
These words, like daggers, enter in mine ears;
No more, sweet Hamlet!

(3.4.80–88)

Clearly, it works *too* well in the opinion of the Ghost, who materializes at this moment, "his tardy son to chide." The Ghost, after all, had warned specifically against this possible outcome of his return from the dead and his manifestation before his son:

Taint not thy mind, nor let thy soul contrive
Against thy mother aught: leave her to heaven
And to those thorns that in her bosom lodge,
To prick and sting her.

(1.5.85–89)

Two admonitions, both of which Hamlet has conspicuously failed to heed. But what exactly is Gertrude confessing *to*? Though the closet scene may have promised to render everything explicit in such a way that the queen would finally reveal the particulars of her inner life, along with a clearer sense of her responsibility, if any, in those possible crimes (incest, adultery, murder, and the like), or at least her viewpoint in regard to them, no such thing happens here.

What, then, exactly *are* those "black and grainèd spots"? Gertrude certainly cops to *something*, but what? I have two answers to this question, which stand in a somewhat jagged relation to each other. The first is that we don't know—and can't know—the answer, that the Mother as she is inscribed by the Son remains a question mark throughout. What she is thinking when she says that Hamlet has gone mad because of "the main" ("his father's death and our o'er hasty marriage"); or what she is thinking when she hears those heavy-handed speeches about second marriages and says, "The Lady doth protest too much"; or what recognitions she is having now as Hamlet forces her to reflect upon her life: This is closed to us. The mother is definitively an enigma to the son.

The second answer to the question what are those "black and grainèd spots" is, on the face of it, a very simple one: Those black and grainèd spots are the mother's sexuality. Elsewhere in this volume, à propos of *King Lear*, I ask what a father *does* exactly beyond the procreative act. That matter is full of uncertainty: *Pater semper incertus est*. The mother, on the other hand, is, on these terms at least, *certa*, in fact, *certissima*. She engages in the sex act and creates the child, after which, at least in the imagination of the son, sexuality is meant to drift out of the picture. The fable of *Hamlet*, though it may foreground power, politics, and dynastic struggle, comes down to being a narrative in which an adult son, whose origins in the sex act are tucked away a few decades in the past and associated with a highly idealized paternal relationship, is now, owing to the particulars of the plot, forced to recognize that his mother's sexuality is as alive as it was when he was conceived. These two answers to the question of Gertrude's "black and grainèd spots" fit together in the sense that once the answer to the enigma is that she was in fact an erotic, desiring subject, then the door needs to be shut on the whole question of her inner life. Shakespeare, one might say, colludes with Hamlet in that shutdown as much as is possible. As, in these pages, do I—and I'm not referring merely to Gertrude.

The truth is, I don't like Hamlet all that much. I don't mean *Hamlet*—the play's a dandy. I mean Hamlet. Part of it is the tortured Romantic soul thing, part of it the Laurence Olivier "This is the story of a man who could not make up his mind" thing. I tend to think that the eighteenth and nineteenth centuries hijacked a deeply problematic narrative in which no one was to be viewed as wholly heroic or admirable (just like the other plays Shakespeare was writing in those years, for instance, *Measure for Measure*) and grafted their own—what shall I call it?—romantic self-hatred on to it. It may be, of course, that my *Hamlet* is merely a relic of the now passé late-twentieth-century *No Exit*, *Waiting for Godot* thing. Perhaps it's just that I feel as though my world and I have had too much experience with manipulative egomaniacs—the kind who hear voices from the beyond and grant themselves blanket permission in the here and now.

Personally, I'm rooting for Horatio. It's nice, of course, that he survives and lives to tell the story, without which there would be no story. But more than that, it's his quietly receptive sensitivity. I confess that this impression of mine is largely built into one moment in the final scene. Hamlet is recounting his miraculous escape from Claudius's plot to arrange for the English king to kill him, and he is clearly very pleased with himself at the cleverness of his strategy in (quite unnecessarily, in my view) substituting Rosencrantz and Guildenstern as victims. All Horatio says in response is, "So Guildenstern and Rosencrantz go to it" (5.2.57). To me, this speaks volumes about the way that ordinary folk, morally speaking neither heroes nor villains, persons like Horatio, like me, or even like the accessories to power politics at the Danish court, can be easily wiped off the map as collateral damage in the operations of charismatic big shots. Hamlet clearly hears something in Horatio's tone that suggests he is being challenged, to which he responds defensively, "Why, man, they did make love to this employment." Did they? Tom Stoppard and I are not so sure.

It's the latter phases of the closet scene, after the Ghost has come and gone, that display a Hamlet who descends into a realm that one might even call despicable. He has already reduced his mother to near collapse on grounds that, as we've seen, are at best ill-defined. After all, the ambiguity of Gertrude's responses to him, in addition to being, as I've suggested, part of the enigmatic quality of her utterances throughout the play, may also be attributable to the fact that it's not so very clear what it is exactly that she has done wrong. The play presents us with not a shred of evidence that she was aware of the murder, let alone that she colluded in it, and throwing around the term "incest" seems like very special pleading indeed. Gertrude's "crime" is that Hamlet cannot bear to think that his widowed mother could enter into another sexual and marital relation, and this sentiment Shakespeare establishes in all its passionate rage with "O that this too too sullied flesh . . ." all the way back in the first act, before Hamlet has even heard that there is a Ghost with a tale to tell about his father's death.

Reflect on this while hearing Hamlet, who has already reduced his mother to staring at the "black and grainèd spots" in her soul, continue in his attack:

HAMLET   Mother, for love of grace,
   Lay not that flattering unction to your soul,
   That not your trespass, but my madness speaks:
   It will but skin and film the ulcerous place,
   Whiles rank corruption, mining all within,
   Infects unseen. Confess yourself to heaven;
   Repent what's past; avoid what is to come;
   And do not spread the compost on the weeds,
   To make them ranker. Forgive me this my virtue;
   For in the fatness of these pursy times
   Virtue itself of vice must pardon beg,
   Yea, curb and woo for leave to do him good.
GERTRUDE
   O Hamlet, thou hast cleft my heart in twain.

$$(3.4.140–52)$$

He goes on to offer her lessons in the practice of sexual detoxification in relation to Claudius. I shudder when I read these speeches; Gertrude somehow buys it, but I don't. If we as readers/viewers have maintained a shred of—what shall I call it?—objectivity, in other words, the ability to see the action of this play through our own eyes rather than exclusively through Hamlet's eyes, then the torture that the son is inflicting upon the mother here becomes unbearable. What is her "trespass"? Which exactly is the "ulcerous place," and what is the "rank corruption"? For what, exactly, should she "repent"? In what sense is Hamlet himself "virtue" and Gertrude "vice," and how could anything in this speech be construed as his begging her pardon rather than, as it actually is, brutalizing her? What circumstances could justify any son addressing his mother in these terms?

That last rhetorical question will perhaps have laid my cards on the table, have justified my own attempt to accomplish what I have described as impossible, that is, unraveling the enigma of the mother.

My mother, as I am able to recall her, which is to say not much younger than age fifty, was barely over five feet tall. She was—again, for as far back as my memory travels—decidedly overweight, like me. Unlike me, she was a heavy cigarette smoker and quite unrepentant about it. I can recall in my grade school years occasions when she got seriously dolled up for some event, mostly courtesy of her impressive gifts at the sewing machine, but actual purchases of dress-up couture or accessories were rare. She prided herself on saving money by never frequenting beauty parlors or nail salons—the money saved, she said, helped pay for my private school. (No pressure . . .) On the first occasion when she attended an evening event for parents at this school and concluded (correctly) that these were likely to be richer folks than us, her accommodation was to purchase a more expensive brand of cigarettes than her regular smokes; how she went on to display this marker of wealth I have no idea. To her credit, though, I know about it because she told me afterward, laughingly, by way of self-irony. That combination—the ineradicable smoking habit, the awkward gesture at class jumping, and the joke at her own expense—is as good an introduction to my mother as any.

It's certainly not a complete introduction, though. There exists a small cache of photographs, many of them with dates in a handwriting not her own, all between 1929 and 1940: These depict a woman with whom I can't say I'm familiar. This lady appears quite glamorous, in terms of her coiffure, her fashion choices, and the milieux in which she gets photographed. She appears in front of vine-covered country cottages or else townhouses with big pre-Depression-era automobiles parked in front of them; in one case she is on the deck of what appears to be a small ship and wearing a costume that evokes a sailor suit while being perfectly acceptable should the vessel's destination include cocktail hour at a chic country club.

At the other end of her life, once she was widowed, she shut down rather decisively; if I am less detailed in my reportage, it's partly because I had left New York and wasn't often with her and partly because even forty years later it's painful to remember. She stayed in the apartment smoking, watching game shows on TV, and religiously reading the *New York Post*, apparently not noticing that it was no longer a liberal paper (as it had stood, solo, among the city's dailies in earlier years) but now the scandal sheet excreta of Rupert Murdoch. Visitors, apart from me, were unwelcome; when I was in New York and a friend whom I was meeting in the lobby asked if he could use our bathroom, I had to direct him to a coffee shop down the street.

I am doing my best here to avoid any gesture of mythmaking, whether in the direction of glamour or that of squalor, knowing that she herself would aggressively shut down the slightest sign of either awe or pity that might have come her way, in the 1930s or 1970s respectively. Then, too, I don't feel competent to write her solo biography. We've already heard about episodes in her life pre-me; now, after this brief glimpse at her on her own, a few glimpses at what it meant to grow up under her care. Whether any of this will lay bare the enigma of the mother, it is difficult to say; at least, though, to bring the matter back to Shakespeare, it may signal why it is, given my own life experience, that I dare to call Hamlet despicable.

A view from three different perspectives.

The first is drawn from a phase of childhood—I hope it was brief, since the act I'm going to chronicle is simply unimaginable to me and I refuse to see carryover to any other phase of my life—in which I shoplifted. Again, it's the summer cottage, so I'm not yet eleven, and I have a new friend, who is a little bit wild. He visits us for a weekend, and since he shows an interest in my mother's china collection, she decides to take us to one of her favorite Westchester antique shops. I'm supposing (though I can't actually remember this) that Ronnie had already boasted to me of walking into stores and slipping merchandise in his pockets. In the backseat of the car on the way to the antique shop I volunteer to him, in a whisper, that in this very crowded and unsurveiled warehouse, which I knew well, it would be easy to get away with pocketing a few choice items. It was, and we did. I won't pretend to remember exactly what I took. I think there were three pieces, one of which was a little crystal dumbbell, which must have tickled my fancy because the idea of a crystal dumbbell struck me as bizarre; the other pieces were probably side dishes from a china service. Ronnie had his own hoard, about which I remember nothing. He was duly dropped off at his parents' house on the way back, and I, with pockets not exactly bulging but definitely encumbered, found myself home again. What was I going to do with these pieces? They weren't useful for anything, and they could hardly be displayed. I hid them in some remote corner of a bedroom closet.

A few mornings later, I awoke to the sight on my bedside table of my three thefts, arrayed (or so it seemed to me) as though in a shop window display of criminality. My punishment, besides a look of speechless rage, I recall as being played out in multiple phases. My mother announced that she would *not* simply return the objects to her friend the antique dealer: That would be too easy (on me? on her?). Instead, she would, with me in tow, return to the shop, where I would confess my crime and apologize. My mother would then ceremoniously pay for the three objects, such that I could witness the economic outcome of my act; allowance would, of course, be suspended indefinitely. The final consequence, upon returning home, was that I was lectured on my terrible taste in antiques: The china was *dreck* of utterly trivial pedigree, nothing like the objects in her own collection (was I raised in a barn?), and as for the crystal dumbbell, which, I learned, functioned as a knife rest, it was many years before my mother ceased to point them out to me in all their vulgar profusion every time we came across them in an antique shop, which was often. None of the stolen property was ever seen again.

Around the time I was finishing junior high school and showing strong interest in my English classes, my mother took me aside when no one else was home and revealed that for some considerable time she had been writing a novel. It was a secret; only I was allowed to know about it, and I was forbidden to speak of it to anyone. Sadly, the manuscript has disappeared, but, in physical form, at least, it remains vivid in my recollection. Even for quite casual communications, say, sending me a recipe for cheese blintzes when I was at Oxford in my twenties, my mother produced something she referred to as her "fine Spencerian hand," a canon of penmanship with an abundance of whorls and loops and capital letters that require many superfluous strokes. It is a handwriting that occupies a great deal of space on the page. Not only did she choose to compose in longhand (though the house possessed a typewriter, which I had mastered already to the limited extent that I ever would), but she also avoided 8½ × 11 sheets, preferring the many many pages of a miniature loose-leaf notebook of a kind that housewives used when they collected recipes. In fact, she *was* a housewife and *did* collect recipes on the very same little sheets of paper—those Oxford-bound secrets of her cheese blintzes, for instance.

Between the loops and whorls, on the one hand, and the constant turning of tiny pages, on the other, reading my mother's novel was not easy. Not that it mattered, exactly: The dissemination of this novel, which was entirely limited to my mother and me, was more like the oral composition that we now understand to be at the heart of the Homeric epics than anything in a form destined for the printing press; it existed as a live conversation between the

The story starts here: Falstaff, Prince Hal, and the chair that has followed the author around for sixty years.

The author's father in plus fours, c. 1927. Impeccably dressed, but not for the beach.

Seeing Peter Brook's production of *A Midsummer Night's Dream* seven times, the author never tired of Bottom's phallus and Mendelssohn's "Wedding March." Photo: Reg Wilson © Royal Shakespeare Company, 1970.

The author in the midst of performing Bottom's Dream: He seems to be missing something.

The author's mother, newly divorced from her first husband, seems to be airborne, but who's the gentleman in the homburg who's keeping her afloat?

The family's summer bungalow. The walkway on the left was the site of *both* the disastrous kiddie bowling match *and* the mysterious revelation that the author's mother was a "flapper." The cowering figure up against the house may, or may not, be the author.

FINAL EDITION

The New Have

155TH YEAR—NO. 333   NEW HAVEN CONN. 06503, MONDAY, DE

Co
In

Mir

CAPE TOWN,
(AP) — A Sout
with the transpla
25-year-old girl
blood announced
feeling much bett
Louis Washkan
nanian-born bus
able to speak 33
medical break-th
tion. The tubes t
were removed fr
permitting him to
words since Sund
But he remaine
period at what
Hospital called th
human heart tran
Heart specialist
world were waiti
Washkansky's bo
cept or reject the
Miss Ann Darvall,
machine operator

Register Photo by Stuart Lander

California Governor Here For Visit

California Gov. Ronald Reagan, accompanied by his wife and Leonard Barkan, an associate Chubb Fellow, walks through Yale campus this morning with Timothy Dwight College Master Thomas Bergin, right. They were en route to press conference at which Reagan defended his record in California.

Reagan Hard | Small Growth Found

"All's Well That Ends Well," but it took too long to get to the end. The author in 1967 hosting a weeklong visit of Ronald and Nancy Reagan to Yale.

The author and his cousin, taking the long view on Shakespeare's *Winter's Tale*.

Shakespeare and Michelangelo on the same page: *Night* in the Medici Chapel. "Not only the stillness of one sleeping, but the grief and melancholy of one who has lost a great and honored possession." Photo: Erich Lessing / Art Resource, NY.

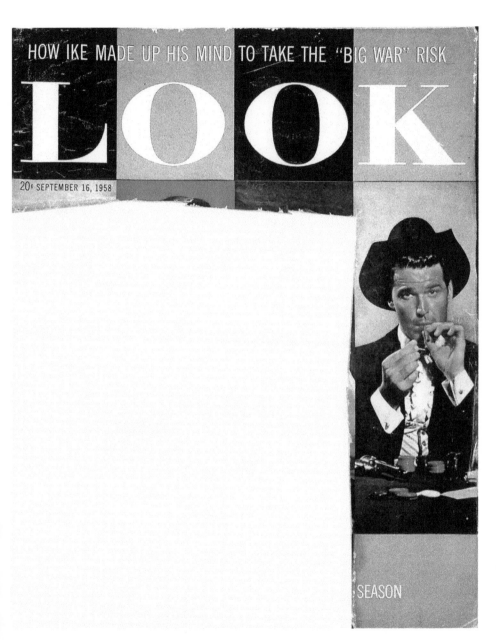

Look magazine cover, 1958, after the author had trimmed it for his viewing pleasure.

Not kings but queens. Coco Montrese and Alyssa Edwards in their full "realness" as Black Swan and White Swan.

two of us. Nevertheless, when I think now of its physical form, I realize that the medium was itself delivering quite a bit of message. This flashy handwriting was, as I now see, letter production such as my mother had been taught when she was an immigrant child at public school on the Lower East Side of Manhattan. Fifty years later and, as it seemed, in exaggerated form for this precious manuscript of hers, she was creating a frozen-in-amber replica of something from her childhood. It wasn't just the replica of an alphabet; it was a replica of the extraordinary distance she had traveled, first from the shtetl to Ellis Island and then from Ellis Island to her own particular version of an aspirational American bourgeoisie.

That handwriting was itself, though my mother probably didn't realize it, telling part of the story. Her novel—and I am recounting it many decades later without direct access to the manuscript or to her for all these years—was all about a man who wanted to live his life entirely as though he had always and even ancestrally belonged in the world of the upper class, which he did not. To whatever extent he passed as such, it was through his own strenuous efforts. He wasn't, in my mother's novel, a particularly good man: These struggles of assimilation were essentially deceptions. She did not credit him for the educational leaps—I think he became a lawyer, maybe even a judge—that made this attempt at assimilation possible (say, learning to write a "fine Spencerian hand"); rather, she blamed him for the dishonesty at the heart of his misguided ambition. Only now in writing this do I realize that she was painting a jagged sort of self-portrait.

What happens to this man in her novel I cannot remember. Perhaps nothing much. Plot is always more difficult than character (dialogue most difficult of all), and it's clear that what fascinated her was the problem of her problematic hero rather than his destiny. And this problem, I now realize, turned into a kind of education for me. She taught me to share her fascination, to be on the lookout for, as it were, would-be aristocrats. This coincided with the moment when I was entering a famous private day school, which was dream territory for the kind of sleuthing that my mother's novel inspired. At my school—I loved it and still do, in recollection—something like 90 percent of the students were Jewish, but the whole place was run in emulation of the kinds of New England prep schools that, at least some decades earlier if not still, would have burned themselves down rather than admit a Bernstein, or a Barkan. My mother never identified her problematic main character as a Jew, but even as a child I understood that this drama of assimilation was about *us*. So a school full of Jewish boys being taught by a bunch of ostentatiously self-identifying Episcopalians in imitation of Groton and St. Paul's, themselves imitating Eton and Harrow, was, depending on how you chose to look at it, either a puzzle box of debatable identities begging to be decoded or a machine designed to instruct boys whose ambition was exactly like that of my mother's hero. Or both. To a kid like me in 1958 none of it was that cut and dried; what I knew, however, was that I had at home a brilliant co-conspirator in decoding at least some of the mysteries of my adolescent existence and reflecting on my own motives along the way. Nor was it only about the enigmas of social class: I was being taught how to look behind—and delight in—all the ways in which projected personalities might be fictions.

There was also the continuing life in *my* life of one particular phrase from the play; it produced a little Shakespearean land mine, call it a delayed explosion, that popped out from this novel *à deux* of my mother's. In speaking of her story and in the words she composed on those mini-pages, she always used exactly the same phrase to describe her main character's goal in life, the object of his quest, which apparently so fascinated and disturbed her. He was prepared to sacrifice everything, both people and principles, so as to appear *to the manner born*—those italics representing an attempt to capture the way my mother would intone that formulaic phrase at the center of her novel. The expression, of course, comes from *Hamlet,* and, very much like "the lady doth protest too much," it's a phrase that has exited from the play and taken on a life of its own. It's the hero expressing his distaste for Claudius's noisy drinking bouts, which, though they are apparently a Danish tradition, do not please the prince at all. By the time a couple of years later when I actually read *Hamlet* closely enough in my English class to notice the phrase, I hadn't been hearing about the novel for a while, and thus I was met with a sudden blast of awareness: So my mother hadn't invented the expression after all.

The antique shop heist was a single episode, thankfully. The conversations about her novel were matters for special confidential exchange. Now I want to talk about a *practice*, in the sense that, for instance, medicine is a practice or meditation is a practice. Or, to quote my favorite book, *The Oxford English Dictionary*: "The actual application or use of an idea, belief, or method, as opposed to the theory or principles of it; performance, execution, achievement; working, operation." I've already spilled the beans by citing the *OED*: My life with my mother was a continuous, passionate, and often uproarious seminar in language, or languages. Part of it was the multilingual past of persons brought up in border territories. Yiddish was the native language of both my parents, but in their pre-émigré childhoods they must have spoken, or at least understood, Polish, Russian, perhaps Lithuanian and Belarusian. I never got beyond Yiddish, and even that got pretty much wiped out once I became fluent in German. (Pause while that sinks in.)

But this gives quite the wrong impression of what I mean when I say that my mother's life with me was a practice of language. There were no lessons, no inculcating of the pluperfect subjunctive, no simultaneous translation. It's rather that in the orbit of my mother, it seems as though every word wasn't just a *thing*, it was also a *word*. (*Use* and *mention*—the alternatives when Helena and the Countess bandy about the word "mother"—were effectively coterminous.) And as a word it could float around in a whole bath of puns and sound-alikes, of slippage into other languages, of memory strings referring to previous usages of the word. When I was quite small—but not so small that I didn't get the joke—we were shopping in some unfamiliar neighborhood, and my mother spotted a little dress shop called Gay Cottons. Readers with knowledge of Yiddish may see where this is going. The commonest expression of casual disdain when someone has said something silly or made themselves look ridiculous, is (translated into English) go *shit on the ocean*. The *ocean* part is often left out, and so in Yiddish it's simply something like *gay kakn*. It wasn't just that my mother found it amusing that a presumably non-Yiddish-speaking dress shop owner in New York (is that even a possibility to begin with?) would name their cute little establishment "go shit" (I should point out that this is well before the wide diffusion of *gay* in the sexual sense, at least so far as we knew). It wasn't enough for her to stand on the sidewalk and be amused; she had to act upon it. She took me into the dress shop, pretended to be interested in their wares, even though—how shall I put this delicately?—there was nothing there in her size, and proceeded to contrive as many ways as possible to get the staff to repeat the name of the shop, by pretending to have forgotten it and wanting (supposedly) to recommend it to all her friends, but for the fact that it kept slipping her mind: "What was it, again . . . ?" "Sorry, one more time . . . ?" "Where is my head today . . . ?" Of course, it was all about me (isn't every-thing?); the real joke was that I (aged, say, seven) had to keep a straight face, at least until a millisecond after we were back on the sidewalk.

Yiddish was not required for this game. In 1960, Britain decided to stop minting their quarter penny. The *New York Times* saw fit to put this on their front page—it was a summer weekend, and it must have been a light news day—and I learned about it because at eight in the morning my mother came running into my room in a state of pretended alarm, clutching the *Times*, pointing to the headline, and shouting, "The British have outlawed farting!!!"

Have I descended too far from Shakespeare? Then permit me to report on the hours spent with the *Times* crossword puzzle and the *New York Post* cryptogram as well as the long consultations with Roget's thesaurus. The cryptogram was her favorite teaching exercise. She would show me a few lines' worth of letters in nonsense arrangement, and I would have to turn it into a familiar phrase or quotation, the only help being that the substitution of letters was always consistent. For instance, in this case what should be a quite familiar quotation:

UZFWCZ R YO TYURBJ ZJAJ YTG UF UZJ OYTTJA MFAT . . .

It looks hopeless, but then you notice certain things. Unless it's a deliberately twisted phrase (which this one is not), you start by noticing the one-letter word followed by a two-letter word: Might that be "I am"? You also notice that there are quite a lot of J's and U's, and you start thinking about frequent vowels and consonants. From that point, the whole thing will open like a flower.

It wasn't all cribbed from the newspaper. There were homegrown word games set by my mother for me, an example of which was the following. All I was told was that the four hints all lead to a logically grouped set of famous names, persons with a profession in common:

Makin' liver for dinner
The guy who sells you loafers
Don't just give me one cookie, I'll take the whole . . .
A mere problem in bovine dermatology [actually, I made this one up;
    you can tell it's not as good as the others]

The only further thing I was told is that in order to solve this, you have to do some really terrible mispronouncing. And that, as I look back on it, is the heart of the exercise, whether in the cryptogram or in the list of famous names. You have to be ready to twist language, to turn words into other words, to break the rules of syntax and pronunciation, to look at nonsense and make it into sense, or to make sense and see how you could break it down into a different or a non-sense. You have to be willing to make mistakes but also to turn those mistakes into creativity. I wish I could show my mother that I now do the *New York Times* crossword puzzle, from Thursday to Sunday, disdaining the early part of the week, *in pen*. She would be very proud of me, which is, after all, the most I can wish for, a small return for her life investment, and what separates me and my mother from Hamlet and Gertrude. Did I signal any of this to her? Or did I just keep saying to myself what I've now said in these pages about Coriolanus: "There is something questionable about a man who has the wrong kind of attachment to his mother"? If I am still making that claim here, without qualification, am I really any better than that despicable Hamlet?

4

Faith Awakened

One evening late in the last century (the phrase has a wonderful Edwardian ring to it, though that would be the wrong last century), I was in Brooklyn attending a Royal Shakespeare Company production of *The Winter's Tale* together with my cousin Jon. I come from a very loosely connected extended family. My father's side is a blank; on my mother's side there was a moderate-sized cast of characters. There were occasional visits, mostly when I was quite young, but what predominated at our end was voluminous and painstaking record keeping as to past behaviors, either wicked or laughable, no other options possible. Jon's family was the exception, and it's fair to say that he, the middle son of that family, became my closest friend, or, more accurately, the little brother I never had. That is in itself a curious development, since we had no time for each other as children or even during the period when we overlapped at Yale. I can't even recall exactly when, or why, this change took place, but at a certain point—I was maybe in my mid-thirties, Jon in his late twenties—we were two people whose lives were wholly intertwined, sometimes tempestuously, but all for the good.

This was a moment of tremendous promise in my life. It was within weeks of my having moved back to New York; taking on a new job about which I was very enthusiastic; and being placed, courtesy of my generous NYU employers, in a quite extraordinary apartment, a penthouse on Washington Square, not so grand in square footage but with terraces on all sides and a kitchen that I had been allowed to design without being asked to pay for it. It also meant that Jon and I could get together via the mere drop of a subway token, and on this occasion we'd dropped those tokens all the way to BAM. Jon, as I recall, was very happy to be joining me but expressed himself as completely ignorant on the subject of *The Winter's Tale*. No surprise. He was very sophisticated in the realm of classical music—he was a pianist turned investment banker—but had been mostly counting on me for the rest of his aesthetic education. Still, I don't think I appreciated the extent of his unfamiliarity with the play until he clued me in as we were sitting down to watch it. Which worried me a little, since it's a difficult play for a newbie and since I had presold it aggressively—splurging on the best seats in the house, for instance—when I suggested we attend the performance.

Watching the first half, then, I not only had to soak it all up (and it was very well done) but also to deal with my anxiety that Jon would give me a big *WTF!* at intermission and even—it wouldn't be unprecedented—suggest we leave in favor of some good food and good wine, should such be available in the Brooklyn of 1994. The lights duly came down for the intermission at the end of the scene where (who can resist citing this line as often as possible?) Antigonus exits, pursued by a bear. Jon turned to me with his most lovable of smiles, his poetically Victorian good looks notably on display, and said, "This play is *you!*" Violent jealousy? Dead children? The seacoast of Bohemia? No, he said, not the events of the play, but something about the language, the tone, the world in which it takes place: It's all the stuff that you write about.

Now, had Jon already seen the entire play and had this taken place five years later, his intuition would have been unremarkable: It ends with a statue coming to life, and I would by then have published a book about ancient statues exhumed and reborn in Renaissance Rome. Jon hadn't seen the future, fortunately, but he had already located *The Winter's Tale* as my spirit animal. And, whether for that reason or on the work's own merits, he loved it. Once the RSC production had come to its statuesque conclusion, and once *Unearthing the Past* had been published, *The Winter's Tale* was able to take its place as one of our common reference points for experiences together.

One other reference point for the play, rather more recent. Students, while making small talk before class, occasionally ask me, "Professor, what is your favorite Shakespeare play?" I am not—or at least I don't want to be—the sort of professor who at that point makes it clear that he thinks it's a stupid question. For some years now, my answer, given without a moment's hesitation, has been *The Winter's Tale*. If it's *still* not time for the class to begin, and they follow up, quite sensibly, with "why?" I answer, "Because not a single thing that happens in the play is in any way plausible. There is nothing in it that remotely resembles real life." For the first-year undergraduates, this functions as a good wake-up call that they're not in high school anymore. So *The Winter's Tale* is *me* (courtesy of Jon), and *The Winter's Tale* is nothing like real life (courtesy of *me*). If Jon required only the first half of the play to identify it so absolutely with me, it's not about statues coming to life, which he didn't know about yet; it's about recognizing me as someone who preferred to live in his imagination. What else, after all, can explain the writing of this book?

Let's keep Jon in the story a little while longer; let's pursue the conceit of Jon as the *Winter's Tale* virgin and imagine ourselves capable of seeing into his mind while he is seeing into the play. In the first ten minutes of the performance, which is about as long as it takes for Leontes to be seized by his violent fit of jealousy, Jon is being asked to swallow an extraordinary series of improbables, or even impossibles. He doesn't know, as many others in the audience do, that everything will change in an instant and revise or even overturn the impressions of these first minutes. Let's pretend that we are as naïve as he is, indeed as naïve as Shakespeare would have presupposed his original audience to be.

For the moment we can glide past the conversation between Archidamus and Camillo that opens the play; they give us some background that will become more significant later, and in retrospect. It's when the main characters sweep onto the stage that we have to imagine our virgin's head spinning. We need go no further than Polixenes's very first words:

> Nine changes of the watery star hath been
> The shepherd's note since we have left our throne
> Without a burthen.

(1.2.1)

This visit of the one king to the other king's realm, about which the two courtiers were moments ago bandying compliments, lasted for . . . how long? Nine months! And, lest one of the implications of that datum chase away the other implication, let's hope Jon notices that we're talking about monarchs, which means that there is a kingdom out there beyond the sea (a very threatening sea, as it will turn out) that has had no ruler for almost a year while he—again, per the two nobles we just heard from—has been engaging in carefree extended holiday with his childhood best friend. Shakespeare (Jon may or may not have the full book on this) is very capable of writing in grave earnest about kings who shirk their royal duty (Richard II, Lear, Prince Hal, *mutatis mutandis*); here there is barely a breath of anxiety on the subject. As for the other implication of this casually delivered bomb, Jon won't require anyone to remind him of the implications of nine months; that unit of time can never be a mere designation on the calendar, particularly not when there is a heavily pregnant woman on stage.

Jon, like any other *Winter's Tale* virgin, is attempting to glimpse the play's central dramatic problem, and, in a slightly misleading sort of way it gets promptly delivered to him. The problem as it presents itself at this moment is an argument over the desire to make Polixenes stay *even longer*. At this suggestion Polixenes does not utter some Shakespearean equivalent of "are you out of your f—ing mind???" He says essentially that he's concerned about things that might be happening back home in his absence, a scruple that apparently hasn't troubled him during the previous three seasons of the year. I'm reducing this on purpose to something as performed by Dan Aykroyd and John Belushi (Gilda Radner as Hermione?), but I think it is important to re-sensitize ourselves to the strangeness of the play's opening premise even before we arrive at the next and bigger premise with its bigger, more catastrophic improbability.

At this moment, Leontes requests backup: His wife, the pregnant lady, can perhaps think of something that will do the trick. To which she moves, as one might say, sideways. First, she says that her husband is speaking "too coldly," which may lead us to expect something more passionate on her part; there will be time for that later. From there Hermione proceeds toward an argument less in favor of staying than of leaving:

> To tell, he longs to see his son, were strong:
> But let him say so then, and let him go;
> But let him swear so, and he shall not stay,
> We'll thwack him hence with distaffs.

(1.2.34–37)

It makes sense that the mother would fix on a maternal sort of reason why Leontes's insistence on extending his friend's stay in Bohemia is inopportune. In effect, she hands him a ready-made excuse, and in the process we are made to notice the absence of this consideration from the discussion so far. This is itself noteworthy in a play that has already installed male children and royal succession as a hot topic, as witness the moment in the previous scene when Archidamus interposes a complete non sequitur from the discussion of the two kings' friendship to "you have an unspeakable comfort in your young prince Mamillius."

Polixenes totally ignores this convenient opportunity to settle the matter in his favor, however, and Hermione, again fittingly, makes a compromise offer: "Yet of your royal presence | I'll adventure the borrow of a week" (1.2.38–39), to which she adds that in return for this week, she'll offer a full month of extended visiting time when, as is projected for the coming summer, her husband will go off to his return visit at Polixenes's court: 400 percent interest on the loan, in effect. This kingdom, in other words, will endure a *ten*-month absence of its king. "You'll stay?" she queries, to which he replies, finishing her pentameter line, "No, madam." We're at line 44; at line 55, he caves.

What exactly intervenes? Once this bizarre problem has arisen, how does it vanish so quickly? There is a little bit of wordplay. Hermione says, "stay"; Polixenes says, "I may not, verily." Hermione teases him about his word choice; perhaps we are to understand "verily" as a girlish sort of locution unsuitable in the vocabulary of a king. She then introduces what appears to be another exercise in terminology:

> Force me to keep you as a prisoner,
> Not like a guest . . .
>   . . . How say you?
> My prisoner or my guest? By your dread "verily,"
> One of them you shall be.

> (1.2.51–55)

To which he replies, "Your guest, then, madam." Hermione has executed a sleight of hand whereby in place of the original binary—*stay* versus *go*—she has installed a pair of alternatives—*prisoner* versus *guest*—both of which belong on the *stay* side of the previous dichotomy. (Cf. me at the VW dealer, when, in the course of half an hour, "Do I want to buy a Volkswagen SUV?" turned into "Do I want to buy a Tiguan or a Touareg?" Subaru had somehow dropped out of the picture.) Perhaps (though it's unlikely) Jon could deep-read *prisoner* and *guest*, the former being decidedly less attractive, though at the same time more evocative. After all, kings *did* keep other kings as prisoners in what counted as a standard element of warfare and statecraft. And passionate erotic desire was also figured as imprisonment, as in the Petrarch/Wyatt "That loseth nor locketh holdeth me in prison." In love with each other, at war with each other: The play's opening is doing its best to instill in us some evocative confusions, even for those who may be better prepared than Jon.

The great dramatic question of the play's opening—one of them, at any rate—has been answered, but a new and more troubling question arises: Why was Hermione successful in getting Polixenes to stay longer where Leontes wasn't? There is a very simple answer, of course, but it's a ridiculous one and is unlikely to occur to anybody—yet. Her mission of extending Polixenes's stay accomplished, Hermione does not report her triumph to her husband but rather opens up a vein of small talk with his friend: "Come, I'll question you | Of my lord's tricks and yours when you were boys" (1.2.59–60). It's no surprise at all that this should lead to a lovely picture of childhood as a quite specifically Edenic condition:

> We were as twinn'd lambs that did frisk i' the sun,
> And bleat the one at the other: what we changed
> Was innocence for innocence; we knew not
> The doctrine of ill-doing, nor dream'd
> That any did.
>
> (1.2.66–70)

Hermione detects from Polixenes's nostalgic tone that he no longer considers himself in this state of innocence. He concurs:

> Temptations have since then been born to's; for
> In those unfledged days was my wife a girl;
> Your precious self had then not cross'd the eyes
> Of my young play-fellow.
>
> (1.2.75–79)

Let us fine-tune our conceit about the *Winter's Tale* virgin and replace 1994 Jon with Jacobean Jon, someone watching the play, say, at the Whitehall Banqueting House circa 1611. The notion that married love might be considered an enactment of the Fall of Man is possibly more shocking than anything that has been said, or will be said, in the course of the play. Married love is the very bond of sacred faith that works to repair fallen humankind. In regard to lust of the Seven Deadly Sins kind, it is not just *different*, it is *contradictory*, designed in fact for the prevention of lust. Hermione, logically, notices this piece of blasphemy right away: "Of this make no conclusion, lest you say | Your queen and I are devils" (1.2.80–81). To think this way is to be fallen, and in his quiet way Polixenes is here committing as grave an offense against holy wedlock as that of Leontes, which will soon follow. If married love is sin, is it really any different from adultery? A question, admittedly, as alien as the world of *The Winter's Tale* itself to the two unmarried spectators whose experience of the play we are shadowing.

Hermione finally reports her accomplishment in persuasion, and Leontes notes (in a tone of voice that has to be left up to the actor) that she "never but once" before had spoken "to the purpose." The "once" was when she consented, after keeping Leontes waiting for three months, to accept his marriage proposal. Is Jon paying close enough attention? You don't have to be a Jacobean to note that we're in a world where Hermione's success in obtaining an extra week's worth of guesting is deemed by her husband to be on the same level as his own success in winning her for his wife. That equivalence is cinched by Hermione's—which is to say, Shakespeare's—choice of words:

> Why, lo you now, I have spoke to the purpose twice:
> The one for ever earn'd a royal husband;
> The other for some while a friend.

(1.2.105–7)

This is the moment of explosion, at least for those who know the code meaning of "friend." The tradition of courtly love, rampant in the later Middle Ages, depended upon the wooing of a married lady by an attractive young suitor-troubadour who would be designated euphemistically as a "friend." In fact, one of the *OED* definitions of "friend" is "a romantic or sexual partner," dating back to Old English; it cites Caxton and Shakespearean usages in *Love's Labour's Lost* (5.2.404) and *Measure for Measure* (1.4.29). No surprise that at this moment Shakespeare finally gives Leontes speech: "Too hot, too hot." Now we know the simple and obvious answer to the conundrum of Hermione's achievement: She succeeded because she and Polixenes have been having a torrid affair that, judging from the calendar, must have begun the instant he set foot on Sicilia's shore nine months ago.

Recollect my rave notice for the play: Nothing in it is believable as real life. But what kind of unbelievable are we going to be asked to believe? The nine-month visit, along with the exaggerated courtesies that accompany it; the hyperboles attached to male friendship; the casual assertion that married love might be damnable; the extravagant self-congratulation that Hermione indulges in over what appears to be a minor social coup. Let's imagine that Jon, with his special respect for Shakespeare, for the alien nature of the past, for me, who dragged him to Brooklyn, has accepted all those premises. How have those suspensions of disbelief prepared him for Leontes's sudden and violent certainty that his wife has been unfaithful?

Jon is being called upon to make some triage in the realm of believing. The realm of believing has in fact complicated itself. Is Leontes mistaken in his suspicion? That appears to be an easy question, to which the answer is yes. Do I credit the fiction of Leontes's precipitous onset of jealousy enough so as to accept it, even in the recognized realm of Aristotle's probable impossibilities, which he prefers to improbable possibilities? I raise this slightly indelicate point—indelicate since fictions are, after all, meant to be fictional—because Shakespeare seems to have deliberately done everything he can to make Leontes's move here unbelievable. And, of course, the matter in question is itself belief—that is, Leontes's faith in his wife's faithfulness, a matter that is familiar from countless premodern narratives as the quintessential proposition that resists definitive proof or disproof. In *Othello*, the game is based on the efforts of a wily manipulator, along with the occasional lucky accident (lucky for Iago, anyway), to create a constant series of *seeming* proofs. Here Shakespeare plays exactly the opposite game: Not only is there no Iago, but the suspicion arises before our very eyes in the opening five minutes of the play, during which we are witness to everything that might plausibly ground these suspicions, all of it completely innocent. Productions, of course, may introduce business to alter this impression, but the script seems to me quite clear. Clear, that is, as to the unbelievability of Leontes's unbelief.

Why create a fiction whose purpose is to be unbelievable? We've gone here beyond what it would be prudent to try to offer for sale to even the most imaginative and receptive investment banker. Except maybe one with whom I had spent happy hours in front of Pollock and Picasso at MoMA or with whom I had, also for happy hours, sat tush-to-tush on a piano bench, me struggling, him breezing through Schubert's Fantasia for four hands in F minor—all of which works *don't imitate anything*. The doctrine of art imitating life, and receiving the highest marks for the most scrupulously photographic, even xerographic, imitation, has to count as more than a *theory* about art; it has to count as an *ideology*. By which I mean a theory that demands adherence to a whole lot of other theories on completely different subjects, thus abridging one's freedom to say, "*Yes*, in this case, but *no* in that case." (This is the iceberg tip of my contempt for ideology, but we'll let that pass.) The ideology of art imitating life owes its origins to a widely held assumption that art is somehow of an inferior status to life—a reasonable opinion (which I don't share) but certainly not a fact. So art is admitted to legitimacy by hanging on to life's coattails. More background that Jon was spared: It goes back to Plato (via his mouthpiece Socrates) and Aristotle, though what I'm calling "Life" Socrates would have called "Philosophy." For Socrates, Philosophy was truth, art was fiction; Aristotle found ways to redeem art via mimesis, or imitation, and ever since that move was made, art has had to defend itself by advertising its place on the grid of true-to-life.

I think Shakespeare by this late stage of his career had done his time in serving the Real, and I think *The Winter's Tale* is his letter of resignation from the whole mimetic brotherhood. Hence my love for the play as containing nothing that resembles reality. Shakespeare wants to announce that Leontes suspects his wife not, like Othello, mistakenly though with enough circumstantial evidence to make it plausible but rather mistakenly *for no reason at all*—except, of course, the necessity of fueling an artistic design, which is a necessity not for Leontes but for Shakespeare. And I think that the absurdly long royal vacation and the absurd attempt to prolong it and the argument against prolonging it that collapses with absurd ease: All of this is an announcement that if spectators want a mirror up to life, they had best pack up their half-gnawed chicken legs and schlep them over to the plays of that clever fellow Mr. Benjamin Jonson, where lots of what they'll hear is exactly the same as what they can hear on the streets of London when they leave the theater.

There is another bit of revolutionary willfulness in Shakespeare's *Winter's Tale* design, this one something like a side joke designed to remind us that cultural pieties may not be any more dutifully observed in the play than the laws of true-to-life. Recollect that as soon as Hermione has secured Polixenes's presence for the extra week, she initiates a conversation with Polixenes about the childhoods of the two bosom friends. Before we get to the disturbingly uncanonical set of implications concerning married sexuality, we are treated to some memorable lines about childhood as a state of innocence. In the design of a play that, among other things, will take us from a corrupted royal court through a pastoral interlude to what is ultimately some sort of harmony, it's vital that we be given to understand childhood as a model for the state of innocence. The play renders that image most vividly, later, in the narrative surrounding Perdita, notably when Paulina obtains the infant's release from Hermione's prison cell by declaring that

> This child was prisoner to the womb and is
> By law and process of great nature thence
> Freed and enfranchised, not a party to
> The anger of the king nor guilty of,
> If any be, the trespass of the queen.
>
> (2.2.58–62)

Even Leontes's harsh law, it seems, must give way in the face of an innocent child.

But what about the *other* child? Things can't be looking quite so kiddie-Edenic when the scene of mother-and-son opens with Hermione announcing to one of her ladies, "Take the boy to you, he so troubles me | 'Tis past enduring" (2.1.1–2). Given the extravagant gestures of inducing Polixenes to prolong his stay, followed by the even more extravagant foiled plot to murder Polixenes, this almost comes as a breath of fresh air. It's probably the first speech in the play that one could imagine hearing in real life (and the last?), and it raises some doubts about "what we changed was innocence for innocence," etc. Even so, Shakespeare is going to channel these doubts in a truly strange direction. Mamillius refuses the attentions of the Lady whom Hermione had delegated to take charge of him; when she asks why, he offers a prompt answer:

MAMILLIUS   Not for because
   Your brows are blacker; yet black brows, they say,
   Become some women best, so that there be not
   Too much hair there, but in a semicircle
   Or a half-moon made with a pen.
SECOND LADY   Who taught you this?
MAMILLIUS
   I learnt it out of women's faces.

(2.1.7–12)

And he proceeds with a few more cosmetic tips. Is there anything more bizarre in all of *The Winter's Tale*? (Don't answer that—*yet*.) This is the future king, aged seven or so, the "unspeakable comfort" of Sicilia's future, as Archidamus declared in the opening scene, who will be martyred as a result of his father's fatal misprision; after this appearance we'll never see him again. Why, if he is being presented as a figure of lost innocence, does it have to be a lost innocence of such banality? Polixenes figured loss of innocence as love and marriage; for Mamillius, it appears to be mascara.

Mamillius in the scheme of things is small fry. If Shakespeare is veering off into the probable impossible, the big question is, what will he do with Leontes? Let's go back to Aristotle and his preference for probable impossibilities as over against impossible probabilities. What I think he means is that it is preferable in creating fictions to invent something that couldn't happen in life as we know it yet make it seem credible, as opposed to dealing in ordinary events (in his terms, probabilities) and to transform them—say, via the mechanisms of plot—into something surprising or unlikely. The poet engages in a higher order of creativity when the ultimate premise is unbelievable yet the manner of its presentation is so compelling that we simultaneously embrace two opposites. No one could possibly enter the state of violent jealousy that Leontes reaches within five minutes of the curtain going up. *And yet*, the performance, or fulfillment of that state, once he gets there, is so compelling within the poetic fiction that the impossible is made to look probable. Which takes us back to Jon's diagnosis of the play as *me*, the would-be disciple of the impossible.

Shakespeare bestows on the madly jealous Leontes a very particular language to fit this condition. He is speaking to Mamillius; Hermione and Polixenes are standing by:

                              Come, sir page,
Look on me with your welkin eye: sweet villain!
Most dear'st! my collop! Can thy dam?—may't be?—
Affection! thy intention stabs the centre:
Thou dost make possible things not so held,
Communicatest with dreams;—how can this be?—
With what's unreal thou coactive art,
And fellow'st nothing: then 'tis very credent
Thou mayst co-join with something; and thou dost,
And that beyond commission, and I find it,
And that to the infection of my brains
And hardening of my brows.

                                              (1.2.134–45)

This is not the incoherence of heroic madness, like Lear on the heath or Othello in the midst of a seizure; it is plain incoherence, for Mark Van Doren "the obscurest passage in Shakespeare." We can read the several pages of commentary in Pafford's edition, we can tally up the non sequiturs, the breaks in syntax, the vaguenesses of "things" and "something," but the real tip-off is Polixenes's response:

What means Sicilia?

Heroic sufferers in Shakespeare are often prone to using propulsive, disjointed language. It's not so common, however, that when one of them orates in that manner, another character responds, in effect, "*huh?*"

Is this the last word on the struggling Leontes? Does his agony—his *self-inflicted* agony—add up to no more than a resounding "*Huh?*" I have an ingenious answer to the question, and I have Jon's skeptical response, delivered energetically over a pair of brisket sandwiches courtesy of a post-theater visit to a Brooklyn institution called Junior's. Jon was kind enough to recognize my authority as a professional Shakespearean but nevertheless asserted that he did not come to this discussion without superior expertise in a field of his own.

All those limits having been established, the case for or against Leontes revolves in my view around two memorable speeches. First, in the scene where he attempts to convince Camillo that Hermione has been unfaithful. Camillo resists energetically, and Leontes reviews what he takes to be evidence:

                    Is whispering nothing?
Is leaning cheek to cheek? is meeting noses?
Kissing with inside lip? stopping the career
Of laughing with a sigh—a note infallible

Of breaking honesty . . . is this nothing?
Why, then the world and all that's in't is nothing;
The covering sky is nothing; Bohemia nothing;
My wife is nothing; nor nothing have these nothings,
If this be nothing.

(1.2.281–93)

Leontes delivers the second speech when he learns that Camillo and Polixenes have sailed off to Bohemia, which Leontes takes—rather improbably—as confirmation of his wife's infidelity, a sentiment that he expresses in a memorable image:

There may be in the cup
A spider steep'd, and one may drink, depart,
And yet partake no venom, for his knowledge
Is not infected: but if one present
The abhorr'd ingredient to his eye, make known
How he hath drunk, he cracks his gorge, his sides,
With violent hefts. I have drunk, and seen the spider.

(2.1.36–45)

What both these speeches say to me, personally, is that I wish I were the actor who gets to deliver them. They are thespian fodder of the highest caliber, and they embody everything about the ways in which performance—and we'll get back to that word—is all about the lie that is made to appear as truth. They must not, cannot, convince us that Hermione was unfaithful, but they must inspire us with the grandeur of what Leontes was suffering while in the grip of his delusion. They must discredit Leontes in one way and exalt him in another.

Jon bought only part of that package. No, that's not quite right. It really goes back to my oft-repeated insistence that fictions are fictional, that they are crafted, that, in this case, we are sitting at BAM not in the grip of Leontes but in the grip of Shakespeare. Of course, Leontes is suffering, but Shakespeare is exposing that suffering for the dangerously self-indulgent performance that it is, just as he exposed him earlier by turning his tragic speech into something so incoherent that even the other characters on stage couldn't understand it. That hammering down on *nothing, nothing, nothing*: It's not the terrible nihilistic vision of *Lear*, where that word gathers horrifying force. It's a reminder that Leontes's suffering is based on . . . *nothing*. And as for that tiresomely self-indulgent "I have drunk, and seen the spider," it's no more than Leontes trying to play the heroics of Adam and Eve in the Garden of Eden. Except that his knowledge is no knowledge at all; you can't have the agonizing knowledge of good and evil if you've failed to figure out which is which.

Lifelong pedagogue though I am, I must confess that I failed to engage Jon on this level, the level of (what shall we call it?) metametacriticism. He was in fact engaged on the least meta level imaginable, and he was in effect confirming Shakespeare's fulfillment of Aristotle, whereby the impossibility of Hermione's faithlessness was meeting up with the probability, or better the authenticity, of Leontes's pain. It didn't really matter whether Leontes had good reason for his agony. Jon was witnessing a sufferer from male heterosexual despair, and his heart went out to him, replete with fellow feeling, doubtless based on personal experience, since Jon had not always chosen well in love.

He had me there. Jon and I had always managed the most loving dialogue possible—"dialogue" isn't a loving enough word, really—across the gap between our sexualities, and considering that this had formed itself at least a decade before our visit to BAM, it really has to be viewed as something that helped save me as a gay man in dark times. Jon was the first person in my life who could give and receive comfort about love, desire, and all the joys and woes attached to them without the slightest sense that homosexuality was a separate case. I fully understand that for many gay people this acknowledgment of separateness is exactly what's needed. That I was in a minority, that I might be victimized as a result: I knew all this without having to be told; that I was extra cool, that I might seize the chance to revel in a separate episteme: this didn't ring true for me. What I needed was to feel that all my impulses of desire, whether toward a gorgeous piece of eye candy on the subway or toward the prospect of a loving life partner, were part of the universal order of things, susceptible to a whole range of affectionate sharing with a true friend who would respond from his location on a fundamentally undifferentiated playing field. Even as recently as 1994, when Jon and I were watching *The Winter's Tale*, this was very hard to find, even among one's most well-meaning heterosexual acquaintances. It's all the more remarkable when I report that Jon was an exceptionally beautiful youth who doubtless must in the past have frequently declined offers from men (and I think he did decline them) but who had no difficulty in balancing the different accidents of desire and maintaining the legitimacy and unity of the thing itself. I've had many intimate friends who are heterosexual—too many, probably—and I'll have occasion soon to mention another, *the* other—but none quite like Jon for the affectionate ease in the face of our difference.

Which—to descend from the plane of love to the plane of literary criticism, a long way down indeed—made it possible, with the last bites of brisket (and another beer), for me to ask some tough questions about sexuality and *The*

Winter's Tale. Was Jon's instinctive sympathy for Leontes a sign that the exaggerated fear of infidelity, of being a cuckold, is a defining feature that is built in to heterosexuality? In a time when most of us feel there is lots more to loving than the legitimate reproduction of the family and the species, is there still a need to retain the atavistic fear of impurity? The folks who play on my team are spared some of this motivation, which, after all, comes in for plenty of attention in *The Winter's Tale.* But when I allow myself to look at Leontes straight in the eye, as though we existed on the same plane of reality, I say, "Dude, you keep talking about the baby's DNA, but what's really driving you nuts is the idea that Hermione preferred Polixenes to you." Which, of course, she didn't. But what about the place that *I'm* coming from? What I say to Jon but probably wouldn't *dare* say to Leontes is, "Dude, who are you really jealous of? Is it because Polixenes had Hermione like you did, or because Hermione had Polixenes like you *didn't?*" Shakespeare has put that bit of symmetry front and center, at least for this reader. On the long, sleepy ride back to Manhattan, discussion trailed off.

Having opened this account of *The Winter's Tale* with such a barrage of affection for the play, perhaps I should admit to some obstacles that it puts in the way of a reader's—*this* reader's—love. There is a moment in Simon Gray's wickedly funny play *Butley* when the title character, a desperately frustrated lecturer at some unnamed college of the University of London, is forced to listen to a student read her essay on *The Winter's Tale*, to which he attends with a mixture of boredom, indifference, mockery, loathing, and self-loathing. We're allowed to hear several samples of the paper, for example, "'So just as the seasonal winter was the winter of the soul, so is the seasonal spring the spring of the soul. The imagery changes from disease to floral, the tone from mad bitterness to joyfulness. As we reach the play's climax we feel our own—spiritual—sap rising.'" At which point Butley interrupts, first questions and then embraces the word "sap," preferring it, he says, to "some others that spring rhymingly to mind." Yes, there is something in the nature worship of Shakespeare's play, particularly as seen through some mid-twentieth-century readings of it, something that veers off into the simplistic and self-congratulatory, which, one might say, rhymes with "sap."

If you're looking for this, you'll probably find it in act 4. I don't think that *The Winter's Tale* runs out of steam once Antigonus is pursued, fatally, by the bear (3.3) and only picks up again when all the surviving cast members stand onstage in wonderment at a statue that comes to life (5.3). That being said, it is the rare production that can make the shepherds and their sheep shearing, or the endangered love affair of Perdita and Florizel, or the plot mechanics of getting everyone back to Sicilia in time for the happy ending quite so riveting as the disasters that preceded or the magic that will follow. (The Royal Shakespeareans whom we were watching, as I recall, did a lot by switching from many umbrellas in the first half to many balloons in the second half; they also had a music-hall-style Autolycus who stole the show.)

Ground zero for my own Butley-esque problem is a passage that seems designed to provide a kind of handy ideological key to unlock the larger implications of a possible marriage between an heir to the throne and a shepherd maid who isn't a shepherd maid. I am speaking of the conversation between Perdita and the disguised King Polixenes, who, along with Camillo (also disguised), has crashed the sheep shearing party, where they are enraptured by the charms of the lowborn (*not!*) girl but show no interest in abandoning their plan to scratch her eyes out should she presume to marry the crown prince.

In the course of the festival, Perdita hands the two disguised visitors rosemary and rue, noting that they "keep seeming and savor all winter long" (4.4.74), from which Polixenes detects that her flower choices are (as we would say) age appropriate. At which point she volunteers that there might be even better flower choices if only she were willing to cultivate them in her garden. The trouble, it turns out, is that these are produced by *grafting*: "There is an art which in their piedness shares | With great creating nature" (4.4.87–88), which renders them, in a memorable phrase, "nature's bastards." This ideology of racial purity hits the fan when Polixenes, himself anything but a product of grafting, speaks up in favor of the bastards:

> Say there be,
> Yet nature is made better by no mean
> But nature makes that mean; so over that art
> Which you say adds to nature, is an art
> That nature makes. You see, sweet maid, we marry
> A gentler scion to the wildest stock,
> And make conceive a bark of baser kind
> By bud of nobler race. This is an art
> Which does mend nature—change it rather—but
> The art itself is nature.

(4.4.89–96)

I get it: Ironically, Polixenes, who is about to threaten that unspeakable tortures be loosed upon a (mistakenly supposed) piece of "wildest stock" for her presumption in being grafted on to the "gentler scion," Florizel, is *pro*-grafting, whereas Perdita, a mere shepherdess who is on the verge of being affianced to a prince, is *anti*-grafting. Hermeneutically suspicious that I am, I can't help seeing a kind of bad faith here. We are to welcome the celebration of simple good country values in a lowly maid, but only if the lowly maid isn't really a lowly maid. And in case that confirmation of the status quo isn't emphatic enough, it's the king, and not the lowly maid, who is permitted the expression of a willingness to mix the lower orders (= bark of baser kind) with the higher orders (= bud of nobler race), when, as we in the audience know all along, no real baser stock is involved in this transaction.

All of this, including my own somewhat jaundiced reception of it, speaks to some larger matters in the history of my profession, not to mention the history of my own operations within the profession. Though the precise dates of the phenomenon can be disputed, it's clear that for a period of ten or fifteen years starting in the late 1960s, there was a torrent of interest, particularly among students of English, in the literary mode of the pastoral, that is, the creating of fictions that are set within the rustic world of shepherds, goatherds, country maids, etc., but whose concerns are not fundamentally or authentically bucolic. I'm calling it a "mode," but even the question of what to call it as a body of imaginative work was open to debate. The same would go for the exact years in which it flourished: Empson's all-important *Some Versions of Pastoral* dates from well before that time, and movements like the New Historicism and Eco-Criticism will translate some similar issues into the methodologies of later decades. What matters for me is that the hegemony—let's call it that—of the pastoral as a literary mode with particular prestige and recognition value coincides closely with my time in graduate school and the beginnings of my career in the academy.

For some reason, a little cache of my typewritten papers from the late 1960s and early 1970s survives (in a shoulder bag on which is inscribed THE BALVENIE SINGLE MALT—itself a mystery, since I hate scotch, which tastes to me like wet dirt). Every one of these papers, produced at two different graduate schools and for three or four different professors, is about—guess what!—the pastoral. "Nature's Bastards," "Milton's Paradise and the Fallen World," and most embarrassing of all, "'Insnar'd with Flow'rs': On the Pastoral and Carpe Diem Modes as Two Sides of the Same Natural Coin." ("Too many metaphors here" is the great Rosalie Colie's scribbled comment next to *that* title, though it counts as a rave notice compared to her note on page 3: "Oh, Leonard, this is impossible to read," with double underlining for "impossible.")

What was it all about? Were we fantasizing our own withdrawal to a simpler life than what was presented to us as the academic rat race? Did we think that maintaining a double vision of (pretended) country and (real) court was somehow political work that would bring down the Nixon administration? Were we gravitating to the reassuringly simple exercise of decoding the dress-up identities of rural swains and maidens so as to reveal that these poems weren't *really* about sheep? Duh! Who knew? Looking at my own papers now (a horrific exercise, about which I can only say I did it for you, dear reader), what strikes me is that pastoral literature seemed to *require* the work of the decipherer (that is, *me*) because, whatever it *might* mean, it couldn't possibly mean the silly things that it *said* it meant.

This is an admittedly harsh and unfair account of work including that done by some of the scholars I most love and respect (I'll name names: Paul Alpers, C. L. Barber, Harry Berger, Louis Montrose, Jane Tylus, and, of course, Rosalie Colie herself). But arrayed against Perdita's dress-up, her debate with Polixenes, and, most of all, the interminable rustic goings-on of such figures as Dorcas and Mopsa, plus the threatened appearance of twelve Herdsmen, which even the Old Shepherd, bless his heart, tries (unsuccessfully, alas) to abbreviate— "Here has been too much homely foolery" (4.4.326–37): The whole package, once so alluring, has for a long time given me grief.

If there was something that I responded to even less than the debate about grafting or the rustic high-jinks of stage shepherds, it was the one alien character whom Shakespeare hurls into the mix. I can't claim that I disliked the wandering thief and rascal Autolycus on principle, say, because he represented a literary mode that had lost its savor for me; it was more that I didn't know what to do with him. All I could manage over the years in teaching the play was to note that in the song with which he makes his entrance he declares that "the red blood reigns in the winter's pale" (4.3.1–4)—"pale" referring both to the colorlessness of the season and to the idea of the pastoral as a kind of enclosure. My interpretive takeaway, however, was that Autolycus's verse might be designed to be misheard as "the red blood reigns in the winter's *tale*." A slender thread, to say the least, but not without some signifying potential. Partly it reveals my own difficulties with the pastoral mode, as established earlier. Transitioning from the tragic materials of the first two acts, followed by the drastic circumstances of the shipwreck, the bear, and the discovery of the foundling, celebrated in the great formulation of the Old Shepherd to his son, "Thou metst with things dying, I with things newborn" (3.3.109–10), the upcoming episode of the sheep shearing is liable to seem rather (what shall I call it?) dainty. And the fact that it is managed by Perdita, who is timorous both about the dress-up and about her relationship with Florizel, while also exhibiting herself so censoriously about grafting—all of this is liable to make us feel that the play has undergone a serious temperature drop. How fortunate, then, that before we've witnessed any of this descent into the realm of the delicate, we've encountered a lusty thief who promises a transfusion of red blood into our anemic theatrical patient.

We might even take the presence of Autolycus as a sign that Shakespeare was as bored with the pastoral as I am. The requirements of the narrative are such that we must enter a world of something like pure nature. What Shakespeare needs out of that is a marked alternative to the corruptions of high civilization—so corrupt in this case that they believe they are corrupt when they aren't, the deepest corruption being of the kind that is in the eye of the beholder—and so we are sentenced to shepherds and problematic flower gardens. Genius that he was, he determined to seek out the energies that can be provided by something more vigorous and disruptive than even the most transgressive shepherd, so he gives us a country rogue who wastes no time in telling us that he drinks ale, engages in a bit of thievery, and tumbles with "aunts" in the hay.

I started to wonder, though, if it was quite enough to say that Shakespeare needed someone among the shepherds who was just a little bit naughtier than the shepherds. I also recollected that I had warned Jon during the intermission that we might be in for a dry patch among the shepherds of Bohemia, but to my surprise he'd whispered to me at one act 4 moment, "Best character in the show!" I was, to say the least, surprised. The moment was Autolycus's long monologue at the end of the sheep shearing episode. Somehow our post-theater conversation never returned to this subject, and I'm left on my own now to reconstruct the sources of that explosion of enthusiasm.

Autolycus begins by declaring, "Ha! What a fool honesty is," and he proceeds to congratulate himself on his many successes with the crowd. "I have sold all my trumpery," he tells us, whereupon he enumerates a long series of products: "not a counterfeit stone, not a ribbon, glass, pomander, brooch, table-book, ballad, knife, tape, glove, shoe-tie, bracelet, horn-ring" (4.4.493–96). Apparently, this success fits under the rubric of honesty because, whatever *Consumer Reports* might say about these transactions, they followed the accepted rules of exchange. The rustics gave him money, and he handed them trinkets. But he concludes the speech with a different sort of self-congratulation: "So that in this time of lethargy I picked and cut most of their festival purses; and had not the old man come in with a whoo-bub against his daughter and the king's son . . . , I had not left a purse alive in the whole army" (4.4.609–14). This would seem to follow a quite different business plan: He steals their purses, and they get nothing.

How do these two commercial enterprises fit together? There is a kind of contradiction, of course. If he stole their purses first, not only would they be unable to purchase his stuff, they would also be alerted to the theft. We've seen a form of that problem already in an earlier scene when Autolycus, in what is surely one of his standard ruses, has presented himself to the Shepherd's son as the abject victim of a highwayman (we'll get back to that). In the midst of his feigned collapse and without detection, he steals the boy's purse. The lad, unaware of the theft, is moved to pity and gestures toward offering the poor self-declared victim some coins. Which precipitates a little comic crisis: Autolycus has to think quickly in order to prevent the boy from discovering that he no longer has the purse that was comfortably in his possession a few moments before and out of which he was about to offer alms.

What we have here is something as alien to the pastoral as can be imagined: a little typology of financial transactions, none of which is precisely legitimate. Buying goods and collecting money for them might be legitimate, except for the constantly reiterated fact that the goods in this case are worthless; charity is laudable, but on this occasion it is not only misdirected but also shut down by the previous intervention of the third kind of financial transaction: theft. What we are seeing, I think, is something more immediate to real experience than shepherds cavorting. Property is theft, said Proudhon two and a half centuries later; here, we have a petty thief who is a (very) petty capitalist. Marx and Proudhon may not belong in social theory available to Shakespeare, but it is certainly within his sights—notably, in *The Merchant of Venice*—to express the kind of anxiety about money that arises whenever it is not clear that there is a real product at the other end of a money transaction. That's one way of describing the sin, as it was understood, of usury, which is to say making money off of money itself, as opposed to, say, making money off legitimate goods. It's even clearer that there is no real product when a bunch of worthless knick-knacks gets exchanged for coin of the realm. From this perspective, it looks as though Autolycus's twin professions—rustic tchotchke salesman and itinerant pickpocket—aren't so very different.

Of course, Jon zeroed in on Autolycus: He was glimpsing a fellow merchant. After all, investment bankers were the economic swashbucklers of the 1990s who moved money from one pocket to another, sometimes other peoples' pockets, mostly their own, with only the vaguest connection to real goods. It's lucky, in a way, that I only see this connection now; it might not have been a good thing, even in jest, to cast aspersions on Jon's profession back in the height of its commercial and cinematic allure.

But let us rescue Autolycus from the world of Oliver Stone and return him to the Shakespearean sweet state of nature that he somewhat discordantly inhabits. During the lovable scamp's first encounter with the Shepherd's son, something takes place that is more peculiar than pickpocketing. Autolycus, as mentioned, presents himself as the victim of a highwayman; the boy asks whether he can identify his aggressor, to which Autolycus responds in the affirmative:

> A fellow, sir, that I have known to go about with troll-my-dames; I knew him once a servant of the prince. . . . I know this man well: he hath been since an ape-bearer; then a process-server, a bailiff; then he compassed a motion of the Prodigal Son, and married a tinker's wife within a mile where my land and living lies; and, having flown over many knavish professions, he settled only in rogue: some call him Autolycus.
>
> (4.1.85–97)

The details of the supposed assailant's résumé are delicious and (one has to assume, given the source) 100 percent accurate, but we must stop to ask, what is Autolycus doing here? Or better, as with any question of motivation inside a literary invention: What is the *author* doing here? (Cf. the repeated mantra to my students, often to no avail: Fictional characters don't have motives, authors have motives.) Why, in other words, create a fiction inside which Autolycus fictionally claims to have been assaulted by Autolycus?

There is no narrative purpose here—Autolycus isn't, for instance, going to be found out as the aggressor upon the Shepherd's son when they see each other again later. Once again, Shakespeare is leading us outside the contract of verisimilitude whereby we do the Aristotelian mimetic thing of equating literary characters with people we know in real life. This is someone who can be himself and outside himself at the same time. He is a shape-changer, but this particular fable of shape-changing is initiated with a narrative in which he held two identities at the same time and managed to reduce himself to rags and abjection. Granted, it's a lie, but what fable *isn't* a lie?

I have been, and still am (I hope), intellectually restless. I have always been more eager to annex materials outside my officially assigned space than to master that space in all its depth and fullness. In case this seems like one of those confessions of inadequacy that really amounts to bragging in disguise, I'll try again. I have a short intellectual attention span. Whenever I am invited to exhibit myself as an "interdisciplinary scholar," I begin by saying that I'm not really interdisciplinary; it's just that I'm easily bored. I'm also lazy: When I swerve into some other professional field, for which I am untrained, I never have the patience or *Sitzfleisch* to school myself in its ABCs; I go straight for the sparkling gem that attracted me there and hope that I can somehow reverse engineer all the disciplinary wisdom that those who are properly instructed in the field take for granted. And if I can't, well, I propose to be providing a "fresh voice," free of the burdens of . . . what? Knowledge?

And yet, when I look back on my sequence of interests, I detect some kind of pattern. I speak elsewhere in these pages about my intermittent engagement in theater as director and actor, definitively concluded forty years ago, and I focus on how it provided a sociable alternative, or, less euphemistically, an erotic alternative, to what I found to be the rather bloodless milieu of practicing the university-based humanities in the 1970s (or any other decade, now that I've seen so many). There was more to it than that. To make the transit from reading Shakespeare or teaching Shakespeare to performing Shakespeare was to move from texts to living, breathing, three-dimensional persons. (Nor did it have to be Shakespeare: My engagements with *Hello, Dolly* and *The Odd Couple* offered me as much sense of bodies rather than texts, maybe more.) I didn't have the methodological education to realize it at the time, but I now understand that it wasn't just my officially assigned colleagues and students and articles and books that were confining; it was the written word itself.

The subject of my first book was the human body as image of the world; I look back on it now and ask whether this was my way of avoiding the human body as . . . the human body. Part of it was, of course, that I was lonely and horny—I've written about that elsewhere, and I can skip it here—but I think I was also feeling that ink marks on a page, not to mention ink marks on a page *about* ink marks on a page, even the spoken word about ink marks on a page . . . all that text can come to feel desperately mediated. The theater wasn't just a sociable space preferable to department cocktail parties; it was a space where the ink marks were not just on a page; rather they were emerging from persons, tall and short, fat and thin, lovely to look at and . . . not so much.

The visual arts represented a different escape from the tyrannical mediations of the word, and it coincided—cause, effect, who knows?—with the moment in the early 1970s when I fell in love with Ovid. Long before I performed the role of Bottom in Chicago, as discussed earlier in connection with *A Midsummer Night's Dream*, I had been strong-armed—as a very junior faculty member—into teaching a Western Civ course that included the *Metamorphoses*. The work, with which I was scandalously unfamiliar, was a revelation that has kept fueling my intellectual life and my imagination ever since. What I discovered in Ovid was that practically everything I loved most about the Renaissance— the worship of beauty, the inextricability of folly and desire, the sensuous materiality of the sacred—could be located on the pages of this poem. Of course, I had to become more of a Latinist than I would have dreamed possible under the censorious eye of my high school Latin teacher, and, in a pattern that would often be repeated, I managed just-enough-plus-a-little-more, so as not to embarrass myself.

But there was another discipline involved for which I had not the slightest preparation. I knew enough to be aware that writing about Ovid in the Renaissance as though it were all poetry and no pictures would be absurd. I had, as noted elsewhere in these pages, some indoctrination in the intellectual world of Aby Warburg and his followers, but I completely lacked what they seemed to possess—the whole of art history, the casual recognition of everything from Apelles to Zurbarán—as though flowing in their bloodstreams. Of all this, I knew nothing. I skipped art history in college because all courses demanded a set of introductory lectures that were delivered at eight in the morning: a no-go for a theater boy accustomed to long nighttime rehearsals. As a consequence, I had never had an art history course. So, like many who were professing literature in the 1970s, I needed to learn a new discipline from scratch. In my case it wasn't Marxism or deconstruction; I chose the discipline that afforded me a grant to travel to Venice, Florence, Rome, Munich, and Vienna, where I was commissioned to photograph every mythological artwork that hung on their museum walls. There were quite a few.

I know that the bodies in Titian's paintings and Michelangelo's sculptures are, at the deepest theoretical level, no more real than those belonging to Spenser's Britomart or the Dark Lady of the Sonnets, but I don't live at the deepest theoretical level. The excitement of entering the discipline of art history as a thirty-year-old kindergartener possessed an erotic charge: The beauty of the figures in *Sacred and Profane Love* or those on the ceiling of the Sistine operated in the very best way to elide the distinction between aesthetics and desire, an operation that words might accomplish, but ever so much more slowly. It wasn't just about bodies; it was about the fact that this was a discipline of material objects, often unique ones, that needed to be measured and described in advance of interpretation. I was thrilled by the sense that this was a field in which, for many of the things it studied, there was a unique final object that held within it everything we might want to know about it, if only we could figure it out, and that this object existed in a certain place, could be accessed properly only there, and was subject to the tenuousness of materiality. All of which gave the field an eros of its own, quite apart from the attraction of those bodies.

Truth to tell, there was something cultic in my encounter with the unfamiliar discipline. Residence in Rome afforded me entrée to a community the kind of which I, at least, had never seen among literature scholars. To join an impromptu leaderless Caravaggio tour from San Luigi dei Francesi to Sant'Agostino to Santa Maria del Popolo or to engage, among friends, in the early morning race through the Vatican so as to have a little quiet time at the end of the compulsory itinerary among the Raphaels: These were sacred journeys in almost the same sense as the faithful might do the pilgrimage route to Compostela because the relics of St. James can be found nowhere else but at the end of that trek.

This materiality was also a sociality, and that counted for a lot in my long bachelor days. We gathered together in front of the art relic, talked about it, went for a glass of wine afterward, then found a favorite pizzeria known only to the cognoscenti, and then went for a grappa, and then . . . ? I know that some English department colleagues led a similar existence in and around the British Museum, but it never happened to me.

There was a problem, however. Ovid and Titian, poet and painter, are indeed two hearts beating as one. The continental literary Renaissance from Dante and Petrarch to Montaigne and Cervantes flourishes inside a shared consciousness that there have been geniuses in another medium, the visual medium, operating for a couple of millennia and continuing into the present day. But cross the channel, and the drop in consciousness of this visual tradition is astonishing. Of course, there are artistic masterpieces produced in the British Isles through the Middle Ages and into the sixteenth century—architecture, portraiture, manuscript illumination—and poets from Chaucer to Spenser to Milton are well aware of the kind of classical literature that inspired visual realization. But for the kind of interdisciplinary cross-cultural argument about words and images that fueled my imagination, the data from the North were scarce.

An exception that proves the rule: Ben Jonson, in a set of rambles that got published after his death under the title *Timber, or Discoveries*, offers up a little history of classical art, pinched from Pliny and Vitruvius, and then, in even briefer form, a list of more recent practitioners:

> There lived in this latter age six famous painters in Italy [he actually lists seven; these are, indeed, rambles], who were excellent and emulous of the ancients—Raphael de Urbino, Michael Angelo Buonarotta, Titian, Antonio of Correggio, Sebastian of Venice, Julio Romano, and Andrea del Sarto.

He cannot even pretend to have seen their work. The sultan in Constantinople negotiated with Michelangelo about building a bridge over the Bosporus, but the learned Ben Jonson more than a hundred years later can hardly get the artist's name right. To be sure, one can pick up a bit of media crossover here and there. Panofsky nourished a forlorn hope that Shakespeare had somehow seen Titian's *Venus and Adonis*, and if you closely read the ekphrases in *The*

Faerie Queene or *Lucrece*, you may get a sense that there is some awareness of what Italian Renaissance narrative art might look like, but mostly these are composed on the basis of earlier literary accounts of visual art and not on the experience of images themselves.

Into this blank space enter those final scenes in *The Winter's Tale*. Where did Shakespeare get the idea of the Hermione statue that comes to life? Though there is nothing like it in the play's principal source, Robert Greene's *Pandosto* (where the Hermione character stays dead), there is plenty of ambient literature, typically based on Ovid's Pygmalion, in which young men fall in love with statues of women that then come to life. That in itself is not so surprising. What is extraordinary and utterly unique is the fact that this statue is credited not to a character out of Greek mythology but to a real Renaissance artist (albeit whose fame rests entirely on his work as a painter) and, equally, that the episode is saturated with the actual language of Renaissance artistic theory. The Hermione statue, in other words, is not just a residue from the world of classical myth; she is a material work of sculpture exhibited in what is essentially an art collection. Which for me made her the golden spike that joins a literary masterpiece in English with the visual arts of the Italian Renaissance.

But there was more at stake for me here than Renaissance art. At the end of the preface to *Unearthing the Past*, which was published in 1999 and written a couple of years earlier, I took aim at the New Historicism, though I was coy about naming it:

> Critics of recent decades, particularly in regard to the Renaissance,
> have brought about a revolution in method, proposing new ways of
> reading the presence of history inside aesthetic objects. Many of these
> scholars have worked under the assumption . . . that history is
> essentially the workings of power in society. I want to separate
> what seems to me a brilliant methodology from what can be an
> underinvestigated set of assumptions. It is not only politics, society,
> and economics that generate the impulses of art; it is also art itself. I
> hesitate to speak up for a New Aestheticism—slogans, after all, are
> better born than made—but perhaps the history that follows in these
> many pages can speak in that language for itself.
>
> (xxxii)

The slogan, as predicted, didn't catch on, but it's well worth repeating the sentiment that aesthetic objects require, alongside whatever else scholars bring to them, aesthetically oriented methodologies. That would sound self-evident only to an individual unfamiliar with the bibliography of scholarship on early modern culture over the last forty years, both before *Unearthing the Past* and since. It is very difficult, in life or in scholarship, to resist the notion that what

I called "the workings of power in society" is *the* master narrative for any account of the past and that it leaves rather little room for other narratives. And the more malign those workings appear in real life (and as I write this, they have been more malign than at any previous moment in my lifetime), the less space there seems to be for other narratives, notably of an aesthetic kind.

I offer two quite different sorts of personal credential for speaking my mind in all of this, and since this volume has "Me" in the title, I'm not ashamed to do so. First of all, I was, in a phrase I never heard until long after I had experienced the phenomenon, a "red diaper baby." Nothing very heroic, I hasten to say. My parents were rigorously leftist-doctrinaire but mostly in decades before I was born or of an age to understand it, nor did they play a prominent role in those movements or come under serious threat as a result. I remember the hateful McCarthy, and I was as a four-year-old marginally witness to riots against Paul Robeson. Even including these bits of biography begins to sound like asking for more special allowances than I deserve. I cite it as some sort of reason—not necessarily a justification—for a certain agnosticism on the political front. For me, membership in the revolution had neither much romance about it nor much sense of efficacy in making things better; there was also the chance, or even probability, that it would help bring on the far deadlier counterrevolution. Of course, the opposite political stance, whatever form it took, emerged, and continues to emerge, as something much much worse.

So the sense that my profession as a humanist scholar might contribute in kind to that master narrative of public life never took hold. On the other hand, I've always known that I passionately love the world's treasury of aesthetic objects for the simple reason that they give me pleasure. I don't pretend to know why this is or even what I mean by it. I know that there are arts that produce pleasure so real as to be instant, unmediated, and corporeal—say, *Così fan tutte* or the Isenheim Altarpiece or a perfectly executed eggplant parmesan—and, as I say this, I find it curious that the art for which I am most particularly credentialed—the verbal art—is, by my own admission, less likely to operate in this unmediated way. But I have attempted through my scholarly career not only to annex some less mediated arts but also to focus my attention on beauty, passion, and form wherever they merit observation, believing that these, too, exercise the "workings of power in society" and that it is worth my time to record the working of those aesthetic forces and worth the world's time to hear about it.

Why, then, *The Winter's Tale*? When Shakespeare elects to resolve the tragic elements of his narrative and turn sorrow to joy by means of a statue, and in particular to give that statue all the credentials of an actual work of art, he is installing the aesthetic at the center of his mimetic world. Further: We can read back from this choice a whole set of ways in which the play replaces mimesis with aisthesis.

We can begin with the space in the narrative that the statue is chosen to occupy. I don't think there is anything else in Shakespeare quite like the resolution of *The Winter's Tale*'s plot, that is to say, the extent to which we are left ignorant of what "really" happened. Hermione dies in act 3; Paulina announces it very emphatically. Perhaps a little too emphatically; perhaps Shakespeare is having Paulina protest too much: When one of the lords upon hearing of the death utters the appropriate formula "The higher powers forbid," which in practice means something like "How dreadful!" rather than "I don't believe you," Paulina seems to take it as an expression of doubt; on that basis, she offers to swear that it is true and, should there be any skeptics, to bring them to the direct sight of the corpse. Perhaps she is, as Gertrude says of the Player Queen, protesting too much. Whether to take all this insistence as confirming the death or as placing it in question, the scene ends with Leontes about to take up Paulina's invitation to experience ocular proof—offstage, of course:

> Prithee, bring me
> To the dead bodies of my queen and son:
> One grave shall be for both: upon them shall
> The causes of their death appear, unto
> Our shame perpetual. Once a day I'll visit
> The chapel where they lie, and tears shed there
> Shall be my recreation: so long as nature
> Will bear up with this exercise, so long
> I daily vow to use it. Come and lead me
> Unto these sorrows.

(3.2.232–41)

If the style of Paulina's announcement leaves a shadow of uncertainty about Hermione's death, this may seem to shut it quite definitively: There will be daily observation by the widower himself, which will have the effect of verifying the death notice.

After the sixteen-year interval, alternative information is offered, however. Immediately after we are told about the statue, the Second Gentleman reports that Paulina "hath privately twice or thrice a day, ever since the death of Hermione, visited that removed house" (5.2.103–5) where the statue is displayed.

"Twice or thrice a day" sounds like mealtimes (the way, much earlier, "Nine changes of the watery star" suggests pregnancy; no surprise in this play that time keeps getting specified), but this contradicts the information about the monument of mother and son in the chapel. Yet another, less precise, account is that which Hermione eventually delivers: "I | Knowing by Paulina that the oracle | Gave hope thou wast in being have preserved | Myself" (5.3.126–28). There is also testimony of a different kind from Antigonus, just before he deposits the infant Perdita and meets his doom on the seacoast of Bohemia:

> I have heard, but not believed, the spirits o' the dead
> May walk again: if such thing be, thy mother
> Appear'd to me last night, for ne'er was dream
> So like a waking.
>
> (3.3.15–18)

And he proceeds to act upon the premise that Hermione is dead and has returned to him as a ghost:

> Dreams are toys:
> Yet for this once, yea, superstitiously,
> I will be squared by this. I do believe
> Hermione hath suffer'd death, and that
> Apollo would, this being indeed the issue
> Of King Polixenes, it should here be laid,
> Either for life or death, upon the earth
> Of its right father.
>
> (3.3.38–45)

The whole matter is very fraught, and well beyond the plot particulars of *The Winter's Tale*, as is evident whenever Shakespeare invokes ghosts, but this spectral visitation has to be marked down at least provisionally on the side of construing Hermione as dead, since, despite some few recorded instances to the contrary, live persons tend not to appear as ghosts. Either way, Shakespeare is playing with us: Hermione may be actually deceased, but Antigonus's conclusion on the subject—that she had been proven adulterous and therefore deserved to have her supposedly illegitimate child deposited on paternal soil— is clearly erroneous. Matters are left indeterminate.

In fact, the question of Hermione's condition during the sixteen missing years is not just a narrative tease but also a cultural quandary. Elsewhere, when Shakespeare restores individuals presumed dead—Claudio in *Measure for Measure*, Hero in *Much Ado*, or Ferdinand and Miranda in *The Tempest*—there

tends to be a single story of a rational (though not necessarily plausible) kind
made manifest to the audience ahead of time. In *The Winter's Tale*, Shakespeare
locates us, first of all, in a state of uncertainty and, secondly, faced with a
difficult choice between one possibility that is almost farcical in its implausibility
(Paulina delivers Grubhub to the garden shed twice a day) and another that is
problematic in its orthodoxy (she died, was resurrected, and in between
appeared as a prophetic ghost). It's Polixenes, of all people, who, very lucidly,
outlines the two possibilities once the statue has been unveiled and the wish
arises to have her speak:

> Ay, and make manifest where she has lived,
> Or how stol'n from the dead.

$$(5.3.114–15)$$

The truth—*my* truth—is that she is neither alive nor dead; she is a statue. The
statue—that is, Hermione as an object of aesthetic beauty—solves the problem. As a piece of sculpture, she possesses enduring life, though frozen into
stillness, as well as enduring beauty, with the significant qualifier of sixteen
years' worth of aging. When the wrinkles are cited as a challenge to the statue's
verisimilitude, they get turned into a signifier of *both* living body *and* aesthetic
object: On the one hand, they reflect the natural process of aging (as marble
cannot), while on the other hand they are credited to "our carver's excellence,
| Which lets go by some sixteen years" (5.3.30).

Before we have our own access to the statue, Shakespeare locates almost
all the major resolutions of the plot offstage. The revelations that emerge from
the "fardel" of the shepherds that Autolycus . . . well . . . shepherded, the fulfillment of the oracle, the identification of Perdita as the king's daughter, the
confirmation of the fate of Antigonus: All of this is presented not before our
eyes as theater but in a long-winded prose conversation among mostly
nameless minor characters who were onlookers to a set of scenes that we're
not allowed to behold. Shakespeare, in short, defies the rule that, doubtless,
every latter-day playwriting teacher would impose; he *tells* rather than *shows*.
This curiously awkward means of transmission does not for a moment allow
us to forget that the life we are watching has been shaped, framed, authored.
On the one hand, this is presented as a limitation. The Second Gentleman,
as it develops, missed out on the scene itself; in response to him the Third
Gentleman says, sorrowfully, "Then have you lost a sight which was to be seen,
cannot be spoken of" (5.2.42). We've been cheated exactly as he was. It's a joke
on theater itself, a parody avant la lettre of the kind of thing Brecht had in
mind with the *Verfremdungseffekt*; Shakespeare insists on reminding us, lest

we be seduced by the presence of real bodies (or statues), that aesthetic labor is being exerted here, all the more so because it is being done awkwardly. It's the "Pyramus and Thisbe" effect all over again: We observe aesthetic production *an sich* when it is flawed, when the labor of imitating reality reveals itself transparently.

These narrators, who, in a manner of speaking, stand in the way of the real and upon whom we are arbitrarily forced to depend, begin to sound like theater critics:

> FIRST GENTLEMAN   The dignity of this act was worth the audience of
>   kings and princes; for by such was it acted.
> THIRD GENTLEMAN   One of the prettiest touches of all and that which
>   angled for mine eyes . . . was when, at the relation of the queen's
>   death . . .
>
>   (5.2.78–82)

Real life is not "acted"; real life does not have "touches" (*OED*, "touch" 10B, which cites the Painter in *Timon* 1.1.38). Life is not arranged for the purpose of bringing tears to the eyes of the observer because it doesn't, in that sense at least, have an observer. Audience in this passage is, in fact, definitive of the aesthetic rather than the real experience. The Third Gentleman reports on the audience reaction: "Some swooned, all sorrowed; if all the world could have seen't, the woe had been universal" (5.2.88–90). It sounds like the wish-fulfillment dream of a Broadway producer.

All of which is preparing us for the crowning instance of life observed, which is the framing of life literally as an aesthetic object:

> The princess hearing of her mother's statue, which is in the keeping of
> Paulina—a piece many years in doing and now newly performed by
> that rare Italian master, Julio Romano, who, had he himself eternity
> and could put breath into his work, would beguile Nature of her
> custom, so perfectly he is her ape: he so near to Hermione hath done
> Hermione that they say one would speak to her and stand in hope of
> answer: thither with all greediness of affection are they gone, and there
> they intend to sup.
>
>   (5.2.92–101)

The naming of Giulio Romano remains an astonishing surprise. Shakespeare, after all, has a virtual interdict about referencing real people of his own time period anywhere in his work. Nor is there much evidence that he was following the history of Renaissance art closely enough to dip into the second rank of masters. It's interesting that Giulio appears on Jonson's list as well; perhaps there was some English source lost to us but known to both of them.

In the end, what may be more striking than the choice of this particular master is that there is a name at all. The citation of a real artist, unknown to most members of the audience but with a resounding Italianate moniker (Julius the Roman: the great Caesar reborn as a sculptor?), summons up a far-off pictorial culture of great prestige. The central datum about this pictorial culture, familiar even to those who had never heard of Giulio Romano or seen a single example of any Italian master's work, was the endlessly repeated claim, common to Pliny in antiquity and Vasari in the sixteenth century, that great artists produced perfect likenesses of their subjects. It is exactly the attribute of the visual arts that inspires envy among those whose medium consists of mere words. Italian Renaissance artists, however much or little the average Elizabethan theatergoer knew about them, were known to possess the summit of this skill. So the magic of the living Hermione is brought to us via the exercise of artistic genius; she is as much a miracle of verisimilitude as she is a miracle of love. True love and true art both result in perfect likeness.

As Shakespeare cunningly phrases it, there is more than one artistic verisimilitude involved here. "A piece many years in doing and now newly performed by that rare Italian master, Julio Romano": As will become apparent when we actually see the work in question, Shakespeare is at pains to use language that refuses to choose a side in the game of statue versus real person. Both sculpture and persons can be said to be "many years in doing." And, as for "now newly *performed*," it is an even bolder stroke in that same game. The primary meaning of this verb in 1600 is, per the *OED*, "To carry out in action, execute, or fulfill (a command, request, undertaking, threat, etc.)." At that moment it is only just beginning to be narrowed down to the specific case of theatrical labor. (One of the earliest *OED* citations for that meaning is, in fact, Prospero to Ariel, "Bravely the figure of this harpy hast thou perform'd" [3.3.84], and even there we can see the overlap between the two meanings, the birth, as it were, of our narrower, theatrical sense of the term out of its original, legalistic meaning. The term is also at the heart of the superficially nonsensical but deeply signifying babble of *Hamlet*'s Gravedigger, parsing the question of Ophelia's suicide: "An act hath three branches—it is to act, to do, to perform" [5.1.11–12], the terminology in this case imported from a famous law case.) At this moment in *The Winter's Tale*, Giulio Romano is, with a wink and a nudge, doing double duty as a theater artist. The statue is Shakespeare's escape attempt from the same limitations of language that I was trying to evade by dallying between two disciplines.

But all that is just the setup. For the real conjunction of mimesis and aesthesis, we must find ourselves in the company of the statue herself. The final scene begins with the delicious detail that Paulina actually has an extensive private art gallery and that at this critical juncture, with everyone reunited and identities reestablished, the group has been (forcibly?) detained by a Paulina-led tour of her lesser acquisitions, rather the way you have to slog through a couple kilometers of papal knickknacks at the Vatican before you reach the Sistine Chapel. It's part of the same game whereby the sculptural identity of the Hermione figure is insisted upon as valid. But the authenticity of Hermione-as-statue doesn't depend on the fact that she is in a museum. It depends on the way Shakespeare has absorbed the classical and Renaissance discourse of the visual arts as locus of perfect mimesis.

These claims are woven into some very concentrated, even metaphysical, language. First, Paulina, just before she unveils the statue:

> here it is: prepare
> To see the life as lively mock'd as ever
> Still sleep mock'd death: behold, and say 'tis well.

(5.3.18)

It is a complex passage, the nodal points of which are, first, a formal analogy that can be expressed as

Art:life :: sleep:death

and, second, the term *mock'd*, which seems to be the engine of the analogy. Just as sleep "mocks" (whatever that means, exactly) death, so art "mocks" life. What we *want* "mock" to mean is, roughly, imitate or counterfeit (to choose the glosses from Pafford's and Orgel's editions), but if we substitute "imitate" for "mock," we end up with a rather banal proposition: Sleep looks like death, but isn't; art looks like life, but isn't. It's the heritage of Plato and Aristotle all over again: Mimesis disparaged as mockery. Which doesn't seem quite enough for this remarkable moment.

But let us step back from the specific language and reclaim the experience. Shakespeare devises a narrative in which persons enter into a gallery and experience the transformation of an art object into a living being. It is a fantasy. No such thing could ever have happened to Shakespeare, and not only because there were no public galleries in England at that time. Of course, he is always writing—and brilliantly, even photographically—about experiences he cannot have had; in this case, he is constructing a metaphor about love. As for me, I walk back along that metaphoric line and find love and art on the same site. I won't say that I never enter an art gallery without entertaining the expectation of art coming to life, but I do think that the Hermione miracle, which I have absorbed in the way that I customarily come to believe the greatest fictions as real, is my answer to and my substitute for all those art history courses that I never attended.

In particular, the Hermione miracle frames my relationship to Michelangelo. I'm not sure what was the first time that I entered a room and found myself in the living presence of Michelangelo: It could have been the *David* in the Accademia or the *Pietà* in St. Peter's or the *Moses* in S. Pietro in Vincoli. There is nothing very original about claiming a transcendent experience in front of masterpieces like these, works so famous as to have been eroded in the imagination by their endless reproduction. For me, it was Shakespeare and the statue of Hermione that scripted a viewer experience that broke outside the clichés:

There is an air comes from her . . .

(5.3.78)

Would you not deem it breathed?

(5.3.63)

Does not the stone rebuke me
For being more stone than it?

(5.3.37–38)

And it was this experience, Shakespeare and Michelangelo together—my two gods of aisthesis, with what has always been for me an uncanny doppelgänger relationship—that has taken me through the writing of three books largely or wholly devoted to a visual artist whom I have no traditional credentials to study other than this sense of an intimacy and a receptivity that owes everything to that fairy tale of Hermione's statue.

I have predecessors in this force field, as it turns out. There was a widely quoted poetic exchange concerning Michelangelo's marble figure of *Night* in the Medici Chapel. The statue is of a massive reclining female, her eyes shut, and her posture arranged such that she is deeply wound up in herself. Even within the Olympian world of Michelangelo's sculptural masterpieces, this work has always occupied an exceptional place. If there is a "real" connection— the historically provable kind—between these geniuses, it comes back to this episode and to its prominent presence in Vasari's *Lives*, published in 1550 and then in an expanded edition in 1568, available in Shakespeare's England, though not in translation. The whole poetic exchange concerning the statue of *Night* is quoted there, and Vasari's own words make it even more tempting to draw the connections:

What can I say of the Night, a statue not rare only, but unique? Who is there who has ever seen in that art in any age, ancient or modern, statues of such a kind? For in her may be seen not only the stillness of one sleeping, but the grief and melancholy of one who has lost a great and honoured possession. . . . In that statue is infused all the somnolence that is seen in sleeping forms; wherefore many verses in Latin and rhymes in the vulgar tongue were written in her praise by persons of great learning, such as these.

The Night that you see sleeping here in such loveliness
Was by an Angel carved in this rock,
and by her sleeping she has life;
wake her, if you disbelieve, and she will speak to you.*

The conceit, which the subject of the statue makes possible, is that the stillness of a marble statue (inevitable, since it's made of marble) is *not*, as the casual observer might assume, a sign that the human figure represented is dead but rather that she is asleep—that is, alive, immobile only momentarily, and capable of awakening in an instant. To translate it into aesthetic terms, the statue is of a verisimilitude that borders on life, once it "awakens." Michelangelo replied to this, as Vasari also records, in the voice of Night and, swerving toward his own preoccupations, referencing the Medici, who were then in power:

Welcome to me is sleep, more so being made of stone.
While crime and shame endure;
Not to see, not to hear is my good fortune
Therefore disturb me not; please, speak softly.

The aestheticizing concerns of *The Winter's Tale* are uncannily present in all of this. Shakespeare's narrative seeks to take us past the point where art requires the metaphor either of sleep or of death and toward a state in which it becomes unmetaphorically life itself. In his story, the loss of "a great and honoured possession" will be remedied, and, as for the endurance of "crime and shame," their epoch is about to be concluded once the statue awakens. What Shakespeare is constructing here, similar in certain ways to the shockingly antitheatrical and tell-don't-show style of the previous scene and to the sly punning on "perform," is a celebration of his own aesthetic medium, which

---

*Giorgio Vasari, *Lives of the Painters, Sculptors, and Architects*, trans. Gaston duC. de Vere (New York Everyman's Library, 1996), 2:682. The verse, left in the original in that edition, is translated here by the present author.

mocks the limitations of "real" (that is, pseudo-real) statues for not being real and depending on mere metaphors to be equatable with life.

Mock continues to be a key term in this conversation:

POLIXENES   Masterly done:
  The very life seems warm upon her lip.
LEONTES
  The fixture of her eye has motion in't,
  As we are mock'd with art.

                                                 (5.3.65–68)

LEONTES   Still, methinks,
  There is an air comes from her: what fine chisel
  Could ever yet cut breath? Let no man mock me,
  For I will kiss her.

                                                 (5.3.77–80)

Mock has now become more a property of the observer than of the object observed. Art, at this stage of the process, is understood not as mocking life but as mocking those who believe in it. Wrong again, Leontes; he will continue to have something to learn until the moment when he fully receives Hermione once more. For now, he imagines that belief in the reality of the artistic object/love object is the kind of credulity that deserves ridicule. His struggle at this point is reminiscent of those much earlier struggles in which, repeatedly, his language became incoherent. Paulina urges him to stop gazing on the statue, "lest your fancy | May think anon it moves":

LEONTES   Let be, let be.
  Would I were dead, but that, methinks, already—
  What was he that did make it? See, my lord,
  Would you not deem it breathed? and that those veins
  Did verily bear blood?

                                                 (5.3.60–65)

Editors have generally shied away from taking Leontes's death wish literally, turning it into the equivalent in our idiom of a throwaway expression like "I'll be damned if I don't think the statue has moved," which doesn't really mean that the speaker expects to spend eternity in hell. Perhaps so, but I take this sudden, rather non sequitur, interest in the statue's maker as a last-ditch effort on Leontes's part to normalize the relation between the viewer and the (safely inert) art object. Giulio Romano—if only Leontes could remember his name—would save him from the terror/joy of a resurrected real Hermione. Like a properly orthodox early modern Englishman, Leontes needs some reassurances.

First, that no "wicked powers" are involved in this operation (5.3.91). That having been established, Paulina can, like her avatar and namesake St. Paul, assure him of the holiness of spirits (cf. 1 Corinthians 12) and utter the magic words, "It is required you do awake your faith" (5.3.94–95), which speaks to Leontes on the plane of love and marriage while speaking to the rest of us— me, at least—on the plane of the mimetic/aesthetic object.

I suppose it is the course of my own life that has made me particularly receptive to this seesaw binary reading of *The Winter's Tale*. When I sat with my cousin Jon at BAM a quarter-century ago, I was a lonely aesthete, hungry on both counts, and the play could pivot in my consciousness at will between the love story and the tale about art, the first because I lacked it and the second because I possessed it but was nevertheless insatiable for more. Now, a couple of decades into a love that has never been subject to anything like the aberration that possessed Leontes, I take the love story, or jealousy story (one and the same, and together occupying the largest share of stage time), a little bit as some kind of formulaic romance narrative that has to find a problem where, on the plane of "real life," there needn't be one. Not that it's impossible to "relate" the main plot to my experience, but—we work with what we've got—I end up with something a little less (what shall I call it?) *hetero-normative*. The fantasy (and that's clearly what it is) of an illicit sexual relationship between one's beloved spouse and one's best friend has a kind of perverse logic. It completes the circle of love and sex centering on oneself, offering a voyeuristic engagement in the friend's sexuality while definitively excluding the fourth individual, who, in this case somewhere out in far-off Bohemia, has the proper right to lay claim to the best friend. And Shakespeare could scarcely have done more to erase the existence of Polixenes's queen, who is nameless and invisible. The entire orbit of desire is made to travel around Leontes.

If, nowadays, I attempt to read *The Winter's Tale*'s main plot as about me, I am forced to tell the saddest story of my love life. For about twenty-five years I had a best friend, ten years younger than me and uncomplicatedly heterosexual, a circumstance that was probably the central enabling factor of our intimacy. Along with Jon, he constituted my life of intimacy. I never wanted to go to bed with Aaron; he never withheld any of the signs of affection that exist in this world outside the bedroom—which are most of the best ones. Aaron, as I think about him, makes me understand why Montaigne said about de la Boétie, *parce que c'était lui, parce que c'était moi*. To say because it was him, because it was me, is precisely to say, there is no explaining our intimacy any more than we can explain our own selves; the intimacy and the selves are inextricable. We could talk about absolutely nothing and amuse ourselves for hours; we could cook or taste wine with an absurd conviction that these were the most important things in the world to be doing. We could face our own individual crises together and find our way through them as though they were jokes. We had completely different styles, but each of us was fiercely loyal to the other; right or wrong, right *and* wrong mattered not so much. The narrative of our lives overlapped very little: We pursued completely different professions, and over the twenty-five years of our friendship we lived in the same city for a total of about six months. There were some massive battles and some enduring wounds, but if he were to appear right now at my front door, I would—actually, I don't know what I'd do. No. I'd say to myself, "Leontes, you are one lucky son of a bitch."

Aaron married a smart, caring, sturdy sort of wife; I was, of course, best man at their wedding. But he never recovered from a much earlier love affair—a person he knew before we had met—and after a while he began a long and intricately staged affair with her, living a lie of a narrative complexity that I couldn't have tolerated for a quarter of an hour and that Shakespeare would have written off as bad theater. I can't resurrect the calendar of all this, but he must have gone on with this arrangement for a decade at least before it finally normalized itself with a pair of relevant divorces. Before all this readjustment was complete he and I simply ceased to communicate. No fight, no scenes of jealousy, no Camillo despatched to assassinate either one of us.

Was there a cause why this love of mine came to an end? The best I can do is to invoke (but certainly not blame) the spouses. He had a fixed and angrily promoted belief that I was opposed to his extramarital affair. There was nothing I could do to persuade him otherwise, and, despite my disclaimers, he may well have been right. The truth is probably that I feared if he concluded his marriage, he would conclude with me as well. If that's what I thought, I was exactly correct; he may have seen all that more clearly than I did. As for my spouse, who came into my life many years into the time of that friendship, his notions of love are far too *oceanic* (I'm using Freud's word; by Freud it's a bad thing; by me it's the *best* thing) to feel he had to displace anyone or to fear that anyone would displace him. The responsibility is mine: I apparently didn't need the turmoil and uncertainty of my Montaignian friendship—*parce que c'était lui, parce que c'était moi*—anywhere near as much as I had needed it before I found the oceanic sensation in love.

That's too simple; it doesn't take into account the sorrow I still feel when I think about the lost friendship. Recently, I was having students stage *The Winter's Tale* statue scene in class—who can resist it?—and, since I didn't want to cheat any of them by assigning a part with very few lines, I stepped in to read Polixenes (interesting, isn't it, that he has so few lines; what is there left for him to say?). They are all standing in front of the statue, Camillo repeats the consolations we've heard before, that Leontes has suffered enough for his terrible mistake and should be easier on himself after all these years. Whereupon Polixenes says,

> Dear my brother,
> Let him who was the cause of this have power
> To take off so much grief from you as he
> Will piece up in himself.
>
> (5.3.53–56)

I rattled it off unthinkingly—the worst thing you can do in this situation is try to look like a better actor than your students—but then I actually listened to what I had just said. It's preposterous that Polixenes should, first, call himself the "cause of this" and, second, promise to unload a share of the suffering from Leontes to himself. (Recollect that Hermione has not yet come to life, so the suffering that Polixenes is offering to shoulder is of unbearable weight.)

This more or less throwaway comment, soon to become irrelevant in the light of the happy ending, nevertheless gave me a glimpse of a fictional future. Even with a happy ending, or *especially* with a happy ending, what will have become of the friendship between the two men? It's always a mistake—again, I tell students this but with only middling sense of having convinced them— to postulate futures beyond the scope of the text. But I somehow could not prevent myself from the absurd act of imagining the two couples, everything patched up, five or ten years in the future, let's say, on the SS *Apollo* taking a cruise in the Greek isles together. Unimaginable: Suddenly the play starts to look a little less like the story of a broken and then healed marriage and a little more like the machine for destroying a dangerously intense male friendship.

The truth is that I had, in the years before what I call my oceanic love, specialized in dangerously intense male friendships, all love, no sex; they were all-consuming for a while—six months, twenty-five years—then they weren't. If I harp on the friendship angle in the play and if even the play's happy ending doesn't satisfy me as much about the future of the two men as it does about the married couple—after all in the classical formula persons released their same-sex bonds when their heterosexual marriages were confirmed—it's probably because my own life has witnessed so many friendships that, quite without apparent drama or cause, simply dissolved. I recently came across a little pre–Palm Pilot leather-bound address book, which flourished in my life around the same time that Jon and I were watching *The Winter's Tale*. Leaving aside the deaths (12) and the names that summon up no recollection whatsoever (9), I find 27 individuals with whom I was once close—anything from multiple evenings spent in their company to more than one soul-searching session together to ongoing heavy erotic vibes to all of the above—who have simply vanished from my life. It's no wonder that I might zero in on Leontes and Polixenes.

My beautiful cousin sitting next to me at BAM is a different story. Once we found each other as friends, as brothers, all the potential differences, beginning with our sexual orientations, made no difference. I don't think it was because we were cousins (I'd certainly ditched most of my other relatives). And it certainly wasn't because we never argued: There was actually the freedom to fight, sometimes bitterly, in the knowledge that there would never be a divorce. And he was just enough younger than me so that I had always felt he'd be there to take care of me, to take care of everything. I was wrong about that. Jon, as I already knew when we were sitting together in Brooklyn, had been diagnosed with a rare blood disorder. Healthy young people like himself, he'd been told, lived on for at least fifteen years under the existing treatments. Jon only made it as far as twelve years. It was he, more than Aaron, who was Montaigne's *parce que c'était lui, parce que c'était moi* intimate friend, stolen away long before his time.

Only in the instant of writing these words does it occur to me that taking Jon to *The Winter's Tale* may not have been entirely accidental, chosen randomly as opposed to, say, making the easier trek to Broadway for *The Glass Menagerie* or *The Flying Karamazov Brothers*, which were playing at the same time. Was I hoping for some Shakespearean sympathetic magic? Was I imagining another draft of the play in which it is Polixenes rather than, or in addition to, Hermione who dies but can come back to life? Perhaps so, but Shakespeare proves infuriatingly unsentimental on this point. Was I trying to repair, as Shakespeare does not, the loss of Mamillius? The play, after all, begins by establishing a kind of risky extremity in the friendship between Leontes and Polixenes:

> Sicilia cannot show himself over-kind to Bohemia. They were trained together in their childhoods; and there rooted betwixt them then such an affection, which cannot choose but branch now.

> (1.1.20–23)

For me, this passage, whose original purpose may involve merely the humdrum necessity of conveying plot information at the outset of the action, is uncannily evocative. Readers may well have noted throughout the present volume that I am drawing parallel and intersecting lines between myself and Shakespeare's works but—here's the important detail—avoiding anything like literal equivalences. There are a few occasions when that breaks down, and I am forced into the naïve, even infantile, position of saying that my reality and his fiction coincide. Jon and I were trained together in our childhoods and (eventually) there rooted betwixt us, etc., etc.

At which point Shakespeare delivers a zinger that will extend the parallel, though with a difference. To characterize the relation between the two kings at the play's opening, he chooses a word—*branch*—that has a set of opposite meanings. What we're principally to understand is that when they were young they were like a pair of saplings that now should be growing into mature trees, producing branches but still entwined, *trained* being a term with reference to both education and horticulture. But to *branch* is also to grow apart, as they will soon do. The implication here, with either meaning of *branch*, is of inevitability; that's the way metaphors from nature always work, particularly in premodern times when human beings looked upon the workings of nature as more mysterious and inexorable than we do. Was it inevitable that Leontes and Polixenes *branch* (in the sense of *separate*)? Or that Aaron and I did? Shakespeare had clearly sworn off writing the kind of play based on the sort of *branching*—the branching by death—that Jon and I were going to suffer. So far as branching with Aaron is concerned, it feels from this distance just as inexorable, as a blood disease. Leontes is too possessive, Polixenes too naïve: That's the sort of thing one would say if the two of them existed in real life. As for my own real life, I am less certain what to say.

But real life is inadequate to Shakespeare anyway. If I hold on to the idea that *The Winter's Tale* is above all about the aesthetic object, clearly it's in part a kind of defense against the *real* in real life. The play *is* the beautiful object, the perfect statue that can heal the wounds of real life. Hence, perhaps, Shakespeare's almost comical insistence that it is a *tale*. Mamillius offers up a *sad* tale; the fabulous denouement is drummed into us to as "so like an old tale" (5.2.28), "like an old tale still" (5.2.58), and, again when the denouement has been fully reached, "like an old tale still" (5.3.117). The central property of a *tale* is that it is false, or so we're being told, and the gathering repetition of this message is like an act of Pavlovian conditioning: For each impossible event, we are reminded with the repeated *tale* that even as the play is promoting the truth of these events there is something false about them. We sit there in the audience fighting this; our empathetic wish is that the tale *be* true, since at this point it's only the happy ending, and never the sadness preceding it, that is characterized as a mere *tale*, a fiction. Happy endings, this play that contrives so many of them is saying, are fictions. At the same time, what the statue helps us realize is that fiction—or artistic representation—is not (contrary, once again, to Plato) an inferior form of reality. The play—at least for *this* reader— is dedicated to the proposition that art is superior to life, that improbable stories are better than probable ones, that Bohemia *should* have a seacoast even if it doesn't, and that, while we're imagining Bohemia, let's give it deserts right next to the seacoast (equally unfactual) where mauling bears abound, that statues can come to life and princesses, though believed to be dead, can come back to life. If princes, on the other hand, do not survive, if love dies, or if loves die, there exists somewhere an artifact, a statue, an evening in Brooklyn, a memory.

5

Queer

In the early 1980s, I was on friendly terms with a colleague who was—*is*—a celebrated essayist and of a staunchly neoconservative bent. It's not much of a tribute to either of us, that is, to his perspicacity or to my forthrightness, that he may well have believed I shared his political views, or at least that I wasn't among the sorts of colleagues who participated in hurling a bloodlike substance at a right-wing campus speaker. (He was right about that; I wasn't.) He was good company, we bonded around a certain sort of vernacular Yiddishkeit, and we didn't talk politics. Around this time, the Yale historian John Boswell published a game-changing book called *Christianity, Social Tolerance, and Homosexuality: Gay People in Western Europe from the Beginning of the Christian Era to the Fourteenth Century.* My colleague, who was the editor of a highly regarded cultural journal, asked me to review it. This was early days in my own career, and such invitations were not coming my way very often. Exactly what qualified me for this assignment in my colleague's mind was not clear to me. He may have imagined that any professional specialty in Western culture whose focus predated, say, the early novels of Saul Bellow was pretty much of a piece; in other words, it may not have been evident to him that a Renaissance specialist was distinct from a medievalist, with a well-defended firewall between them. And as for the other area of expertise that Boswell's book summoned up: This was never discussed between us.

As I started to read the book, which is as breathtaking in its scholarly display as it is aggressive in its argumentation, it dawned on me, considering the source of the invitation to review it, that it was just possible I was being set up to trash it. In other words, that my colleague, who was in the habit of preaching to his own choir, was hiring me to chant a few like-minded hymns of my own directed against what he may have assumed was scholarship from the hard left. I pled insufficient expertise, outlined the difference between Lorenzo de' Medici and Charlemagne, and the whole thing got cordially dropped. The book, however, made an enormous impression on me, and for reasons that, paradoxically, might have gladdened my colleague's neocon heart, had I ever fulfilled my writing assignment. Boswell's book isn't simple at all, but my reaction to it was: Here was a politically engaged, even activist scholar writing learnedly about his own—*my* own—community in the remote past who . . . now we get to the big point . . . was *not* telling us how appallingly we had been victimized by history.

It doesn't matter that this particular argument for an enlightened treatment of my community—the reading, for instance, of medieval church rituals so as to foreground some that bound together men in the equivalent of same-sex marriages, or the cheerfully promiscuous use of the term "gay people"—turned out to be the most factually and methodologically controversial aspects of Boswell's book. That would matter to (a) medievalists and (b) members of the methodology police. I was, and remain, neither. But the experience left me with the sense that I could do what I wanted to do—write about the European cultural past, which I loved—without having either to ignore or to wallow in the unspeakable sufferings of people like me.

It's no coincidence, therefore, that if you look at the work I have done in regard to groups who have historically suffered (and to which I belong), whether it's Jews or homosexuals, my subject has always been geared far more toward their triumphs than toward their oppression. Doubtless in both cases there has historically been a lot more oppression than triumph, and if it's the case that I am therefore painting myself into a tiny corner of their histories, I'm willing to accept that limitation, probably for the not-so-respectable reason that, since I have not myself been gravely limited by my membership in these groups, I do not wish to ground my own intellectual authority in sufferings that I have not undergone. This may be controversial; what, on the other hand, seems to me absolutely undeniable in the path I have chosen is that I am demonstrating my solidarity with these groups at least as much by chronicling their achievements as by bewailing the wrongs that they have suffered. There is room for both.

So my "gay" book pursued a Platonic reading of the Ganymede myth that associated the love between men and boys with the highest levels of wisdom and rapture. And I wrote my "Jew" book about the extraordinary flourishing of Berlin's Jewish community before 1933 and the ways in which the culture that Jewish and non-Jewish Berliners shared for a century before that fatal date remains visible in the city of today.

It's easy enough to think of *As You Like It* as Shakespeare dipping his toe into the dark waters of Queer. We'll never know the exact chronology of those fin-de-siècle romantic comedies of his, including *Twelfth Night* and *Much Ado*— all three of them, interestingly, with a gesture of self-deprecation in their titles—but among the things they have in common is the subject of disguise and, more often than not, cross-dressing. (Absent from *Much Ado* but, on the other hand, present in the subplot of *Merchant of Venice*.) In *Twelfth Night*, the gender dance raises the most profound questions about identity. In *Merchant*, where it's relegated to the sidelines, it is connected with the grim issues that are raised by the cross-dresser's father, Shylock. *As You Like It* is the site where cross-dressing is all about *play*. Indeed we might (playfully?) say it is the work that best justifies the lexical fact that the term with which we designate a work of dramatic literature is a noun borrowed from a verb that refers to the ludic activity that is performed by puppies, kittens, and children. (Full disclosure: the *OED* suggests that both meanings go back as far as English usage can be traced; it's nice to know that they have shared semantic space for so long.)

A boy actor plays a woman who dresses up as a man (or boy), who then impersonates a woman who becomes the mouthpiece for all the traits that (presumably male) antifeminists conventionally assigned to women, particularly their supposed crimes in relation to love, notably fickleness and infidelity. In itself, the action embodies the quintessential material of Shakespearean comedy: the world up for grabs, gender in a state of confusion, hardships real or feigned that put young people to the test so as to prepare them for the happy ending at which point they will be mature and properly paired off.

Where exactly does such a text leave the . . . (what shall we call him?) . . . aspiring homosexual, who, Shakespeare-nut that he is, was familiar with the play from a quite young age? For all of its narrative gender bending, this is perhaps Shakespeare's most insistent contribution on the wrong side of the gay marriage debate: *Marriage should be between a man and a woman!!!* No fewer than four such couples are ritually united in the closing minutes of the play, and in case we don't get it that such pairing off is not merely a human practice but rather a heavenly law, Shakespeare introduces Hymen as the god of marriage to cinch all these bonds. "Wedding is great Juno's crown . . .'Tis Hymen peoples every town" (5.4.136–38), she sings, but she wasn't going to be peopling my town until about 2013.

The perfectly reasonable counterargument as regards the play's underlying conservatism—and it's an argument that has some truth on its side—is that it allows us to glimpse alternatives even though none of them is enshrined in the ending. What a pity! Wouldn't it be delicious if Jaques, instead of gloomily trudging off at the end to join with the formerly bad Bad Duke in some kind of penance project ("Out of these convertites | There is much matter to be heard and learned," he declares [5.4.179–80]), announced that he and the above-mentioned Duke were taking a summer cottage together in P-Town? That would tie up all the only loose ends; alas, it is not to be.

What we *do* have—and it is not to be underestimated—is some truly radical thinking about the category that we call gender, by which I mean a way of thinking about sexual identity that isn't necessarily fixed and binary and that isn't focused on the genitals. Rosalind's disguise—the whole roller coaster whereby she cascades from boy actor to girl character to disguised boy, etc.— can stand as virtually exemplary for the notion that gender is performance, that the way persons—let's call them males and females—operate in the world is learned, rehearsed, perfected, much in the way that theatrical roles come into full operation. I'd love to declare that this procedure as fictionalized in the play amounted to sexual liberation for our young viewer, who was, in fact, dazzled by a Stratford, Connecticut, production of the play when he was in high school. And I've given a lot of thought, retrospectively, to why he wasn't. The best I can come up with is that the whole "performing gender" thing—which of course did not exist as an intellectual topic, even to grown-ups, in 1961—puts an extraordinary burden on the subject. Me, aged seventeen, in other words. I think that this particular subject didn't want to be told that he could invent his own sexuality; he wanted to find one that was preexisting and that he could slip into with all the comfortable fit of a favorite sweater. Far from showing the way, *As You Like It* was telling me that I had to bring heavy construction equipment to build the way—and then I might be the only person traveling on it.

As I've already suggested, this is a reconstruction from a great distance. It may or may not be true of the boy that I was, but I would argue that it captures something true about the play, that is, about the way it illustrates a certain escape from the tyranny of binaries but frames it with such grand embellishment as to leave the viewer helpless to follow its example. On the other hand, it seems to me now—though it certainly didn't in 1961—that there are a couple of moments in the play when some kind of liberation can be glimpsed.

When Viola in *Twelfth Night* dons male attire for reasons roughly similar to Rosalind's—that is, protecting herself from a world of uncertainty and danger—she takes the name Cesario. There is nothing particularly striking about the choice: At the risk of over-reading, one might say it seems to contain a little bit of Caesar and a suffix that adds a touch of miniaturization. She wants to be the biggest guy of all, but all she can manage is a diminutive. Rosalind's choice, "Ganymede," bears a good deal more weight, however. She herself glosses her alias as referring to "Jove's own page" (1.3.124), but that is a highly sanitized take on the rich traditions associated with the boy whom Jupiter, in the form of an eagle, abducted from earth to Olympus. Ganymede runs the gamut from the cognate *catamite*—the passive figure, typically a boy, in anal intercourse—to the ecstatic embodiment of Platonic wisdom (indeed, he is in those terms the hero of the book referenced here earlier as my "gay" book). Ganymede, Jupiter's desire for the boy, and the whole classical tradition surrounding such a liaison as invoked here, seems to me radically different from cross-dressing. That there is a sexual relation between the king of the gods and a beautiful Trojan boy: On the revolving wheel of desire, that's a quite different spot from dress-up.

The other moment comes in the final seconds of the performance. The action of marrying all those girls to all those boys having been concluded, the highest ranking character, Duke Senior, announces the beginning of revelry. There is a dance, then all but one of the performers leaves the stage. The individual who has played the role of Rosalind remains and begins with "It is not the fashion to see the lady the epilogue, but . . ." Which turns out to be absolutely true: We have no recorded previous instance in the Elizabethan theater of a female delivering a play's epilogue. Phrased that way, of course, it's a trick statement: There could be no female delivering an epilogue, since no females appeared on the stage. This boy actor thus begins—in case we didn't notice it—by calling attention to the matter of gender and continues by specifically dividing his message between the women in the audience and the men: "I charge you, O women, for the love you bear to men . . ." and "I charge you, O men, for the love you bear to women . . ." (Epilogue, 11–13), even though the two messages are essentially identical.

Only near the end does the speaker come out of the closet: "If I were a woman, I would kiss as many of you as had beards that pleased me" (16–18). It may be the most deliciously tiptoeing bit of gender-as-performance in the whole play, if not in the whole canon. This is a boy actor, who by playing Rosalind for the last couple of hours, has epitomized, literally, gender-as-performance. The offer that is being made here is itself exquisitely gender-precarious. My womanness is in the realm of contrary to fact ("if I were . . ."), but my proposal to kiss members of the audience is specifically limited to those with beards, and even that is in some way modulated by ". . . that pleased me," which introduces a sense that the erotic connection referred to here will be made by the choice of finding someone attractive, which—who knows?—might well supervene the particulars of officially constituted gender. "If I were a woman," which means, but does not say, "I am *not* a woman," enunciated after two or three hours of performing Rosalind and proposing an erotic connection that (as we would express it in the modern theater) breaks the fourth wall—all this as the very last thing that the play, which has been focusing upon no fewer than four heterosexual couples joined together by the goddess of a rite that is the unique prerogative of such couples, leaves us with—what can one say?—maximal uncertainty on a very important subject. It will be recalled that this is the play, courtesy of Touchstone, with that lovely conclusion to a bit of tangled discourse, "much virtue in if" (5.4.98): The biggest *if*, it turns out, is the one about gender. I leave the theater with the possibility of an open invitation.

Granted, this is quite a lot of baggage to hang on the hook of a single word. The Sonnets, with many thousands of words, are brimming over with challenges to sexual orthodoxy, yet, for me at least, they too present themselves as something of a problem. Perhaps it all comes down to the fact that I like narratives better than lyrics, and although this is a set of lyrics that definitely encompasses narrative, whenever I feel obliged to read a serious chunk of them in sequence and in bulk, I always say to myself, "Why didn't he just put this on stage?" Or perhaps it's just that I am uncomfortable about the claims of the first person, in particular its relation to the truth. Earlier in these pages, I cited St. Augustine, Dante, and Montaigne as authors who set an example and gave us permission to write about ourselves, indeed to write about the *self*. This great trio of the first person composed their work in different genres: autobiography, sacred epic, essay. But there is one literary genre that far outdistanced these in disseminating the writing of the self. Born in the thirteenth-century Sicilian court of the Holy Roman Emperor and launched massively upon European letters by Petrarch a century later, the sonnet became for three or four hundred years the essential template for poets in which to bare what they represented as their inmost thoughts and feelings. Curiously, these feelings turned out to concentrate on one theme almost to the exclusion of everything else: the expression of unfulfilled erotic desire. Which, at least for many decades, certainly worked for me.

There are certain consequences to this focus, apart from the amorous narrative itself. When Virgil composes the *Aeneid*, he may work very hard to impress upon his readers the reality of the events that he chronicles, but he makes no declaration that he witnessed them with his own eyes; the flight of the defeated Trojans toward Italy didn't happen to him. When Dante creates the fable of his universe-spanning journey during Easter weekend of 1300 and when Petrarch composes 366 poems devoted to one particular love story, they are not only making a truth claim about their own experience, they are also choosing to narrate a set of experiences (inward for Petrarch, inward *and* outward for Dante) for which there can be no authority but themselves. We sophisticated moderns and postmoderns may view *everything* as a fiction, but there are many indications that even in past epochs these particular first-person narratives occupied for their readers an uncomfortable space between reality and fiction. Early readers of the *Divine Comedy*, which, after all, made astonishing, even sacrilegious allegations about the author's personal experience, worked assiduously to prove or disprove the veracity of the poet's claims by carefully measuring the time frames and the astronomical indicators in the poem. As for Petrarch, even within his lifetime he found himself attacked on the grounds that the endlessly celebrated object of his desire, Laura, was a fabrication.

Is the *I* of the Sonnets in fact Shakespeare? It's a deceptively simple question. For a certain kind of reader who loves poetry but hasn't had the opportunity of being trained in multiple methodologies, the answer is obvious: yes. The speaker of the poems is apparently named "Will," and his experiences can be without too much trouble correlated with those that Shakespeare might have had. For that other, methodological kind of reader, the answer is just as obvious: of course not. Everything set down on a page diverges from the straightforward replication of experience the moment that it is crafted in language, and even for those who don't swallow all the terms of late-twentieth-century deconstruction it's clear that a document that makes autobiographical claims but frames them in the very artificial building requirements of a sonnet sequence must have traveled a considerable distance from raw experience.

The problem is complicated by the fact that it's about *Shakespeare*. By the late eighteenth century, and forever after, Shakespeare counts as an icon; for the English-speaking world and beyond, he is the Bard. Unlike certain other Bards—for instance, again, Dante and Petrarch—his bardic work is in the medium of theater, where the author appears to be completely submerged inside the personalities of his fictional characters and never managing to speak for himself. So, absent the Sonnets, the question "who *is* Shakespeare?" would be maddeningly impossible to answer. Thus, when we tire of wondering whether he was Hamlet or Lear or Prospero or Cleopatra or . . . fill in the blank—all very shaky equivalences indeed—we need only turn to this slim 1609 volume and find the truth there. Except that the slim volume is itself infuriatingly evasive on this very subject. Coincidental? Maybe not. The famous dedication ("To the onlie begetter of the ensuing sonnets Mr. WH . . .") that fails to nail down the identity of the parties involved; the almost farcical circumstance that so many poems are devoted to the idea of immortalizing the young man when in fact his identity has turned out to be definitively undecipherable; the sense that the whole narrative might be rather scandalous, whether on grounds of sexuality or of social class: It might almost appear that the maker, or makers, of this book were trying to confuse us. In other words, that the 1609 volume, rather than laying bare the inner life of the "real" Shakespeare, were intent on wrapping it in even more enigmas than the plays do.

Not only is it about *Shakespeare*, it also presents itself—no surprise in a sonnet sequence—as some kind of erotic autobiography. And even pursuing the most sanitized reading of these 150-odd poems, of a kind in which same-sex desire gets somehow explained away, there can be no denying that this is an act of fairly edgy public exposure. And that, in the end, may be the key to my problem with them, particularly in the framework of this book, where I read *King Lear* and *The Winter's Tale*, which are manifestly fictions produced at arm's length from the author's experience, and massage them into my own real experience. What happens, in short, when the poet's own self-exposure is jammed up against my personal truth-telling, also subject to question? And what if, as it happens, this self-reflexive practice à deux is bound to light upon matters of personality and experience that seem to bind author and reader (*this reader*, anyway) in some sort of special brotherhood across the gap between fiction and autobiography?

That may be the heart of the problem. I have already intimated on a number of occasions that I consider my capacity to suspend disbelief so absolute as to border on the delusional. Now the world literature of love and desire, with some notable exceptions, is heavily heterosexual, Shakespeare included. No problem: If I can massage my own inner voices such as to be deeply moved by Dante's arrival in Paradise or horrified by the success of Satan in *Paradise Lost*, none of which circumstances have the remotest place in my notions of reality, I can certainly embrace fictions of heterosexual desire and perform the necessary operations so that they reach me where it counts. What happens, then, when a piece of poetic fiction, brilliantly composed and with every sign of emotional authenticity, demands none of these exertions by way of adaptation into the contours of my own experience, my own map of desire?

What happens is, first of all, that I feel exposed. The fable of Shakespeare's Sonnets, in which a person of mature years desires a younger man, is, so far as male same-sex love stories are concerned, the quintessential ur-narrative. For a couple of thousand years, it's virtually the *only* such narrative; in antiquity, and sometimes later, it can shade off in directions that we (rightly) find abhorrent. Happily, neither I nor the Shakespearean speaker shows any signs of going there. The love object in the Sonnets is clearly of marriageable age, though of a younger generation than the speaker; such an arrangement is not unfamiliar to me, to say the least. This exposure is something like the demon that lurks threateningly at the center of this book itself. Reading Shakespeare and reading myself are intriguingly parallel operations; their aggregate pleasure arises out of the fruitful distance, the sparking gap that separates them. Otherwise, I really am like those naïve youngsters who can only read fictions narcissistically. Otherwise, I am just like those well-meaning but (let's face it) unsophisticated interlocutors who hear me talking about the Sonnets, raise their hands, and ask, "Was Shakespeare *gay*?"

For sure, Shakespeare wasn't gay. *Gay* is a historically specific designation, having over the last couple centuries veered off in part from being a simple equivalence to terms like "light-hearted" or "flashily dressed" into directions that were less complimentary, for example, "promiscuous" or even "engaging in prostitution." About a hundred years ago, its referent starts to be narrowed down to homosexuality, and in the twenty-first century it has become impossible to use the word "gay" in any of its older senses without explanation and apology. All this counts as more than the lexical pedantry of someone with an unnatural attachment to the *OED* because, like many histories of words, it tells us about the history of things. That narrowing of meaning for the word "gay" corresponds to the narrowing of the thing it designates. Shakespeare wasn't *gay* because he lived about 250 years before homosexuality itself was coming to be understood as something like a fixed category of human identity. One looks back on this development—to simplify greatly the work done so persuasively by David Halperin in *One Hundred Years of Homosexuality*—as a kind of good-news-bad-news story for us gay people, offering us the possibility of a certain sort of legitimacy but also framing us with a set of predictable traits, as though homosexuality were equivalent to left-handedness or AB-negative blood type. Hence the revival and repurposing of *queer*, which stands at the head of this chapter so that I can execute the matter of reading Shakespeare and reading me, as regarding sexuality, without forcing either one of us into a fixed space or necessarily even the same space.

The first time I ever fell in love—the kind of love where you think about them all the time, want to be in their company all the time, and count every minute with them as precious and worthy of close introspection afterward—it was with a couple. I was seventeen, he and she were a year or two older, and (pause for the weight of cliché to sink in) we were in Paris. They were newly, and, as it turned out, quite temporarily, a couple; he had someone else back home. For me, they divided between them what anyone would most desire in a love object: He was imposingly beautiful in a manly-but-tender sort of way, given to soul-searching that veered off into European philosophy; she was a musician and an ocean of welcoming sensitivity, too young to be an earth mother, more like an earth daughter. I contrived shamelessly and successfully, when we were being assigned living spaces in the Sorbonne foreign student residence, to hover next to him in the queue so that we would automatically become roommates; somehow (how is this possible?) there never seemed to be an awkward time when either of them wanted me out of the room so they could be alone together.

The whole summer was entirely too *Jules and Jim* to be believed. I loved them both, but not in the same way. I would have given my life for him; she probably would have given her life for either of us, though perhaps for him a little more enthusiastically. At the end of the summer, there was a break when we all had ten days free in which to travel before meeting up again for the charter flight home. I had never wanted anything so desperately as to be asked to spend it with the two of them. It didn't quite work out that way. They invited me to a dinner-powwow at a favorite bistro and announced their decision on the subject of the break: I would be spending the ten days traveling with *her*, while *he*—but I've forgotten exactly what he did. She and I made the absurdly romantic Rhine journey (I wanted to show off my German), at the end of which we arrived in Heidelberg and climbed all the way up to the absurdly picturesque castle, from whence we hitchhiked northward, encountering drivers variously amusing and terrifying, thus affording much anecdotal material for what we expected to be our long future (as *what*, exactly?); we parted in Basel, where she met up with a family friend. Alone on the train back, I wept all the way to the Gare de Lyon. I never made love with either of them, and I don't really know whether they made love with each other (when would they have had any time alone together?), but it took some years before I felt that one person alone could ever be quite sufficient for all the purposes of desire.

About ten years after that Paris summer I was working as a stage director. The leading man in my first production was breathtakingly handsome. A twenty-year-old budding movie star. As may be typical among people who look like that, he had a rather forbidding personality; nobody in the cast, certainly none of the males, liked him, and some, quite vocally, hated him. I had a good instinct with such persons, however. I wasn't frightened by them; I knew how to treat them with affectionate respect at just a slightly warmer temperature than guys were supposed to use with other guys. It helped when, as in this case, I didn't want to go to bed with him. I wanted his Friendship, no, I wanted his Love. He had married very young, before I knew him; his wife was solid and level-headed and rather plain, a rung or two down the ladder of social class from him, a perfectly worthy and, in this context, a somewhat incongruous figure.

I don't recall how it is that I reached with amazing swiftness the stage of being brought home to his extended family, but that changed everything. They turned out to be incredibly glamorous—rich and accomplished and charming and with all sorts of cultural bloodlines in literature and the arts. From the first Christmas, which I spent in their sprawling Midwestern home (there were other homes to which I developed regular entrée), I was family. It had a lot to do with the mother, who possessed a very significant New York literary pedigree but who had married a Midwestern doctor and been exiled to a milieu very far from the Algonquin Round Table. For a time, I simply belonged with them: Christmas in Vermont; summer on a boat; a brilliant older sister married to a dashing newspaperman; a beautiful younger sister, who was my great pal and never anything more. There was an occasion when the parents were for some reason distributing among the five children equal shares of some country property. One of the children refused her share, wanting the money instead. My friend's mother, I learned from him, had a dream—a night dream? a daydream? that would make a lot of difference—in which she bestowed the unwanted share of the property on *me.*

Like most dreams, it didn't come true. As my friend entered deeper into a Hollywood orbit, I began to see him as somebody quite different, either from what he used to be or from what I had imagined him to be. By some secret magnetism, as I began to see him differently, at a certain moment the family and I simply ceased to be in touch. It's hard to believe, looking back, that the whole thing flowered and withered within the space of two years.

Before that, however, one evening sticks in my mind. I was rehearsing with my actor friend well into the evening, and by the end of the rehearsal it was just the two of us. Our town was felt to be a little unsafe at that hour, plus it was raining hard, and so, even though I had a relatively short walk to my apartment, he said, why don't you hop on the back seat of my motorcycle, and I'll take you home. I'd sat there before—he had a passion for motorcycles and even gave me a few lessons in riding them solo—and I was familiar with all the sensuous immediacy of being helped on with the helmet and then sitting behind him with zero space between us. On this occasion, during our ten-minute rain-soaked drive he had something he wanted to tell me. Of necessity, he was shouting it forward, and I was listening from behind. I heard it nevertheless. It seems that he and his wife had just learned late that afternoon that they were going to have a baby. He had rushed off to rehearsal so fast that he hadn't even told his family yet. I was the first to know, even sooner than his parents.

So this is not a story about my falling in love with a man and a woman; this is a story about falling in love with a man and his family. Either way, it helps me understand why Shakespeare, faced with the fact that as of 1609, when his Sonnets were published, the vogue for Petrarchan lovers agonizing over their woes fourteen lines at a time may have been getting stale, might feel the need for an extra character, another love object, in *his* sonnet sequence, kind of the way years ago family sitcoms that ran out of material after a couple seasons resorted to the invention of wacky neighbors.

I've represented the Petrarchan sonnet as a vehicle for self-consciousness and introspection, but there is another purpose, more overt, though somewhat fictive. The poet longs for the lady's love; that she does not bestow it upon him—she doesn't fancy him, she is married to someone else, she is dead, she is imaginary—is axiomatic. The onrush of amorous suffering in fourteen-line stanzas will win her over: Poetry is persuasion.

What Shakespeare does with this widely practiced formula is to redistribute it. The lady in question, who makes a brief appearance at an early moment in the sequence and then takes center stage much later, requires no persuasion. Quite the contrary: She does not physically resemble the many descendants of Petrarch's Laura—famously, her "eyes are nothing like the sun" (130), etc., nor is she "fair," which means both not pale and not (conventionally) beautiful; and her attitude toward male desire is pretty much the more, the merrier. In a brilliant stroke, Shakespeare, now that he has increased the sonnet population, focuses the persuasion not on the woman but the man. In this process, the objective of the persuasion both is and isn't transformed. The poet, as in the whole preceding tradition, is still arguing passionately in favor of love over against the claims of chastity, except that this goal is situated at one remove from the customary erotic pairing.

Except that it can't be. No amount of careful contextualizing in past history with what are assumed to be different ways of thinking can erase the central fact of the plot that gets hammered into our consciousness from the opening of the sequence: The poet-speaker is addressing a young man whom he passionately loves for the purpose of persuading him to marry someone else: a woman. Far from sidestepping this set of erotic paradoxes, Shakespeare immerses himself in them. The opening sonnets focus upon two arguments that are supposed to convince the Young Man to marry and procreate. On the one hand, there is the negative argument: By refusing to take this advice, the Young Man demonstrates that he is in love with himself:

> Thou, contracted to thine own bright eyes,
> Feed'st thy light's flame with self-substantial fuel,
> Making a famine where abundance lies.
>
> (1)

The direct allusion to Ovid's Narcissus—*inopem me copia fecit*; "plenty makes me poore," in Spenser's translation—from the first moment of the sequence nails down the crime of refusing to marry as narcissism. A similar line of thought, but grittier, is to be seen when the speaker asks the Young Man, "why dost thou spend upon thyself thy beauty's legacy?": A nonmarrying narcissist is, figuratively or literally, a wanker. Alternatively, there is the positive argument. "The world must be peopled" (as Benedick says in a similar context). To stand apart from the duty of procreation is to be complicit in the terrible curse of universal mutability—day turning to night, violets withering, hair turning white, trees losing their leaves, etc. (12). And it is the special duty of the beautiful—the *eugenic* duty—to procreate beauty; to fail in that is to be complicit in universal decay.

In fact, if we permit ourselves to understand the speaker of these arguments as someone with a more than usually strong attachment to his addressee—the hell with lexical correctness, if we understand the speaker to be *gay*—then these arguments that he is offering up to the Young Man with such persuasive energy reveal themselves to be exactly those that turn back on himself and on his kind. Narcissus was in love with his own reflection; you do the math: Ergo, homosexuals are narcissists. Furthermore, within their own erotic circle, they cannot procreate. To the conventional two-person sonnet population Shakespeare has added what the Italians call a *terzo inconveniente*—usually either the mistress or the male lover as viewed in relation to a fixed married couple, except that in this case that role is doubled, as it were, between the imaginary future wife whom the speaker is promoting and the real woman who will eventually bear the sequence's heteroerotic charge, once it finally kicks in. With this expansion of the cast of characters, the whole system winds in upon itself. Each of the characters in this triangle, quadrangle, rhombus, whatever, is, in fact, a *terzo inconveniente* in relation to the others; the expectations of either gender are undermined, and gender itself mutates into something that can best be called *queer.*

That ought to be the cue for saying something about my own intellectual investment around the turn of the century in queer theory, but the truth is that I, though an interested party, watched these developments from the safety of the sidelines. How a sternly sectarian politics inspired by the AIDS crisis and fanned into real-world opposition by movements like ACT-UP somehow paradoxically morphed into a set of intellectual positions that challenged the whole notion of binaries: This is a story for others to tell. I can only note as demurely as possible that Shakespeare prewrote some version of this narrative. Don't get me wrong: I love Petrarch and all his followers, but I am capable of exhaustion as I contemplate the relentless heterosexuality of Petrarchan love, which, as it happens, owes a great deal to medieval traditions that were far less rigid in their gender categories to take us back to John Boswell, with whom this chapter began. I've already suggested that Shakespeare may have been tired of the two-person love story; more specifically, he may have been tired of the fact that the two persons had to follow the Noah's Ark proportions of one man and one woman. I believe that the Sonnets are as queer as it was possible to imagine anything published in 1609 and that the rejection of binaries as the only structure in which to frame desire is displayed *passim* on the seventy-odd pages of that little volume of his.

Sometimes this wish to destabilize comes out into the open in Shakespeare's language. At the end of a sonnet that is particularly aggressive on the subject of the young man's refusal to procreate, the poet declares, "Make thee another self for love of me" (10). It's often pointed out that this is the first mention of the speaker's own love for the Young Man, as distinct from what are merely his expressions of general admiration. That being the case, this love is introduced in the queerest possible way: as though the procreation in question is not, in the normative biological sense, between a male and a female but somehow between two males. A different sort of entanglement emerges from the famous reference to the Young Man as "master mistress of my passion" (20). If making another self in Sonnet 10 united the triad in procreation, here they seem united around the sexual act. It's a startling epithet for the Young Man, in itself bringing out into the open the radically unorthodox erotics of the sequence, while maintaining quite orthodox power relations (there are frequent suggestions that the Young Man is aristocratic). And what is compressed in that memorable phrase then gets drawn out in that sonnet's curious narrative of a mythical history in which (female) Nature first created a female, fell in love with her beauty, which, being female, would have been sexually useless to Nature, as a result of which she added a penis. The poem ends with the duly normalizing gesture of asserting that the resulting penis is useless to the (male) speaker; hence in place of a forbidden sexuality, a purer love obtains. By this time, however, the queering of gender has been let out of the box too aggressively for any such happy ending to remove all the attendant ambiguities.

Just when we thought that nothing queerer could be introduced into the erotic tangle, Shakespeare deals us the Rival Poet, who turns out to be a yet more peculiar *terzo* (*quarto? quinto?*) *inconveniente*. It's doubtless a tribute to the passionate vitality of the verse in this segment of the sequence that we tend not to ask ourselves why should the fact that another poet is celebrating the same young man produce such passionate jealousy. What underlies the conventional story—conventional since the beginning of literature, it would seem, though decidedly antiquated in the twenty-first century—of male jealousy? Some notion of pollution, of territorial invasion: Again, all of these things seem nowadays almost too embarrassing to set down on paper. Whatever they may be, they graft strangely on to the notion of a rival whose operation in regard to the common object is the composition of verses about him. Clearly, the writing of poetry, especially given the power of poetry to immortalize its subject matter, is a significant theme in the sonnets, and it's reasonable that our sonneteer might worry that the rival is a better poet. And he does: "A better spirit doth use your name . . . my saucy bark inferior far to his" (80). But as Shakespeare presents it, there is no mistaking the fact that he is turning this competition into competitive sexual preening. "The proud sail of his great verse" (86), "he of tall building" (80), "a modern quill doth come too short" (83). In fact the efforts of the Rival Poet disable our sonnet speaker's performance: "My love was my decay" (80). How often has that line been uttered by a passionate but underperforming lover? And:

> . . . when your countenance filled up his line
> Then lacked I matter, that enfeebled mine.

(86)

This is a universe in which eros is polymorphous, binaries have ceased to structure its operations, and celebrating individuals in poetry functions as some sort of equivalent to having sex with them.

I wasn't cut out to be a poster boy for gay manhood. Though I was born in Manhattan, I was too young for entry into the glamorously closeted nightclubbing world of Broadway and too old—or at least I felt too old—for full participation in the liberations of the 1970s. I also fell deeply in love with a girl when I was nineteen: another borderline moment, not quite puppy love, not quite a prudent age bracket for a middle-class lad to marry. The sincerity of that love on my part (her part is a little harder to gauge) is a historical fact about my life, not an anxious striving after normalizing heterosexuality or a cover while I undertook more exciting experimentation elsewhere. I loved her and wanted to marry her—she was resistant; we'll get back to that—but I also had what was even by then a long history of carefully collecting materials, both words and pictures, that did not feature girls.

This latter activity can be dated quite precisely. I have before me, courtesy of the internet, the cover of *Look* from September 18, 1958; I am therefore thirteen, going on fourteen. (Bar Mitzvah time, "now I am a man," though no such thing was allowed to take place in our house.) I don't recall that the family subscribed to *Look*; if that's the case, then I saw this cover at a newsstand and—since it was safely outside the embarrassing cliché of porn acquisition— purchased it without fearing shame. The big story, besides "How Ike Made up His Mind to Take the 'Big War' Risk," which interested me not at all, was the fall TV season. The cover is divided into four stripes, each headed by one of the four letters of **LOOK**, each framing a TV celebrity with a show to plug. Garry Moore, in a sweater holding a jacket jauntily over his shoulder; Jackie Gleason, with his patented cynical smirk; Dinah Shore, in a low-cut pinafore dress, lurching forward into the frame. None of those three merited my twenty cents. The final, or "K," stripe of the **LOOK**, on the other hand, displays James Garner as Maverick. He is seated at a poker table with abundant piles of chips and his shiny revolver at the ready. His trademark Stetson is rakishly angled upward. He is in the act of lighting his cigarillo as he moistens it between his lips, and he stares with a look of limitless, defiant self-confidence directly into my eyes. I kept this document for a very long time at the bottom of a dresser drawer into which others were unlikely to pry; after a while—propelled by I'm not sure what need to concentrate or purify the experience—I took a pair of scissors and carefully amputated Garry, Jackie, and Dinah. This is a boy with, it would seem, the most unimpeachable credentials of early onset homosexuality. And yet. . . .

I met Ellen when I was in my third year of college and she in her first. I had a job as a teaching assistant in language labs for French and German; partly I ran the equipment (incredibly out of date, even for 1962), and partly I checked up on the students' pronunciation. Normally, they attended in small groups, but this young lady was so clueless in executing her nasals that I suggested, with no shred of enthusiasm and still less of a romantic agenda, that she come on her own for extra attempts at *un bon vin blanc*, the magic phrase that, with an extra bit of Gallic panache, encompasses all four nasal vowels. One thing led to another. She was "kooky" in a late 1950s manner, she was attentive but also assertive, she had long blond hair. And she had a boyfriend back home on Long Island.

There's no need to chronicle the succeeding six or seven years in detail. I was an extremely—in her frequently expressed opinion, excessively—attentive boyfriend. I led her through the challenges of being an English major; she introduced me, very tentatively, to sexuality of a mutual kind (well, partly mutual); we traveled together in France; she continued to have the boyfriend, who was devastatingly handsome; there was an abortion—the boyfriend, not me—which I learned about years later from a casually dropped remark made by a mutual friend. I asked her to marry me; she said no, no reason given.

None of which quite "gets" Ellen; certainly none of it captures the gifts she bestowed on my life. There was, for one thing, playfulness: She introduced

me to a life lived in a continuous state of adventurous amusement, of whimsical-
ity, of private language, of (thank you, Oscar Wilde) *not* being earnest. She
certainly didn't learn this at home: She hated her father, adored her mother
(judgments in which I roughly concurred), she had two much older brothers,
twins with developmental difficulties, one at home, the other institutional-
ized; the atmosphere in her family, in short, was none too jocose. Playfulness
was thus a work of her own genius, before which I was an enraptured acolyte.
The other gift, different yet closely related, was cooking. In my childhood
home, there was always plenty to eat, and it was always pretty good; sometimes there was even a sense that the production of nourishment and flavor
merited serious effort. But for Ellen and her family, good food was a creed,
one that merited the most passionate and painstaking forms of commit-
ment. Looking back on it all, I would say that nothing that happened to me
in my late teenage years, including my elite academic education, has been
more important to who I am as an adult than the door that Ellen opened
upon the kitchen. On both grounds—playfulness and cuisine—I owe Ellen
some of my best lessons in how to conduct a happy life. And it is no coincidence that both recur so prominently in my now twenty-plus joyous years of
marriage to a man.

It's difficult to assign a moment when all this had come to an end in much
the same way it's difficult to weave the fact of my homosexuality into the story.
I remember, rather late in the game, bringing my Hollywood actor friend and
his wife to meet Ellen at her rather squalid Bronx apartment; the moment we
were out the door at the end of a rather charmless visit, the two of them almost
in unison and with pitying faces said that there wasn't the slightest sign of spark,
even an old extinguished spark, between Ellen and me. I concurred. On the
other hand, they both admired the spotless array of Le Creuset pots hanging
on her kitchen wall.

Then, at four- or five-year intervals a letter would appear, one of them
completely casual and newsy, the next one, now more than a decade since we
were by any definition together, declaring that I was the only man who had
ever really loved her. The interlinear of this remarkable assertion is that almost
from the beginning our love dynamic was that I gave and Ellen received.
(That's my story, anyway.) She received also from her old boyfriend, she
received by choosing far-off places (even farther than the Bronx) to live, she
received—in what way one was never sure—from several girlfriends. So I wasn't
surprised at the idea that I was the only man who ever loved her; I was surprised
that she had finally noticed it.

A couple more years of silence go by and there is a kind of summons: Ellen
needs to see me in order to review the past; in reply, I say that I don't have

such a need myself, but if she did, then I would be willing to meet with her on my next trip to New York. It was a brief stay, most of it spent with my cousins in Connecticut, where we were going to roast a Christmas [sic] goose that I would bring up from the city. It was duly ordered for pickup at Balducci's, and I arranged that the meeting with Ellen would take place at a nearby pastry shop, where I recalled that there were a few tables. I didn't mean for the setting to be so antiromantic; I couldn't have known ahead of time that we would spend the whole two hours' worth of discussion in a crowded and noisy setting where the nearly frozen goose from Balducci's had to occupy the scanty floor space, cradled tightly between my shivering legs. But so it was.

Of all the narrative strands in Shakespeare's Sonnets, each of them making the claim of autobiographical authenticity, there is only one for me that completely transcends the formulaic qualities of a trope and leaps off the page as "real," that is, emerging from a genuine experience in the speaker's life. I understand that this claim, however cautiously I make it, stamps me as a naïve reader. So be it: The naïve reader is, after all, the hero of this book, the person who experiences fiction as real. The thread in question occupies in total merely six (some might say eight, but I disagree) out of the 154 sonnets. The shadow it casts over the whole narrative, however, is so great that most readers, I think, will find it hard to believe that it occupies so little floor space in the sequence.

Sometimes citation is the best analysis:

Addressed to the young man:

Take all my loves, my love, yea, take them all;
What hast thou then more than thou hadst before?
No love, my love, that thou mayst true love call;
All mine was thine before thou hadst this more.

(40)

. . . thou art forced to break a twofold truth,
Hers by thy beauty tempting her to thee,
Thine, by thy beauty being false to me.

(41)

That thou hast her, it is not all my grief,
And yet it may be said I loved her dearly;
That she hath thee, is of my wailing chief,
A loss in love that touches me more nearly.

(42)

Addressed to the Dark Lady:

Me from myself thy cruel eye hath taken,
And my next self thou harder hast engross'd:
Of him, myself, and thee, I am forsaken;
A torment thrice threefold thus to be cross'd.

(133)

Thou usurer, that put'st forth all to use,
And sue a friend came debtor for my sake;
So him I lose through my unkind abuse.
Him have I lost; thou hast both him and me:
He pays the whole, and yet am I not free.

(134)

I love both a man and a woman. My two loves are of a different kind. I love the man in the deepest spiritual sense; his beauty connects my life to all the perfections that Plato talked about in the *Symposium*; our relationship is a joyful meeting of minds and souls; I know that I approach the divine because I love him and he loves me. (By the way, he's gorgeous.) I love the woman because she tempts and teases and satisfies and unsatisfies and makes me forget to struggle for Platonic perfection, which is, after all, rather exhausting anyway.

It all seems quite perfect for that lucky "me," who both relishes these complementary joys and has the intellectual and verbal wit to lay them out in their full taxonomy. *Until* my two loving beloveds turn out to love each other. No, that's not quite right: not love each other; have sex with each other. It's upon that circumstance that the entire system crashes and burns. The words that underpin the whole narrative—*love, beauty, self*—develop double meanings that might just be innocent wordplay were it not for the fact that they map the disintegration of that ego-satisfying triangle. Is *beauty* an ideal or is it the word designating a (possibly quite fallible) person? Is *love* an emotion or, again, the name for a dangerous yet irresistible object of desire? Is *self* just a word for *me*, or is it a now obsolete metaphor for the *other* whom I had mistakenly named as part of my self? Have I fallen from membership in a trinity to being a solitary nonentity? From Platonic perfections has this story collapsed into a sordid piece of money-lending and worse: whoredom ("he pays the whole . . ."; yes, it's *that* crude)?

The final narrative of this tortured triangle, Sonnet 144, seems a deliberate attempt to simplify and compartmentalize:

Two loves I have of comfort and despair,
Which like two spirits do suggest me still:

The better angel is a man right fair,
The worser spirit a woman colour'd ill.
To win me soon to hell, my female evil
Tempteth my better angel from my side,
And would corrupt my saint to be a devil,
Wooing his purity with her foul pride.
And whether that my angel be turn'd fiend
Suspect I may, but not directly tell;
But being both from me, both to each friend,
I guess one angel in another's hell:
Yet this shall I ne'er know, but live in doubt,
Till my bad angel fire my good one out.

The two loves are now tucked comfortably into the roles of angel and devil, which bespeaks the most traditional narrative structure for the wavering soul confronted with a binary choice. And the punchline, operating from a very different realm of consciousness, provides an answer to what has apparently been a burning (so to speak) question: I'll know if the two of them had sex (was it ever in doubt?) when I discover that my friend has caught a venereal disease from her. Who infected whom, according to this model? And will I "know" the answer to this question by his symptoms, or by mine? And if I am symptomatic, to which of them do I owe it? It's clear, in short, that there is a register, the none-too-savory register of bodily disease, by which the three persons of this trinity are as one. Not in a good way.

Ellen declared that she wanted a full sharing of why we hadn't managed to make a life together, where we had gone wrong. I repeated my unlovely mantra: I didn't need to do that, but if she needed it, I would try to participate. The theme of my being the only man who ever loved her had receded; she told me that she'd been unable to face a lifetime with me because she pictured us endlessly giving dinner parties. (She must have offered more than that; it's doubtless a key to my own culpability that that's all I remember.) Then she declared it was my turn to provide the equivalent reason for our sundering. I said the only thing I could think of to say: "Probably it's because I'm gay." She stared rather blankly back at me and said, "Don't you remember? We worked that all out." I didn't remember.

Another couple of years went by, and I received from her a copy of a paper she had published—she had become a clinical psychologist—about ways of treating persons who were convinced from birth that they were innately bad; no knowing what her personal stake may have been in this subject. Along with this, she was returning to me two items whose very existence I had forgotten: my high school class ring and my Phi Beta Kappa key. A few months later, her name appeared in the necrology of our college alumni magazine. I know nothing about the cause of her death; I have made no effort to find out.

In time, of course, I made some progress, slowly, from magazine cover pictures to the real thing, quite a few of which were themselves moving uncertainly among the possible orientations. It all has a very happy outcome, though it took decades and isn't necessarily an exciting story to tell. The truth in all this is that I always wanted to be married; now that I am, I love being married. I don't require Shakespeare to have been gay in his plays or gay in his sonnets. I don't even need to look for the subtle cues that he deconstructs gender, though I *do* look and he *does* deconstruct it. I hesitate to put myself in the shoes of anyone in the tangle of the Sonnets. Having said that, though, I experience by memory and with more immediacy than I should, the whole thing being four hundred years old and fictional, the agonies of sharing a beloved with someone else whose claim is liable to be better recognized in the world. Even so, I say again, I don't need a gay Shakespeare. When I see even the most rudimentary production of a Shakespearean romantic comedy and the couples all come together in the right order at the end, I literally weep for joy. In the making of that response—which I feel may possess more authentic weight in the category of "interpretation" than anything I or any other Shakespearean scholar can put down on paper—the fact that the fictional parties are heterosexual and I'm homosexual is utterly, totally, irrelevant. What proportion of that circumstance is Shakespeare's own pansexuality (which is undeniable) and what proportion is mine—that, too, is probably irrelevant, except to say that I may have learned to be who I am in these regards because of early and constant exposure to the work of a dramatist who looked upon gender and saw far beyond simple binaries, a dramatist who was, in short, *queer.*

If you ask me—and since you're reading this, you *are* asking me—the gayest moment in Shakespeare isn't in the Sonnets, though they are overflowing with the poet's assertions about his love for the young man, nor is it in *Twelfth Night,* despite all the gender-bending when Orsino starts to have erotic feelings for his male (*male-esque?*) servant Cesario. It's the opening of *The Merchant of Venice,* when the title character, Antonio, confesses to his friends that he is depressed but has no idea why. The friends have a ready answer: He is, after all, a merchant with lots of risky commercial ventures among ships that were sailing across the oceans to previously uncharted shores. He must be sad, they assert at some length, because he is risking bankruptcy if his ships go down. Antonio quickly discounts this explanation, making it clear that he is a far more prudent merchant than they might imagine; he has (as we would say) diversified, with so many ventures across the newly navigated world that the prospect of a general crash is remote The friends come up with another answer: "Why, then you are in love." We all know we're at the beginning of a romantic comedy, which makes the love hypothesis very tempting; nevertheless Antonio flips them off instantly with a dismissive but nonspecific "Fie, fie." The subject of Antonio's sadness gets abruptly shut down. A few minutes later, some more friends enter, including a certain Bassanio, and shortly after that, the group thins out, leaving Antonio and Bassanio alone together—on purpose, it seems. Once that has been accomplished, Bassanio reveals the reason for his visit: He wants to borrow more money from Antonio so that he can cut a truly elegant figure when he goes to woo the beauteous Portia.

We all know the expression "the love that dare not speak its name," deriving from a poem by Oscar Wilde's lover Lord Alfred Douglas (and made use of in the trial that ensued from this love affair). The poem itself is a piece of rather treacly Victorianism, but the phrase is indelible and, for long periods of history both before and after it was composed, pretty apt as a not-so-secret code for homosexuality. In effect, it enacts the paradox of its own meaning, both naming this long anathematized aspect of human experience and *not* naming it, or pretending not to name it. And I can't help feeling that that is exactly what Shakespeare is doing in the opening of his comedy. However we may come to understand the relationship of Antonio and Bassanio in the fullness of the play—we'll get back to that—it seems to me a certainty that Shakespeare is delivering to us a question—why am I so sad?—and failing to resolve the problem explicitly but maneuvering the circumstances such that the true answer is manifest before us. Show, don't tell (not to be confused with "don't ask, don't tell," or perhaps in this case they're the same thing) is a prime slogan of playwriting, and we are being given here a little lesson in that technique, with emphasis on the "don't tell." Since we are specifically in the kind of play defined by romance, of course the answer to Antonio's perplexity *is* that he is in love, and that explanation is cinched when the object of that desire presents himself almost immediately before our eyes—and asks for money.

In the early 1980s I started to become friends with a very distinguished academic some years senior to me; he was (still is) a gay man who, at least to all appearances, has never felt the need to closet himself, which, if true, is pretty astonishing for a man half a generation older than I. Some of it probably has to do with luck—a childhood spent among prosperous and worldly people—and some of it is simply in the nature of his own personality, characterized by the forthright and lovable self-confidence he is capable of exhibiting within his own skin. In those days he was together with a somewhat younger, also distinguished, fellow academic. They summered together in New England, and one year they invited me to spend a bucolic week with them. For a while it became an annual appointment, and the whole milieu, which included other gay men and women, along with cultivated European intellectuals of whatever persuasions—became pretty much seven days' worth of Eden for a young person like myself. What I did by way of recompense was to cook, insistently and intricately, for the whole gang—for instance, getting up at 5:30 to bake croissants that I had made from scratch and allowed to rise during the night.

One day, my friend said, "Shall we take a walk?" I was delighted to accept, though a little nonplussed since, although in general this region of upper New England was quite scenic, the area immediately around their summer place was, I have to say, rather drab. No matter: We ambled for a while along dirt-and-gravel roads lined with nothing more exciting than scraggly trees and power lines. There must have been some academic talk—it was a period when I was about as contented with my profession as with my love life—and then he said, "Would you like to be together with a man?" Or words to that effect. I can't pretend to be quoting verbatim, but what I can say was that it was a quite perfect expression of affection. There wasn't a shred of sense that he was propositioning me, or that he was intent on invading my privacy, or that he was engaged in some particular act of matchmaking. He was simply asking me, quite gently, to open up the deepest, most vital place of secrecy in my life. "Well, yes, I would," I replied. Recollecting it after forty years, it occurs to me that being gently coaxed "out" by a wholly committed gay man in a very private conversation didn't exactly amount to some kind of heroic personal Stonewall. Yet for whatever reason, this proved to be the moment when I started to be comfortable not just with my own identity but with the act of sharing it among my friends in much the same way, and with at least some of the same pleasure, that I shared my handmade croissants. Not that Antonio's sadness was thereby lifted from me. But it provides a counterexample: This is what can happen when the love dares to speak its name on a country road in Vermont.

Not so easy on the Rialto, however. The plot that is attached to the title character in this play turns out to be Shakespeare's great masterpiece of silence and sadness. Forget for the moment Portia and her flotilla of suitors, forget Lorenzo and Jessica, even, so far as possible, forget Shylock, except for his instrumentality in Antonio's near-death experience, and you have an exquisitely sentimental tale of the love that dare not speak its name. Don't be fooled by the opening scene's "fie, fie": Antonio's feelings for Bassanio fit every definition of love, even the most heroic, despite the fact that against his own interests he furnishes the means for Bassanio to woo Portia, encumbering himself to an individual whom he despises and has publicly denounced, along the way authoring what will be the catastrophic conditions of this financial arrangement. Shakespeare even throws in a curious circumstance whereby it's Antonio, suddenly in the role of roving weatherman, who rushes onstage with the news that the wind is favorable for sailing to Belmont without delay; God forbid that Bassanio might be late for his appointment there. With a woman.

There is, to be sure, an exquisite account of parting between the two men:

> Bassanio told him he would make some speed
> Of his return: he answer'd, "Do not so;
> Slubber not business for my sake, Bassanio
> But stay the very riping of the time;
> And for the Jew's bond which he hath of me,
> Let it not enter in your mind of love:
> Be merry, and employ your chiefest thoughts
> To courtship and such fair ostents of love
> As shall conveniently become you there:
> And even there, his eye being big with tears,
> Turning his face, he put his hand behind him,
> And with affection wondrous sensible
> He wrung Bassanio's hand; and so they parted.

(2.8.37–49)

Possibly the most touching scene in the play, except, of course, that it's *not* a scene in the play. The "affection wondrous sensible" (in Jay Halio's note, "emotion amazingly evident") between the two men is "amazingly evident" to us only through the filtering screen of third-person narration. Onstage with our own eyes we see nothing of this. Tell, don't show.

Yet again, silence and sadness, and this is followed by another device whereby the expression of emotion is tucked offstage, a letter from Antonio to Bassanio: ". . . all debts are cleared between you and I, if I might but see you at my death. Notwithstanding, use your pleasure" (3.3.316–19). Clearly, Bassanio knows at least how to follow *that* instruction. The pound of flesh and the miscarrying merchant ships are almost marginal in this love story, which, I would hazard to say, emerges as far more sentimental than the heterosexual love story in the play, itself embroiled with finances (not to mention thefts) and lacking the kind of playful love scenes to be found in Shakespeare's other romantic comedies. When Antonio seeks to assert his rights as lover in the trial scene, it is via yet another matter that points offstage—or what would be offstage, except that Portia is present in disguise:

Commend me to your honourable wife:
Tell her the process of Antonio's end;
Say how I loved you, speak me fair in death;
And, when the tale is told, bid her be judge
Whether Bassanio had not once a love.

(4.1.270–74)

Had not *once* a love? Is Antonio saying once upon a time (in a mythical past), or once *only* (not, in other words, with Portia), or is he declaring first dibs, making a case for prior rights? Portia will in any event shut all this down. She has already made it clear to Bassanio that the rite of the marriage ceremony must be celebrated as a condition before she participates in any happy resolution of his friend's little pound-of-flesh problem. And once it is solved, thanks to Portia, she nevertheless prolongs the agony of the game with the device of pretending that the young men gave their promise rings away to the lawyer and clerk (Portia and Nerissa in disguise, of course) who secured Antonio's release; in this whole painful comedic episode, Antonio—a long silent *terzo inconveniente* in the midst of these proceedings—is forced to say, "I am th'unhappy subject of these quarrels" (5.1.238), which is followed by a rather curt reassurance from Portia. Nor does he quite seem to have learned his lesson: "I once did lend my body for his wealth; | Which, but for him that had your husband's ring, | Had quite miscarried: *I dare be bound again*" (5.1.249). The play ends before any necessity arises to take Antonio up on this risky offer.

Granted, not everyone will appreciate the fact that this is made into a story all about silence and sadness; we might legitimately tax Shakespeare with producing an all-too-familiar narrative in which same-sex desire fails to achieve a happy ending. (Not to mention the fact that the play will expose Antonio to the possibility of vastly unhappier endings than merely failing to get the guy.) For myself, I understand how limiting it is to all our lives—LGBTQ and others—if gay characters are never allowed happy endings in fiction and how influential that message may be on the endings in nonfictional people's lives. At the same time, my own experience causes me to have a certain personal stake in the reality and dignity of Antonio's sadness, alongside my own, such that I feel the pleasure of fiction, which is to say the pleasure of recognition (which is the principle of this whole book), just as much when he is solitary and melancholy as when some other gay character (not, perhaps, to be found in Shakespeare) meets the perfect gay love.

The postscript to all this has to be the *other* Antonio. I have nothing to contribute to the wacky theorizing about whether there was in late-sixteenth-century England some sort of gay tip-off in naming a fictional character "Antonio." (In

my youth, I believe that "Bruce" played some such role among the unenlight-
ened.) Be that as it may, the role of Antonio, with whose help young Sebastian
is rescued and brought to Illyria in *Twelfth Night*, exhibits uncanny similarities
to his Venetian namesake. An older man rescuing a younger man, a happy ending in which almost everyone is suitably paired off while Antonio is left solitary:
The framework in the two plays is identical. What is not identical is the kind of
language that the older man uses. For instance, at a moment when Sebastian
has just left the stage, on his way to reconnoiter the situation in Illyria, and
Antonio is, fittingly, making his love declaration to empty space:

ANTONIO

    The gentleness of all the gods go with thee!
    I have many enemies in Orsino's court,
    Else would I very shortly see thee there.
    But, come what may, I do adore thee so,
    That danger shall seem sport, and I will go.

                                               (2.1.39–43)

Or, this time in the presence of Sebastian, who has rather obliquely suggested
that he might have preferred to explore Illyria on his own rather than in his
rescuer's company:

ANTONIO

    I could not stay behind you: my desire,
    More sharp than filed steel, did spur me forth;
    And not all love to see you, though so much
    As might have drawn one to a longer voyage,
    But jealousy what might befall your travel,
    Being skilless in these parts. . . .

                                               (3.3.4–9)

Then, in a time-honored way, when the going gets rough, love turns to hate:

ANTONIO

    Thou hast, Sebastian, done good feature shame.
    In nature there's no blemish but the mind;
    None can be call'd deform'd but the unkind:
    Virtue is beauty, but the beauteous evil
    Are empty trunks o'erflourish'd by the devil.

                                         (3.4.357–61)

The whole Platonic equation of the beautiful and the good is threatened as
Antonio witnesses himself denied by the young man on whom he has staked

so much. Of course, it isn't the young man who has failed to acknowledge him; it is the identical sister who doesn't know him from Adam. This need not matter in the usual logic of romantic comedy: We're at the most tangled-up stages of the intricate plot; all identities will be cleared up in act 5, and happily ever after will reign supreme. Not, however, for Antonio, no more than for the other Antonio. The best that either of them can hope for is the removal of a terrible threat hanging over their lives: in Venice, the pound of flesh; in Illyria, the liberation from a prison sentence for prior service against Orsino.

What is more interesting to me, though, is the difference between the two Antonios. It's always risky to place too much weight on the chronology of Shakespeare's plays, since dates are uncertain and since the entire career was relatively brief (about twenty-five years). That being said, I feel comfortable placing *Merchant* and *Twelfth Night* in that order at some four or five years' distance, time enough perhaps for the boiling up of authorial resentment at the obligatory heterosexual formulas of romantic comedy. With that in mind, I think it's safe to say that the *Twelfth Night* Antonio is the return of the repressed in relation to the *Merchant of Venice* Antonio. It pleases me to imagine the Illyrian Antonio—either a sea captain or a pirate, depending on whom you believe—as a mirror double to the Venetian Antonio. As a sea captain, he might well be in the employ of his namesake across the Adriatic; as a pirate, he would be his namesake's worst enemy. Both Antonios are catalysts of a happy ending in which they do not share, rescuers of a sexually ambiguous young man whom they are preparing for heterosexual union. The difference is that the Illyrian Antonio is afforded—to a limited extent, at least—the opportunity to express his rage and loss, compensating for the imposed or offstage silence of the other Antonio and perhaps more Antonios sprinkled through the audience. Nowhere in Shakespeare does this kind of love emerge as forcefully as in the circumstances necessitated by the plot of *Twelfth Night*. If Shakespeare—to enter perilous territory—really knew what it felt like to love a beautiful younger man and suffer the surrender of him to heterosexuality and marriage, it is this slender thread in the fabric of *Twelfth Night* more than the Sonnets where we can hear about it. "Thou hast . . . done good feature shame," declares Antonio to Sebastian: You have betrayed your good looks with your rotten soul. It's aching to be translated into the brilliant lyrics of a Cole Porter or a Lorenz Hart, though they spent their careers pretending that the love object was a woman. Shakespeare, briefly, didn't pretend. All those circumlocutions and silences and love scenes shunted offstage in the *Merchant* are allowed their moment in *Twelfth Night*, where, finally, the love does dare to speak its name, though quite softly, and tucked into a subplot.

6

The Royal and the Real

The summer before I turned seventeen has, in recollection at least, a magical glow for me. Nothing that would remotely interest Hollywood: no sex, no love, no drugs, certainly no rock 'n' roll. On alternate weeks my father manned his lower Fifth Avenue drugstore until midnight; my mother would drive down from the suburbs to take him back home. Which meant that if I undertook the long subway ride downtown at the end of my school day up in Riverdale, I had the whole evening to play in Greenwich Village and could be safely chauffeured to Westchester and tucked into bed there at the end of it. Granted, "play" has to be defined in terms that would be unrecognizable even to most of my quite homogeneous schoolmates, let alone to Middle America: the Eighth Street Bookshop, where I spent hours not browsing but *reading*; Marboro, full of remaindered books that I could actually afford to purchase on my allowance; the unbelievably highbrow Discophile, where the Highest Fidelity met the latest avant-garde classical performances in an ongoing seminar to which, nonplussed, I was occasionally granted admission.

Once in a while I even ventured above Fourteenth Street. How it happened that I made the trek uptown to see Shakespeare in the Park I can't quite remember. It certainly was not yet the grand cultural institution that it has become. At this early moment it was mired in an ongoing dispute between Joseph Papp (the angel) and Robert Moses (the devil). "Mired" is indeed the right word: Papp had not yet won the battle, the Delacorte Theatre hadn't yet been built, and the whole thing took place in the rather sloppily adapted Wollman skating rink. I'm not even certain how I knew that there *was* free Shakespeare uptown; it must have been because I'd appointed myself the drama critic of my high school newspaper, and occasionally the publicity staffs

176

of even quite fancy Broadway theaters imagined I was worth comping for their shows. No need, of course, in the case of Joe Papp's Shakespeare, where everybody was comped. I was, as has been documented in these pages, already a Shakespeare buff, but I doubt I knew anything about the rather off-center play they were producing at that moment. What did it matter? It was free; it was Shakespeare; I was a kid with several hours during which no one watched over him. *Richard II*? How bad could it be?

Several things happened that night. First of all, I was hypnotized by the play. I don't think I had ever considered the possibility that mere speech, even when scripted by Shakespeare, could be as purely sensuous as music. (Of course, I am speaking the language of myself sixty years later. I can't pretend to translate all this back into the dialect of adolescent mental life; that's the pleasure and pain of remembrance.) I do remember my awe in hearing speeches that went straight to my emotions without even needing to *mean* anything. True, I must report, having now dug up the *Times* review, that the production may not have been of alpha quality. King Richard was played by a soap opera actor, James Earl Jones was assigned a bit part, and John of Gaunt—it's this, more than Shakespeare, that makes me wish the performance were preserved in amber—was, I now learn, played by Abe Vigoda, later immortalized in the role of Fish on *Barney Miller*. Imagining "This royal throne of kings | This scepter'd isle, this seat of Mars, | This other Eden, demi-Paradise . . ." rendered in the voice of a perpetually pissed-off Lower East Side pickle merchant is a fantasy to live for.

My own review of the production, back in 1961, can be summed up very simply. I had seen it on a Monday night. I returned on Tuesday night, Wednesday night, Thursday night, and Friday night. That was the end of my father's late shift for the week; otherwise I might well have just kept going. This is what it means to say "*Free* Shakespeare."

Another thing happened that first night. In my memory, at least, there were two separate exits from the space where the audience was seated, and, in the westbound direction at any rate, they turned into two quite separate streams of patrons heading out of the park. At some distance from the theater itself these two streams merged. When I reached the exact merging point, a middle-aged man who was suddenly shoulder-to-shoulder with me turned in my direction and, as though we had spent the whole evening together, said, "Well, what did you think of it?" Now, if I were a character in an André Aciman story—and I recommend these stories highly—this would have been the beginning of a decade-long affair ending very sweetly when he passed me on to a lover of my own age. As we are in my reality rather than in André's fiction, I can only report that I answered his question with great enthusiasm and offered a similar response when he followed up with "Shall we get a cup of coffee?" In a snack shop just off Central Park West we had a lively little seminar—mostly me—on Shakespeare and *Richard II*. Nothing more. I was so innocent that I reported this encounter to my mother in the car on the way home. With some alarm, she said, "Did he try anything?" Only at that moment did my dim light bulb illuminate. I reassured my mother in a superior man-of-the-world tone, and I was left to ponder the distance between *Richard II* and forbidden sex.

The distance is considerable, at least to the naked eye. I was indeed enthralled by my encounter with the play, but the estimable old-style newsman Arthur Gelb, who wrote that *Times* review, was, if anything, even more dubious about the play than he was about the production. Joseph Papp, he suggested, deserved "commiseration" for having attempted it; he referred to it as "one of Shakespeare's drier histories" and suggested that the audience engaged in an "uphill battle."

He has a point. The play opens with the grandiose ritual of two high nobles formally accusing each other in the presence of the King as judge, but it's not at all clear what they're accusing each other *of*. Maybe the original audience would recognize the background, but, given that it took place two hundred years before the play was written, I'm not so sure. Throughout this opening scene Richard isn't doing a good job of getting at the truth, and neither are we; nor is Shakespeare. When Bolingbroke says that "all the treasons for these eighteen years | Complotted and contrived in this land" owe their origin to his current opponent Mowbray, it's almost a joke on the murky nature of the problem underlying this heavily ritualized passion (*all* the treasons? *what* treasons? please enumerate). We finally do hear about the murder of Thomas of Woodstock, which is in fact the immediate issue, but the information that Mowbray furnishes on this subject is so ambiguous—"I slew him not, but to my own disgrace | Neglected my sworn duty in that case" (1.1.133–34)—that we can't tell whether this neglect consisted in murdering Woodstock or *not* murdering Woodstock. And who is Woodstock, anyway?

The scene in which the trial by combat is actually to take place, and then doesn't take place, pushes all of these forces several steps further along the same blurry lines. The frozen purity of the ritual is intensified at the same time as the sense of authentic purposes or passions seems to recede even further from the theatrical experience we are actually having. The moment when the King throws his warder down and prevents the trial from going forward, besides signaling the beginning of the end for his reign, though we don't know it yet, has been appropriately read as the break between a world of divinely ordered kingship and one characterized by politics and manipulation. Bad for England maybe, but a potential boon for us, a moment we've all been waiting for, when the glittering surface of the ritual becomes transparent, and both combatants finally say what is really on their minds, expression of which was previously impossible. Bolingbroke urges Mowbray, now that their cases have been adjudicated and they are sentenced to (unequal) banishment,

> Confess thy treasons ere thou fly the realm—
>   . . . bear not along
> The clogging burden of a guilty soul.

(1.3.198–200)

And, more significantly, since it's Bolingbroke whose purposes really interest us, Mowbray makes the parallel move of postritual truth-telling:

> What thou art, God, thou and I do know,
> And all too soon, I fear, the King shall rue.

(1.3.204–5)

Truth-telling, but what exactly *is* the truth? In this case, those with some knowledge of royal English genealogy may be able to figure things out and deduce what was really at stake for Bolingbroke—and for Shakespeare. Not cleansing the eighteen years of corruption, nor exposing the murder of Woodstock, but the ambition to supplant Richard as king. The fact that this cannot be said directly (at least at this early moment in the action, which is in fact just when we need it most) is partly political: Shakespeare is not welcome to present Bolingbroke as a schemer with a long-laid plan. But it has theatrical consequences, both here at the beginning and throughout the play. What characters cannot say, audiences cannot hear. The playwright, of course, is in charge of all this. Soon there will be occasions when bystanders tell us things about which the royals are silent; at this point, however, we're given no such assistance.

I've chronicled all this as a problem about the gleaning of information, but that's only the entry point to a bigger problem for the audience, a yet steeper uphill climb for Mr. Gelb and the audience on whose behalf he is speaking. OK, so we've figured out that it's probably going to be a play about two mighty antagonists fighting for possession of the throne. That's simple enough, but who are we supposed to be rooting for? Of course, we all know that Shakespeare is a master of complex characterization, that (at least in the historical and political plays) no one is 100 percent good (though some are 100 percent bad) and that he loves to mix black and white with a lot of gray (or even brighter colors). When it comes to who should be king of England, however, he operates under certain constraints, which have to do with a particular reading of history promoted by Queen Elizabeth's Tudor dynasty. The moment of Richard II's reign is understood as pivotal in this story, leading to nearly a century of dynastic chaos that Elizabeth's dynasty would eventually resolve harmoniously. Richard was, by all odds and not just through the eyes of Tudor propaganda, a bad king; on the other hand, to depose a legitimate monarch was a crime comparable (and often compared) to disobeying God's command in the Garden of Eden.

Now we begin to see why the play presents so many difficulties just when—I make my customary allusion to the hypothetical Playwriting 101—it ought to be setting up the elements of exposition such that issues and persons are crystal clear. The other history plays, particularly in the so-called Lancastrian tetralogy, which opens with *Richard II*, certainly include characters who are not all good or all bad. We may love them or hate them or love to hate them, but we tend to know exactly what we want to happen to them. Prince Hal spends a wicked (though delightful, both to him and to us) adolescence but will transform himself upon ascending the throne; Falstaff draws our attention magnetically, but we know that his hegemony cannot outlast Hal's youth; Henry IV (the Bolingbroke of *Richard II*) will reform the excesses of his predecessor and triumph over rebellion, but, given that it was rebellion a generation earlier that got him on the throne, he must end unfulfilled.

What do we *want* to happen to Richard and Bolingbroke? The uncertainty of that proposition—both the question itself and the possibility of a clear answer—is reflected in all the ways Shakespeare alienates us in these opening scenes. We may say that matters are unclear and indecisive in the way he arranges his fiction because they were in fact unclear and indecisive in their historical reality. Or—better, in my view—we may say that these murkinesses, including the vagueness of information and the refusal to deliver conclusive dramatic action, function as a sort of audience conditioning. Before we ever get to the question whether to root for Richard or for Bolingbroke we have fair warning that simple binaries are not going to be the way to go. In that sense, cutting short the trial by combat (understood as a device in which God determines guilt and innocence) is as much a gesture of the playwright as of the historian: We have graduated beyond a moment when the all-powerful (be it author or divinity) can provide us with straightforward answers.

Several years before my encounter with *Richard II* and the impromptu coffee shop date that followed, I am with my mother in a small, private, theater-like space somewhere in the bowels of Rockefeller Center. I cannot recall anything about how we got there; it may have had something to do with one of her attempts to connect herself or me to show business, though in this episode we were definitely being understood as audience rather than performers. It was, though I had neither the concept nor the words at that time, an exercise in test marketing. There were thirty or forty of us in the audience, and we were shown an hour-long TV movie that must have been under consideration by NBC. Every seat was equipped with a bulky object that housed a dial on which there were readings from one to ten; our instructions were to turn the dial from moment to moment in the course of the movie so as to match our level of enthusiasm, or emotional engagement, or (presumably) lack thereof. I don't remember much about the film: something centering on a cute Asian child who either might or might not get adopted by a nice white American couple; there was also a lot of noisy warfare framing this heartwarming saga. The Korean War may have been involved. I was prepared to take my dialing job very seriously, but the movie was, even to my early adolescent sensibilities, pretty terrible. (My mother later announced to me that she'd found a way to turn the dial to zero and just left it there. My dial didn't have a zero; maybe she unplugged hers from the wall.) All I could think of to do was to rotate it to ten whenever there were explosions and hover in careful gradations between two and three during the gushy bits.

The movie may have been terrible, but the device has remained fixed in my imagination. During my subsequent lifetime as an audience member—movies, theater, opera, whatever—I have always wished that I were in possession of that magical dial. And when I have been engaged in placing something before an audience, I have wanted to get my hands on the readout from *everyone's* dial. In fact, every theatrical presentation is a continuous imposi-tion on the emotions of each person in the audience, a minute-by-minute assault that says, "look at me, look at me," "laugh now," "cry now," or, alter-natively, "you have permission to worry about what you did with your car keys now," etc., etc.

The truth is, I've wanted to have that audience response device with me in life as much as in the theater. I longed for it constantly, for instance, during the months I spent going out on a series of internet-generated blind dates after a painful breakup. What numbers would I have assigned to the sad-sack high school librarian who only wanted to talk about his long-deceased parents? Or the TV tech director who seemed to have a glamorous job but couldn't be induced to stray from the recounting of soap opera plots? And for that matter—turnabout is fair play—how good were *my* numbers when I couldn't begin to keep up with the conversation of the Comme des Garçons–clad gallery owner who seemed to spend his life shuttling between the Centre Georges Pompidou and the Venice Biennale?

Long before that, though, the handy little device inspired me in another direction. There was a period of a few months (children don't measure time very well) when some sort of business war erupted in which my father was a combatant. Later I came to understand the details—he had a younger partner in the drugstore who was trying to squeeze him out, something like that—and the result somehow converted itself to a continuous battle between my parents. Even as an adult I never understood how the hostilities could have shifted to the home front: Could my mother have somehow taken the side of the usurper? I ask that question now, but my mind could not have traveled that distance then. What I did experience was a period of regular, daily rage behind closed, and sometimes slammed closed, doors. That little machine to measure audience response was fresh in my memory back then, and I remember having a vision that, when I think of it now (if small things can compare with great), was my pint-sized equivalent of James Watt, the bubbling tea kettle, and the invention of the steam engine. The dial that NBC had placed in my hands measured the precipitous ups and downs of emotion: What if, instead of just *measuring* them, it could actually *control* them? If I could move the dial downward and lower the emotional volume of my father's anger or somehow erase the even more fearful silences of my mother? It might even work in the other direction: During the long stretches of (quasi) only-child domestic boredom, maybe I could get some action going by just dialing up from, say, 3 to 9. With many decades of retrospection, it begins to look as though Shakespeare became my handy pocket 10 or, when necessary, my 3.

I have to stop for a moment on "if small things can compare with great." *Si parva licet componere magnis*: Virgil coins that expression in the *Georgics* as part of a beautiful account of the beehive, which he wants us to understand as a model for the commonwealth of human beings as it should ideally operate. The fact that commonwealths, whether in Virgil's time or ours, do not always operate so ideally may suggest that Virgil was allowing for the possibility that it was the bees who were actually "great" and not the politicians. For me, the phrase has always been the kind of thing that, if this were the Renaissance and I a grandee of some sort, I would have some gifted craftsman inscribe on a medal surrounding my portrait in profile. This book, after all, operates in the most fundamental way under the permission of "si parva licet," and in this case I hope I never mistake which are *parva* and which are *magna*. In fact, that motto, as it operates for me, always requires another Latin tag: mutatis mutandis, "changing what needs to be changed." This one can't be credited to a great classical poet. It appears to be a notion that developed in medieval law, and a very useful one it is. Where would the law be, not to mention intellectual life of any kind, if we weren't able to make comparisons between different things? But when we do that, we are obliged to recognize that those things are, indeed, different; in other words, that whatever they hold in common may well be exceeded by everything that they *don't* hold in common. I'm well aware—to bring this back to me and *Richard II*—that my father's struggles with his younger partner in the drugstore *might* be compared with Richard and Bolingbroke; it's just that the *parva* is so far from the *magna* that I choose not to draw the connection. There was just too much mutatis that had to be mutandis.

We can agree, I think, that throughout those ritualized early scenes of *Richard II* the dial is pretty much stuck in the 2's and 3's. It's not just that the formalized version of what is, after all, active violence done in the past and threatened in the future diminishes its theatrical excitement in the present moment but also the fact that the King, titular hero of the play, is being constrained into at least seeming impartiality, and impartiality doesn't bring out the high numbers. More than that, Shakespeare has him speak as a sort of anger connoisseur in the face of the two combatants' rages. When Bolingbroke lets loose his accusation and Richard comments, "How high a pitch his resolution soars!" (1.1.109) or when Mowbray declares his passionate loyalty to the crown and Richard comments, "Surely I espy | Virtue with valour couchèd in thine eye" (1.3.97–98), the King's lines seem to beg for a coolly detached reading that, once again, lowers the temperature on the whole scene. Again, of course, there are reasons of political expediency for Richard's detachment here, but that does not alter the fact that if we're looking for our titular hero to bring passion onstage, we will be disappointed. So far.

The emotional seismographs will indeed soon get some considerable exercise, but not perhaps as we might expect. As early as the scene that interrupts the two stages of the Bolingbroke-Mowbray quarrel, the widow of the murdered Woodstock lets loose on her husband's brother an eloquent tirade concerning the murder:

Edward's seven sons, whereof thyself art one,
Were as seven vials of his sacred blood, . . .
One vial full of Edward's sacred blood,
One flourishing branch of his most royal root,
Is crack'd, and all the precious liquor spilt. . . .
Ah, Gaunt, his blood was thine! that bed, that womb,
That metal, that self-mould, that fashion'd thee
Made him a man; and though thou livest and breathest,
Yet art thou slain in him.

(1.2.11–25)

The recipient of the Duchess's passionate anger, her brother-in-law John of Gaunt, will soon unleash his own eloquent rage in lines that are almost too famous to quote:

> This blessed plot, this earth, this realm, this England,
> This nurse, this teeming womb of royal kings,
> Fear'd by their breed and famous by their birth,
> Renowned for their deeds as far from home, . . .
> This land of such dear souls, this dear dear land,
> Dear for her reputation through the world,
> Is now leased out, I die pronouncing it,
> Like to a tenement or pelting farm. . . .
> That England, that was wont to conquer others,
> Hath made a shameful conquest of itself.
>
> (2.1.50–66)

Shortly thereafter, it is the Queen's turn to send the audience's dial toward the high numbers:

> Some unborn sorrow, ripe in fortune's womb,
> Is coming towards me, and my inward soul
> With nothing trembles, at something it grieves
> More than with parting from my lord the King.
>
> (2.2.10–13)

So, emerging out of the chilly and ritualized struggle with which the drama began, where both political truths and private passions had to be suppressed, Shakespeare has unloaded upon us a barrage of expression testifying to all the ways that his story, whether in its dynastic, nationalistic, or personal aspect, can reach the high points of both emotion and rhetoric (which, as we'll see, are two of the play's cardinal points).

Except that one character stands conspicuously apart from this torrent. Richard is offstage for the Duchess, out of the country for the Queen, and, when present with Gaunt, he delivers the same kind of aloof critique that he handed out to Mowbray and Bolingbroke in the first act's trial scenes. We're just shy of halfway through the play, and it looks as if our hero is never going to get high numbers for dramatic intensity.

Then that alters with a bang. Shakespeare does something that he will later do, with varying purposes, in *Hamlet* and *Lear*: He sends his tragic hero away, creating a space in which change is possible. For anyone whose dial is set where mine is, which is to say, anyone who has found Richard chilly and impassive throughout this first half of the play, then the words he utters upon his return from Ireland—"I weep for joy"—should make a distinct impression. These contraries of emotion, expressed in such simple monosyllables, are precisely what we have not seen from him; now, perhaps, the audience having fought Mr. Gelb's uphill battle, will start to see some interesting high ground. The poetic lexicon available for the conveying of powerful emotion on stage in 1595 tends not to rest with such simple terms as "weep" and "joy," nor does it stay that way for long here. Particularly when the monarchy is involved, as it is in this instance, it appropriates a vast metaphoric system through which, in the course of these scenes, Richard will channel his passionate response to the dangers surrounding him. The facts of the case, which we learn at the same time that Richard does, are that rebel groups have formed during his absence, and in the course of the scene there are sequences of bad news that provide a rising inflection of impassioned yet insistently metaphorical responses from the King.

At first, Richard is a mother, and England is his child. Then, confronted with the first round of bad news, he shrugs it off with an extended metaphor of himself as the sun who has been shining on the other half of the planet (= his trip to Ireland), during which time "murders, treasons, and detested sins" are committed, but now that he is rising again (= returned to England) Bolingbroke's "treasons will sit blushing in his face not able to endure the sight of day" (3.2.50–52). It is a standard part of the poetic ideology that surrounded the monarchy that the king was the sun, but we are starting at this moment to see that what makes for powerful poetic imagery may be unreliable as political science: The sun will certainly rise tomorrow, whereas Richard may or may not. At the next run of bad news, when he learns that the Welsh forces have presumed him dead, he turns to something more directly sacred: For every one of Bolingbroke's soldiers, Richard has an angel, he claims. In the search for grounding his claims to power, he has traveled from the natural world to the supernatural. His realm of metaphor is getting a little more risky, as he seems to be appropriating heaven, declaring it personally at his service.

Next, Richard puts his faith in his title: "Is not the King's name twenty thousand names? | Arm, arm, my name" (3.2.85–86). Unfortunately for him, names cannot take up arms. In fact, names are far more the business of poets than of kings. Just when we may be swooning (as I was in my Central Park experience of the play) at the magic of the words, it starts to become clear that this susceptibility may be a risky business. Shakespeare is delivering to us a Richard who doesn't know the difference between words and things, doesn't know that even the loftiest of all earthly words, *king*, can't hold a rebel army at bay. So it's not just that Richard is a poet stuck in the role of king—a familiar reading of the character—but that Richard wants to be a poet but doesn't understand the most fundamental thing about how the poet's weapons—words—actually operate. "Poetry makes nothing happen," said Auden in his dirge for Yeats; he goes on to say, "It survives," which is exactly what Richard doesn't and what Shakespeare did.

Then the problem of words and things and kings gets more heated:

> For God's sake, let us sit upon the ground
> And tell sad stories of the death of kings;
> How some have been deposed; some slain in war,
> Some haunted by the ghosts they have deposed;
> Some poison'd by their wives: some sleeping kill'd;
> All murder'd: for within the hollow crown
> That rounds the mortal temples of a king
> Keeps Death his court and there the antic sits,
> Scoffing his state and grinning at his pomp,
> Allowing him a breath, a little scene,
> To monarchize, be fear'd and kill with looks,
> Infusing him with self and vain conceit,
> As if this flesh which walls about our life,
> Were brass impregnable, and humour'd thus
> Comes at the last and with a little pin
> Bores through his castle wall, and farewell king!

(3.2.155–70)

I'm sure that this speech counted as the very climax of my adolescent sense that the play's words operated as music to swoon by. In later life, however, I begin to hear discords. It's *my* job, not yours, says Shakespeare to his hero, to tell sad stories of the death of kings; you do the king business—you know, maintaining your land in peace, justice, and unity—and leave the tragic grandeur business to me. This is more than a matter of professional rivalries. Shakespeare is treading upon a delicate paradox that has an impact on both of them. It may not be good for a king, if he is to be a good king, to have this cosmic perspective (in this case, in fact, to wallow in it), to see past and future so clearly, so eloquently, through a lens that ultimately reveals a deep nothingness at the heart of the whole grand enterprise of king and nation, for the monarch, in other words, merely to *monarchize*. It's a vision that flips back on the poet, who is stuck with a formula whereby a tragic king must in some fundamental ways be a bad king. I'm not sure Shakespeare ever quite escaped this formula—or that he wanted to. I do know that a play he will write ten years in the future revisits this exact territory in a grand style. In order to evade the possibility of having his royal hero tell this all-too-accurate story about the void at the heart of the system, Shakespeare arranges that Lear be driven mad, with speech that is closer to nonsense than it is to the rhapsodies that I was hearing in Central Park.

All this language that calls attention to itself *as* language—exquisite yet futile, indeed put in the service of displaying its own futility—counts in some sense as phase two of the same self-consuming emptiness that turned the first two acts into sequences of nonevents, of combats that don't take place, of past wounds that don't get cauterized, of cleansings via banishments that have to be rescinded. Presented with the historical material relative to what might be considered equivalent to the Fall of Man as regards English history, the crucial dividing line between simple antiquity and complex modernity, Shakespeare has realized that it all happened with nothing happening. He has already, in plays from a decade earlier, written the latter half of the story, in which wagonloads of things happen: a hundred years' worth of dynasties pitted against dynasties, of murders and battles, of hunchbacked monster-kings and crazy French witches, all tied up with a providential happy ending that would gladden the heart of the present monarch and her loyal subjects. The piece of this long story occupied by *Richard II* looms as nothing but the narrative of a king so weak that he performs as little more than a vacuum into which, rather undramatically, his monarchy implodes.

The recurrent fiction to which I've given the name Playwriting 101—a straw man if ever there was one, who produces logical and consequent fictions that deliver what audiences expect—would probably have fixed on Bolingbroke to rescue things, triumphing in the end over the supine figure of a weak king, though unfortunately without the handy device of a decisive battle (or indeed *any* battle) in which Richard got killed and Henry rode away in majesty. Bolingbroke, however, is the great cipher of *Richard II*, at least until he becomes Henry IV, and perhaps even then. Ultimately, it will be part of his larger cipherdom, as mentioned earlier, that is, the difficulty of assigning him a role in the so-called Tudor myth. It's a risky business, as I often tell my students, to draw interpretations from things that *don't* happen in fictions, but occasionally it is worth following Sherlock Holmes's dog that *didn't* bark, which becomes the key to solving the murder. And *Richard II*, with its lopsided relation between language and action, is a good place to listen for that dog. I am thinking in particular of two things, one that Bolingbroke *doesn't* say and the other that he says, but with astonishing nonchalance.

The thing Bolingbroke doesn't say, even later, when it is about to become real, is that he has the ambition to become king of England. The matter is contained, with an obliqueness that makes it even more occulted than silence, among the claims that his enemy Mowbray lays at his charge back in the opening minutes of the play, when the two are insulting each other, as quoted earlier: "What thou art, God, thou and I do know, | And all too soon, I fear, the King shall rue." The secret known only to those three parties (Richard not being one of them, as Mowbray implies) is that Bolingbroke is bringing this private argument before the king as a step toward deposing him. Whether this is true or not Shakespeare doesn't know, and the play doesn't say. From the point when Bolingbroke returns to England—illegally by Richard's understanding and legitimately only on the theory that, as he expresses it, "I was banish'd Hereford; | But as I come, I come for Lancaster (2.3.112–13)—Shakespeare never gives him the chance to say that he wants, or expects, to become king. Regarding what everyone else on both sides of the struggle believes and asserts, Bolingbroke is silent.

All of this is confirmed by the thing that Bolingbroke says with astonishing casualness. At the moment when, on the level of real power—that is, armies that have the capacity to crush opposing armies—it is clear that Richard has lost what we would call his "base," York declares quite formally, as though the succession were normal, that England now has a new monarch. "Ascend his throne," York declares to Bolingbroke, "descending now from him, | And long live Henry, of that name the fourth" (4.1.112–13). (*Ascend* and *descend* are heavily weighted terms, referring to up and down but also to the fiction that Bolingbroke was the *descendant* of Richard, when the very important truth is that Richard has no descendants, more of which anon.) To that official pronouncement, Bolingbroke replies: "In God's name I'll ascend the regal throne" (4.1.114). That's his whole speech, surely the most offhanded declaration of assuming royal authority that has ever been uttered, in life or on stage. "In God's name" is already in Shakespeare's time an expression of casual emphasis rather than necessarily a sacred oath. So, although we might take it as a grand reference to the divine will, more likely Shakespeare is teasing us with a throwaway.

So we have one protagonist who loses a kingdom to the accompaniment of logorrhea in blank verse and the other protagonist who gains a kingdom by saying, essentially, "OK, I'll take it." The truth is that, at least in these middle phases of the play, and perhaps beyond, Shakespeare relentlessly sidelines Bolingbroke: He is calling his play *Richard II*; he has slipped in a tragedy in place of the expected chronicle plays, aka Histories, that were the box office triumphs of his early career; and, at least for the moment, he is not looking back. In a real coup de théâtre he stages the play's first real face-to-face meeting between the antagonists as, in fact, *not* face to face. By taking advantage of the theater's rarely used upper stage—sometimes called the heavens—he forces the soon-to-be-anointed king, stuck at more or less ground level, to bend his neck upward as Richard makes his grand entrance almost from the sky. No surprise, as Bolingbroke squints aloft (Elizabethan outdoor theater was performed in the afternoon), that he is given his only chance to talk like Richard:

> See, see, King Richard doth himself appear,
> As doth the blushing discontented sun
> From out the fiery portal of the east,
> When he perceives the envious clouds are bent
> To dim his glory and to stain the track
> Of his bright passage to the occident.
>
> (3.3.61–66)

Partly cloudy is better than no sun at all.

The message is a simple one. Bolingbroke doesn't depose Richard, Richard deposes Richard, beginning with the moment when he descends from his lofty perch on the upper stage:

> Down, down I come; like glistering Phaethon,
> Wanting the manage of unruly jades.
> In the base court? Base court, where kings grow base,
> To come at traitors' calls and do them grace.
> In the base court? Come down? Down, court! down, king!
> For night-owls shriek where mounting larks should sing.
>
> (3.3.177–82)

Once both of the protagonists are on ground level, the scene is rather anti-climactic. The two trade a few comments about Bolingbroke's reasons for returning to England (he's still saying, "I come but for mine own"), and as close as they get to actually acknowledging that there might be a shift of kingship is Richard saying to Bolingbroke, "Set on towards London, cousin, is it so?" (3.3.206), acknowledging, in other words, that Bolingbroke is headed for the seat of power, whereas Richard remains atop some backwater citadel. "London" is a sort of euphemism for taking possession of the throne, as though regime change is the act that dare not speak its name.

The real action is the deposition that Richard enacts by himself and out of Bolingbroke's earshot:

> What must the king do now? must he submit?
> The king shall do it: must he be deposed?
> The king shall be contented: must he lose
> The name of king? o' God's name, let it go:

I'll give my jewels for a set of beads,
My gorgeous palace for a hermitage,
My gay apparel for an almsman's gown,
My figured goblets for a dish of wood,
My sceptre for a palmer's walking staff,
My subjects for a pair of carved saints
And my large kingdom for a little grave,
A little little grave, an obscure grave. . . .

(3.3.142–53)

This has no force of law, of course, as will be made clear in a later, more decisive, scene when Northumberland requires a public confession of Richard's crimes in order to make the regime change official. That distinction itself should help locate for us where Shakespeare's heart really lies in this story. The play's first act took the form of official public discourse, with an endless array of ritualized, often repeated, language; it absolutely enshrined the uphill battle that Mr. Gelb quite rightly diagnosed in the Central Park audience. Now, however, Shakespeare offers us a completely different ritualized language, that of human loss. To arrive at that point, it is necessary to imagine a kingship that undoes itself from within the soul of the king.

A confession, or maybe an apology: I'm always a little uncomfortable when I arrive at the point in my literary interpretation where I am, explicitly or implicitly, saying that the work is itself *about* language. Clearly, the work is *in* language, language is its essential instrument; how could it *not* be "about" language? How much analytic mileage, therefore, can I claim by making such a point? Is the Sistine Ceiling *about* brushstrokes or brushes or wet plaster or paint? Is the *Well-Tempered Clavier about* the musical scale? (Actually, it *is*— never mind that one.) It seems I can't let go of Abraham Maslow's deceptively simple observation: "It is tempting, if the only tool you have is a hammer, to treat everything as if it were a nail"; he goes on to call it the "law of the instrument." We know very little about what else Shakespeare might have done other than write plays and sometimes perform in them. Over the centuries, especially earlier ones, readers have been so amazed by the specialized terminologies that he puts into his characters' mouths—the standard example is the precision of nautical terminology in *The Tempest*—that they've invented stories about his apprenticeships in a slew of nontheatrical trades. Such explanations are unnecessary: His trade was language itself. That's his hammer, and it turns out that everything *is* a nail for that particular tool. And it should come as no surprise that his relation to language should come in the form of theory as well as practice.

Which is a good place for me to turn to my own tools, *si parva licet componere magnis*. About fifteen years after my adolescent encounter with *Richard* in the park, I found myself poised to write my very first scholarly article. My doctoral thesis, suitably improved (so I hoped), was at this point on its way to print; it had only a small section on Shakespeare, and the work as a whole pursued a History of Ideas itinerary that I didn't anticipate as constituting the bulk of my future intellectual production. As emerges elsewhere in this volume, I had done and was continuing to do quite a lot of theater, as both actor and director, circumstances that neither the dissertation nor the book in any way betrayed, doubtless for strategic professional reasons, though in fact I was beginning to notice, for instance in my teaching, that theater was a rich creative and intellectual vein for me and also that it might not be (I can't resist quoting *Mommy Dearest*) "box office poison" in literature or English departments after all.

At some point, then, in the early '70s, it came to me as a revelation that it should be my destiny to make an academic career out of combining my lifelong passion for Shakespeare, my training as a recently minted literature PhD, and my work in the theater. This really was a very good idea, and even now it's tricky to piece together the exact reasons why no such thing happened. I spent six months sitting in the old British Museum Reading Room (may its memory be a blessing) doing nothing but reading every work I could locate from 1850 to the present in which Shakespeare's work was addressed from the perspective of theater. I apologize to any present reader of these pages who might have been within that bibliography, but I have to say that it was for me a very uninspiring experience. Sometimes when one takes notice of a lack in previous scholarship—the proverbial "much-needed gap"—it is the perfect inspiration for one's own work, which is then projected as a remedy for that lack. At other times, such as this one of me at my desk in the British Museum, the lack appears so vast, so structural, so constitutive, that the wish to propel oneself suicidally into the void simply fizzles.

All that having been said, I finally cobbled together the makings of a little niche for myself. Though I have always enjoyed performing, both on stage and off, my favorite work in the theater has always been as a director. The most thrilling and demanding task has been that of shaping an overall concept for a text and then working out the minute and varied ways that such a concept might express itself in the physical circumstances of a production and in the nuances of each performance. Why, then, might there not be a scholarly and critical form in which I might deliver this combination of concepts and realizations on pages rather than stages? I never really succeeded, and I'm not sure it is possible, perhaps because the director's work is as a mediator, with a text on one side and, on the other, a host of individuals, materials, and mechanisms that implement the director's conception while contributing to it with every bit as much creativity and imagination as the director possesses; half the subject was necessarily absent when I was sentenced to do this in print all by myself. The residue of all this thinking, the one tiny point of interest on the road not taken, was an article entitled "The Theatrical Consistency of *Richard II*," which I managed to publish in a 1978 issue of *Shakespeare Quarterly*. Once again, as in Central Park, *Richard II* was for me a play of initiation.

"Theatrical consistency" was a clumsy phrase burdened with too many tasks. "Theatrical" was to make sure everyone knew I was talking about effects that emerged via performance, though I was careful to say that I was interested in what the text itself seemed to demand of the performers. "Consistency" was forced into double duty: at once in the sense of *texture* but also in the sense of *uniformity* (or lack thereof). In other words, I was asking what was the emotional "feel" of the play *and* how that "feel" mutated from scene to scene or moment to moment. Only now do I realize that I was in fact back in the NBC studio with my intensity dial, except that I was using it as a metric not only for the aggregate of each moment but also as a way of measuring the emotional tone of each character; think of it as one of those newfangled fever thermometers that operates simply by being pointed at the forehead.

I started to notice that early in the drama every scene was in one way or another being played out as an encounter between passionate or violent emotions, on the one hand, and some kind of supervening restraint on the other. At the opening of the play, the violent emotions, themselves arising out of an act of violence, are constrained both by the rigid structure of the ritual trial and by the aloofness of the king. In the next scene, the Duchess of Gloucester expresses herself in the mode of grand poetic rage, but she is up against John of Gaunt, who says, basically, that it's God's problem and we can't do anything about it. The trial by combat is itself the promise of violent action, but the king terminates it. Gaunt rages against Richard, both in his absence and to his face, but Richard remains unmoved. The Queen plays out another passionate lament, which her courtiers attempt to rationalize into scholastic structures. The Duke of York acts as the embodiment of this mechanism: He is buffeted by the wills of both sides in the dynastic struggle and can only declare to Bolingbroke, "I do remain as neuter" (2.3.158). Rage on the one hand, neuter on the other.

What I realize now, but I don't think I did then, was that I was trying to rescue *Richard II*. I was recollecting my own adolescent version of the play as I experienced it in Central Park—the long Mahler-esque symphony of the hero's inexhaustible speech that had carried me along without quite needing to mean anything, all of that wrapped up in a performance style that was less theater than holy ceremony. Wonderful for a teenage Shakespeare virgin, but there needed to be more. I blame Gielgud: In the 1960s, if you paid any attention at all to *Richard II*, you had probably heard the recordings of that golden voice pronouncing, "For god's sake, let us sit down upon the ground . . ." I had to find a way to dig up that ground.

Shakespeare, as I see it, cooperated, as witness a couple of crucial moments in the last part of the play where he aggressively breaks the decorum that the play had so carefully established. Bolingbroke, attempting to succeed where Richard failed, interrogates some six or seven lords who had knowledge concerning the murder of Gloucester. But instead of an orderly trial proceeding, it turns into a free-for-all of challenges and cross-challenges among the lords, accompanied by the ostentatious hurling of gloves to the floor. Bolingbroke begins with Bagot; Bagot involves Aumerle; Aumerle involves Fitzwater; Fitzwater involves Surrey. Aumerle wants to get in on the act a second time but discovers that he has run out of gloves and tries to borrow one, perhaps looking longingly at the pileup of gloves on the floor, which are, unfortunately for him, one use only. Any time that serious and abstract issues are channeled through a physical object (in this case, the purity of the monarchy versus bulky gloves), comedy lurks. By way of scientific research, I have now watched several videotaped versions of the play, each in front of an audience. In one case, the scene was played for laughs, and it got them to excess, which itself demonstrates how eager a *Richard II* audience is for relief/release. In another case, it was played very seriously, but by the end of the episode, with seven or eight gloves on the floor and Aumerle clueless and gloveless, there began to be isolated pockets of giggling in the audience, quite at variance with the solemnity that the actors were attempting to deliver. A third instance simply cut the scene altogether, which demonstrates the director's discomfort with anything as potentially farcical in the midst of holy poetic tragedy.

A different piece of subversive comedy arises in the fifth act, centering once again on a quite serious matter. A rebellion of King Richard diehards against the new king is brewing, with hapless Aumerle (the one with insufficient gloves) once again at the center of things. He is discovered by his father, the Duke of York, to be taking part in the conspiracy. York is determined to reveal his son's treason, even though he knows that it will likely mean the young man's execution; the Duchess, Aumerle's mother, is, not surprisingly, desperate to prevent this from being revealed to the King. Once more, the subject could scarcely have more gravitas: the sacred bands of family versus the sacred bands of monarchy. But the whole thing is laboriously delayed when no one brings the Duke of York his boots; without boots he can't ride his horse; without his horse he can't confront the king; without confronting the king he can't help quash the counter-rebellion. And once all three members of the family finally get to the king, they indulge in a game of kneeling and counterkneeling so farcical that Henry himself turns into a drama critic and comments (in what I would play as an audience aside, possibly Groucho-style), "Our scene is now alter'd from a serious thing. | And now changed to 'The Beggar and the King'" (5.3.78–79), wink, wink. It's almost needless to point out that both these scenes—first theater of the absurd, then family sitcom—in addition to producing a tonal shock in the play's *consistency*—deliver to us a Bolingbroke who does *not* exhibit himself as the master of action. If he doesn't possess Richard's words but is also inept on the plane of deeds, what good is he?

However raucous in spirit one may imagine scenes revolving around gloves and boots, they are both in significant ways segregated from the grand throughline of the play, whether one imagines that as history or as tragedy. Richard, after all, appears in neither of them. Tucked in between them, however, are a couple of moments with Richard in the spotlight and where something of this absurdist spirit clings to the epicenter of tragedy. Both of them, once again, involve props.

Some background. Over the course of acts 3 and 4 we're dealt a variety of signs that Richard will be deposed and Bolingbroke become king, but like so many things in the play the grand gesture keeps being evaded. There is, for one thing, no battle (a circumstance virtually unique among the history plays). We have seen Bolingbroke as judge, but it's not really suggested that he is therefore the monarch; even when he places all those glove-throwing lords under arrest, it's not made explicit under what authority he does so. York, as we've already seen, names Bolingbroke as Henry IV, but whose voice really possesses that authority?

It will be no surprise that, as was the case earlier, the individual who most grandly announces the fall of Richard is Richard himself. It was he who first used the term *deposed* back in act 3, when he divested himself of jewels, gay apparel, etc. That was autodeposition via the word; in act 4, he will, in the full legal and theatrical senses, *perform* it. (Recall the resonances of that term in *The Winter's Tale*'s statue scene.) Performances require props, and props will take us back to that strange space of the comic, or even the absurd, which was occupied by the gloves and the boots. The theatrical experience of the whole play rises or falls on Richard's protracted self-undoing in act 4, scene 1. There is every reason why Mr. Gelb may have found it one more strenuous climb in the uphill battle that he and his readers were undertaking; for me, it was, and remains, exhilarating. There is no further plot, at least as regards the central question of the play up to this point, which is who shall occupy the throne of England. It's all aria, though the tunes may be changing.

It's also where props come back in. York, whose job it apparently is to certify the legitimate monarch—no surprise, Bolingbroke—is, by way of that office, actually holding the crown. He is not holding the *abstraction* of the crown, which, for over three acts of the play, has been the predominant medium in which monarchy has been presented to us; he's holding a shiny circular golden material object. The point of the present encounter is that Richard officially resign his kingship, as has been agreed. In spite of that, however, it is he who says to York, "Give me the crown." Surprisingly, York hands it over to him. Perhaps just as surprisingly, Richard immediately hands it to Bolingbroke, but (is this also a surprise?) does not himself let go of it. The political essence of the play, which, through three-plus acts of Richard's performativity, has been turned into flights of abstraction, is suddenly literalized—and rendered mobile. Which holds more reality: monarchy or a prop? (Before you answer that, remember we're in the theater.) Who is in possession of the object, and who is in possession of the abstraction? Bolingbroke, as we should have expected, is incapable of operating at a level appropriate to these metaphorics. "I thought you had been willing to resign," he says to Richard, in the tone of a man whose secretary has interrupted a meeting to inform him that his next client, perhaps a more important one, is already waiting in the outer office. Does Bolingbroke let go of the crown? Surely yes: His time is valuable; he won't waste it playing games. He looks at his watch and says, with some exasperation, "Are you contented to resign the crown?" (Understood: *or not??? I haven't got all day.*)

Later in the same scene, Richard is ordered, by Bolingbroke's hatchetman Northumberland, to read publicly a list of his crimes, an exercise that, understandably, he finds humiliating. Instead of agreeing, he asks that someone bring him a mirror. Northumberland says okay, but at least while they're fetching the mirror, you have to read the list of your crimes. Unlike the crown, this prop has no fixed place in the rituals of monarchy. Richard is now pursuing his own script, with his own metaphorics. The mirror—it's the oldest metaphor in the book—is, of course, himself, or, in a usage that is already coming into being in 1600, *his self.* Mirror in hand, Richard delivers his penultimate piece of poetic eloquence, embodying in remarkably simple words (for him, anyway) his royal power, his metaphorical sublimity, and his downfall:

> Was this face the face
> That every day under his household roof
> Did keep ten thousand men? was this the face
> That, like the sun, did make beholders wink?
> Was this the face that faced so many follies,
> And was at last out-faced by Bolingbroke?

(4.1.281–86)

Whereupon Richard commits the terrible act of smashing the mirror: Has he destroyed himself, has he fragmented himself, has his self already been fragmented, such that the broken mirror merely embodies that condition?

I sometimes teach a course called "Learning Shakespeare by Doing," in which we cover only four plays in a semester and spend our time working on performances of selected scenes, pursuant to the principle that no close reading of Shakespeare's text can possibly be more informative than that in which the students themselves actually have to stand up and speak the lines. (I try to have students with some theatrical experience, but I've found it's not absolutely essential.) In the class a few years ago, for this scene I assigned the role of Richard to a young woman who possessed some real stage presence. I also brought a prop from home. It wasn't an actual mirror, of course (the last thing I need is seven years of bad classes); it was a vaguely mirror-shaped wooden pizza paddle from my kitchen. The student captured perfectly both the intensity of emotion and the slight sense that Richard—the king, not the actor—might be overplaying it. She delivered the lines "a brittle glory shineth in this face | As brittle as the glory is the face" and proceeded to hurl the prop to the floor. The pizza paddle shattered into a mass of splinters. We all learned how powerful a *thing* can be, especially when it is wielded amid a forest of abstractions. I don't know exactly what fractured selfhood looks like, but the sound and sight of the fragmented pizza paddle sticks in the mind. Richard's end—for now—was made manifest as both metaphor and object. The class froze in awe.

Fourteen drag queens—white, black, Asian, Latinx—in full costume enter the set one by one. Each has a moment to establish herself (I use the preferred pronoun) with, besides her "look," a character gesture, a tagline, some either catty or faux-affectionate recognition of the previous entrants. So the season of *RuPaul's Drag Race* begins. Each week's show puts the contestants through various challenges—games, comic performances, and a runway spectacle in which they exhibit their most extravagant drag. There are contests where they insult each other and others where they play games of concentration involving the recollection of which colors of underwear the members of a group of well-built young men known as the "Pit Crew" are wearing. (The Pit Crew is one of the few residues from the first couple of seasons, when the idea of "drag race" involved more automotive imagery. Now, presumably, *RuPaul's Drag Race* is actually more famous than any actual speedway, though perhaps with little overlap in their constituencies—or perhaps a lot.) A favorite challenge midway through the season is the "Snatch Game," patterned on the old "Match Game." RuPaul asks questions dripping in double entendre; the queens answer while enacting over-the-top parodies of the celebrity whom they are impersonating. Among the immortals: Maggie Smith, Judge Judy, Cher, Edie from Grey Gardens, and, in a rare act of trans-trans-gendering (sort of), Little Richard.

All the drag queens are biological men, though very occasionally one of them will tearfully reveal himself to be in some stage of transitioning. It is taken for granted that every one of the men is gay: All erotic interchanges are based on that unquestioned assumption. Once all fourteen have entered, RuPaul appears; she will perform, variously, as cheerleader, confessor, shrink, peacemaker, sower of discord, sarcastic fault finder: in short, as a Mother (mine, at any rate; see elsewhere in these pages). Each week a judgment is made of their performance in the challenges and their runway appearance. Some contestants are "safe," one is the winner, and the "bottom two" (every possible double entendre heavily exploited) have to fight it out in a procedure that Ru intones in an echo-chamber-aided voice as requiring them to *"Lip synch for your life."* At the end of that exercise Ru focuses her attention on one of the pair and says, "Chantay you stay"; the other will be told to "sashay away." Once all but three or four have been eliminated as the weeks go by, there is a grand finale, the winner of which is crowned "America's Next Drag Superstar." If ceremony is both brandished and withheld in *Richard II*, no such restraint characterizes *RuPaul's Drag Race*.

What is not so easy to explain is the level of pleasure that this gigantic confection of silliness produces in our house. Two middle aged–to-elderly gay men who have never had the slightest interest in wearing women's clothes or in going to venues where others do so (nor have they ever found it erotically stimulating) cheerfully wipe their social calendars clean on any evening when there is a new installment of any version of the *Drag Race* (and there are many versions—English, Canadian, All-Stars, etc.), and we quite frequently watch reruns with no noticeable diminution of pleasure. We spend serious time debating the merits of the queens and subreading the ethos that emerges from Ru's choices among them. We speak Drag, for example, *to read* (to unleash a sequence of insults, typically to a person's face, as in "I read her for her booger drag," that is, I criticized her for her ugly drag appearance), *serve* (to present oneself a certain way, as in "she's serving fish" = looking especially authentic as female), *T* or *tea* (a tricky one: It can mean gossip, but it can also mean truth; the question "what's the T?" can cover either possibility), *shade* (the casting of aspersions, as in "No T, no shade" = what I'm telling you is not merely malicious gossip, so you'd better believe it), not to mention more specialized things like *tuck* (to arrange oneself so as to hide the lump of male genitals) or *kai kai* (to have drag queen–on–drag queen sex while both parties are in drag).

I fear that I'm sentenced to an all-too-highbrow set of explanations for this pleasure of ours. For me, the show is an act of revolutionary liberation wrapped up in a package of rough-hewn comedy. What the great break-through documentary *Paris Is Burning* did in the key of anthropological/activist investigation thirty years ago, RuPaul is doing as seriously naughty entertainment. Being homosexual, cross-dressing, performing as a drag queen, contemplating gender reassignment: *RuPaul's Drag Race* introduces us to this set of border territories with a patient sense that we may not, even after watching a whole season, become entirely comfortable with the terrain, but we can't fail to notice that some very striking personalities live there and that they make us laugh, give us pleasure. (Bigots, of course, will not be converted by this or any other instrument; I don't expect such an outcome from a TV show.) I describe it all with careful equal time to various alternative expressions of sexuality, but perhaps the best shorthand is to borrow, as I have already done in regard to *As You Like It*, from the great theorist of sexuality Judith Butler, who gave us the expression "gender as performance." There is much complex theorizing in Butler's argument, but the bottom line is that it is designed to liberate us from a sense that we all live in a lock-up determined by a powerful alliance of biology and custom. If you watch a season of RuPaul, or even a couple of weeks, you will at least know what it means to see gender *performed*. In its campy, extravagant way, the *Drag Race* is dedicated to bringing on a revolution through laughter, which makes for much more appealing company in my view than any of the other revolutions—American, French, Russian, Industrial—that take up more space in the history books. No T, no shade.

Justin Dwayne Lee Johnson, also known by his stage name Alyssa Edwards, is an American drag performer, choreographer, and business-person. Alyssa Edwards famously won the *Miss Gay America* pageant in 2010 but was stripped off of the crown shortly after. . . . [She] was dethroned after winning *Miss Gay America* in 2010 by the Miss Gay America organisation, which conducts national pageants for female impersonators. It has been reported by various media outlets that the reason for this dethroning was that Alyssa Edwards conducted some business dealings that conflicted with the Miss Gay America organisation's policy. Her crown was hastily passed over to Coco Montrese, who happened to be the runner up.

There have also been speculations that there could be other possible reasons to Edwards' dethroning. Some media outlets reported that Edwards kept missing major club events and other public appearances for Miss Gay America. Hence, the organisation decided to strip her of the crown. It has been reported that Alyssa Edwards and Coco Montrese were close friends before the 2010 Miss America travesty. Fans of the show at the time were speculating that Coco had played a role in snatching the crown. The speculations suggested that Coco did so by revealing to the Miss Gay America organisation where Alyssa actually was while she was missing from her appearances for them.

—*REPUBLIC WORLD*, LAST UPDATED JUNE 17, 2020

RuPaul's people must have known they were scoring a brilliant coup by managing to include as competitors both these Misses Gay America in a single season, a circumstance that was exploited by pitting them against each other in every possible way throughout the run of the show. We weren't more than a couple of weeks into the season when Nick, my spouse, decided that the Alyssa-Coco story was perfect material for a screenplay. The sequence of two best friends coming in first and second at "Miss Gay America," followed by the rescinding of Alyssa's title and its reassignment to Coco, culminating in the pair's appearance on RuPaul: This was going to be Nick's inspiration. He also determined, without any pressure from me, that his film should have some kind of Shakespearean framework. Something like the *Hamlet* supertext in *Strange Brew*, which envelops a Canadian equivalent of a stoner farce—beer instead of weed—with a narrative about the attempt to dethrone the president of the Elsinore Beer Company. I told Nick that I didn't see much of *Hamlet* in the Coco-Alyssa story but that there was a work of Shakespeare's that did involve a very direct rivalry, in fact, over a crown. Through our twenty-plus years together, Nick had been exposed to a lot of Shakespeare, but he knew nothing about *Richard II*. Before long, however, breakfast had turned into an ongoing seminar on the play, Nick became as conversant with it as I, and within a few months he produced the completed draft of a screenplay.

Alyse Richards, having been named Miss Everything in a national contest, is ruling over her drag bar—called the Crown—autocratically, forcing her two rivals into a Drag Duel, but then she interrupts the action, strips them of all their finery, and declares that they may never appear in drag so long as she is queen. (There's a Mother Woodstock subplot behind all of this.) Covert forces begin to gather that would strip her of her Miss Everything crown, and they gain strength when Alyse goes out of town (to Dublin, Ohio) with her army of drag children, from which she returns bedraggled and in disgrace. A crowd gathers at the Crown to denounce her, at which point she rises to her most spectacular drag queenly impersonation, but to no avail. Imprisoning her rivals and forcing them to dance in cages also does her no good. Ordinary people in a flower shop gossip about her fall. Supporters on both sides defy each other by throwing down their gloves, then go on to discharging other, more interesting parts of their costumes. The officials from the Miss Everything contest determine that the runner-up, Mocha, should now be declared queen, but as they prepare to hand her the crown Alyse snatches it back; there is a tug-of-war. Alyse is ordered to *read* her crimes, but she is too tearful. She calls for a mirror and then proceeds to *read* (in the drag sense) her face. Now that she is dethroned, some of her followers start to mount a counterinsurgency; it is uncovered, and a Drag Mother kneels in front of Mocha to beg for a pardon. Alyse is left all alone to declare, "There is no one here but me in this prison of a body where I live" (Shakespeare, *Richard II*, 5.5.1, roughly; see below). But then she is reconciled—this is one *Richard II* with a happy ending—when she confesses, on air to RuPaul, "It's just that . . . I thought Miss Everything *was* everything. I didn't know how much more I was neglecting." Admittedly, at this point there's a whiff of Queen Lear about the whole thing.

That's the fun part, and I long to see this all on the silver screen. But there's also a real Shakespeare part—not Dublin, Ohio; nor the drag queen, named Harlot, on her knees (!) as the Duchess of York; nor, for that matter, the fact that Shakespeare himself dressed all his boy actors as women and fiddled with gender identity possibly beyond the wildest imaginings of RuPaul. Rather, this is something quite particular to *Richard II*, and it has nothing to do with boy actors dressed as women. Nick entitled his screenplay *Realness*. It's become virtually a throwaway term in the drag world, made famous by *Paris Is Burning* and thence colloquialized as a compliment to any performer who has mastered the regendering of male as female in a particularly convincing way. But it's also an expression that, as the late twentieth century theorized things, undoes itself. The *real* real is simply real. It does not possess *realness*, nor does it have any need of this commodity; the *realness* of a drag queen is the re-production, the re-presentation, of the *real*. *Real* is also in the language of Shakespeare's time *royal* (the two words are etymologically related), as in the archaic racket game known as Real Tennis, which does not mean *authentic* tennis but rather tennis as played by *royals*.

Richard's struggle through Shakespeare's play is a struggle with *realness*, with the *real*, and with the *royal*. He *is* the genuine king (I'm running out of synonyms here), with all the authority of unbroken patrilineal genealogy, unlike Bolingbroke. But there is something about Richard's nature, as Shakespeare imagines it, that compels him to *play* the king rather than simply *being* the king, something that induces him to impersonate the *royal*, or the *real*. Hence all his grand performance of kingliness (*performance* being another term that maps the distance between an authentic phenomenon and a simulacrum; see elsewhere in these pages the statue of Hermione in *The Winter's Tale*, another drag performance in its way, complete with use of the verb *perform*). Richard wears kingliness the way Alyssa Edwards wears gowns and mascara and mile-high wigs. The tragic irony is that Richard *is* a king, whereas Alyssa is *performing* a queen. At his best, Richard accomplishes this performance superbly, just as, say, a winner of *RuPaul's Drag Race* impersonates a glamorous woman superbly. (Alyssa, alas, didn't win; she went home in week five, Coco in week six—the two of them adjacent to the last.) But the tradition for kings of England is not the same as it is for queens on *RuPaul*, and all the external and internal struggles of Richard testify more to the miseries than to the splendors of *realness*.

•

I have been studying how I may compare
This prison where I live unto the world:
And for because the world is populous
And here is not a creature but myself,
I cannot do it; yet I'll hammer it out.
My brain I'll prove the female to my soul,
My soul the father; and these two beget
A generation of still-breeding thoughts,
And these same thoughts people this little world,
In humours like the people of this world,
For no thought is contented.

(5.5.1–11)

"I have been studying how . . .": That opening of Richard's final scene always stops me in my tracks. Actors *study*, literary critics *study*. Tragic heroes don't study. Lear hasn't been *studying* how to say "I am a man more sinned against than sinning," and Hamlet, though he may have been at university, isn't *studying* how to say "To be or not to be." Nor is Macbeth *studying* how to say "a tale told by an idiot signifying nothing." They have aced the course, earned the degree with honors. Richard is *studying*.

To do justice to Richard as he appears here for the last time requires a little context within the arc of Shakespeare's career. It is generally agreed that the play was written around 1595, which locates it among his early—though not earliest—works for the stage. He has written chronicle histories and romantic comedies; what he has not yet written is the kind of complex, psychologically driven tragedy that will occupy him at the beginning of the new century and that, almost from the moment they were written, have counted as his supreme masterpieces. We call *Richard II* a "history" because it fits in the chronological line of his plays that cover the monarchy from 1399 to 1485, but it is nothing like any of the other history plays, and History is not even a dramatic genre in the same sense as Comedy or Tragedy. All of which is a way of saying that in a certain important sense *Richard II* is Shakespeare's first tragedy, particularly if we think of Shakespearean tragedy as focusing on a complex central figure of mixed moral and ethical nature who faces massive and ultimately insurmountable conflicts in both the public and private arenas of his life. If that is the case, then this soliloquy of Richard's, particularly because of its placement at the opening of the final scene, which suggests not a grand conclusion but rather the beginning of a process, must count in Shakespearean terms (with apologies to Nietzsche) as the Birth of Tragedy.

Or at least the birth of the tragic hero. I've already suggested, à propos of "Let us sit upon the ground | And tell sad stories of the death of kings," that Shakespeare is personally invested to a high degree in the nature of the tragic hero. Shakespeare, to put it in old-fashioned terms, *identifies* with Richard. Shakespeare's Richard is, in his fantastically powerful language throughout the play, writing his own life. The real author, in a brilliant stroke, not only creates that circumstance but also weaves it into both the character and the fate of his hero. It would be better for Richard, as king, if he were not given to the practice of writing his own life; it would be better for him just to live it, as, for instance, Bolingbroke does. But it would not be better for tragedy. Back in act 3, as I suggested earlier, Richard was proposing to tell stories of kings, thus placing himself in parallel and in competition with his own author. Here at the end of his life and the play Richard is reflecting on the success of the enterprise. This finally *is* the sad tale of the death of kings, only it's just one king, and the king is the tale teller himself.

It's no coincidence that the scene of this "study" is one of radical solitude. Shakespeare has found a spot where the narrative arc of the monarch coincides with the narrative flatline of the poet. Kings normally conduct their lives in public, even when they may wistfully talk about telling stories of kings; writers conduct their lives—at least their *writing* lives—alone. This king is at the present moment, exceptionally, quite alone. Richard attempts to diversify the enterprise by reference to a fundamental act of creation—*the* fundamental act—that cannot be done alone, the making of offspring; he imagines a male brain and a female soul, both within himself, that can make babies who will in turn make more babies: "a generation of still breeding thoughts." Wishful, wistful thinking for a monarch who has not produced an heir to the throne. One cannot overestimate here the contemporary resonances in 1595, with the childless Elizabeth in her sixties, of these parallels. It is famously reported that the queen, in reference to works treating this period of history, declared angrily, "I am Richard II, know ye not that?" This fury is generally ascribed to the circumstances of the Essex rebellion against Elizabeth, seen as parallel to Richard's deposition, and there was indeed a commissioned performance of the play on the eve of the earl's attempted coup. But her reaction is equally relevant to the parallel between their respective lack of offspring. There are grave dangers to the realm when lineal succession is interrupted. And—to return to the matter of the monarch and the writer—it is widely understood that writings are a form of offspring. Again, though, not perhaps the best kind for a king.

Nor is the writing project going so well for Richard:

> . . . no thought is contented. The better sort,
> As thoughts of things divine, are intermix'd
> With scruples and do set the word itself
> Against the word, as thus: "Come, little ones,"
> And then again,
> "It is as hard to come as for a camel
> To thread the postern of a small needle's eye."
>
> (5.5.11–17)

It's all very well to say "in the beginning was the word," which is a good motto for a writer at the inaugural moment of an enterprise, but what is the trickle down to this writerly undertaking if the divine word contradicts itself? For a Christian awaiting death, there is only one word that really counts, that which assures salvation. On this all-important subject Shakespeare has Richard place before himself the most notorious of scriptural contradictions, between the idea of an all-inclusive heaven accessed by innocent children and the kind of heaven that decrees impossible entrance requirements for rich men, said to be parallel to threading a camel through the eye of a needle. Richard has every reason to feel that he is likelier to be in the rich man's waiting line, which moves ever so slowly, rather than that of the children, who move through the gate with the ease of those in possession of Global Entry.

So much for the *better* sort of thoughts. As for the other kinds of thoughts, those that tend toward ambition have, according to his imagery, led him precisely to his present incarceration, in which his "vain weak nails" cannot scratch through prison walls. The final kind of thoughts—those "tending to content"—can do no better than reflect on the fact that others have suffered as he is now suffering: not much comfort there. No surprise, perhaps, that he is finally reduced to a couple of summations that seem to be designed precisely to compare his own abilities as a dramatist with those of the dramatist who created him. First, "thus play I in one person many people," and then the truism that "any man that but man is" can be satisfied only by death. Surely, the comparison is not favorable to Richard's capabilities as a poet of himself, nor should it be a surprise that the most powerful account of his tragedy that he himself can offer is also the simplest: "I wasted time and now doth time waste me" (5.5.49). All his eloquent speechmaking gets traded in for that near-monosyllabic near-palindrome.

Each of the four plays to which I have dedicated a full chapter in these pages occupies that featured position because, underneath all the Shakespearean particularities, it feels as though it belongs to me. Not that it's nobody else's, though I may occasionally wish that were the case. Rather because I feel as though it became part of my life from an early moment and thus became part of who I am. It wasn't, in other words, just that a person was encountering a text but that a text was helping form the individual who was reading it. A *Midsummer Night's Dream* has been a leitmotif of my biography. *King Lear* became the cautionary guidebook to life inside a complicated family. *The Winter's Tale* is the chartering document, the authorization for my choice to lead a life centered on the aesthetic rather than any of the more immediately rewarding alternatives. The place of *Richard II* is not so easy to describe, and its role in my life may be more about contradictions than about summations. If *The Winter's Tale* gives me permission to be an aesthete—the word is not in fashion, I know—then *Richard II* presents itself as the record, for better and worse, of a life ordered via its expression in language. As should be clear from the way I have presented it here, it does not frame that linguistic vision with anything like the golden glow that surrounds the aesthetic in *The Winter's Tale*. Richard lives by language but also dies by it, and his language dies with him. And any careful reading of the play will take note of the fact that the beautiful speeches—the very ones that enraptured me as I sat in Central Park sixty years ago—run the risk of becoming more part of the problem than part of the solution.

My careful reading isn't so sure of that, however. When I described my evening with *Richard II* in Central Park, I left out something that, now, having unpacked my understandings of the play, seems both important and relevant.

I was young and inexperienced but, with regard to my new friend in the coffee shop, not so naïve as I may have implied earlier in this chapter or allowed my mother to believe. The bookshops and record shops of Greenwich Village, after all, had always offered the prospect of more than books and records. Remote prospects, to be sure; given my level of inexperience, fleeting glances, and nonmutual ones at that, had to be the rule. I knew that something different might be in store on this occasion, though my companion was, so far as I could judge or can now recall, absolutely scrupulous in the correctness of his behavior. Correctness in this case meant that our conversation never strayed from *Richard II*: That was the text and pretext that licensed a late-evening encounter between a teenager and a middle-aged man. As I now look back on this experience over the years and over the time of writing this book, I've come to feel that the Shakespeare play we had witnessed provided both the eros and the restraint that characterized the occasion. What if we had been watching *Twelfth Night* or *Romeo and Juliet*? The passions offered up in such lush display, whether they finished happy or sad, would have rendered us too bashful, too inadequate in the face of the Shakespearean example. And a big booming dynastic tragedy—a *Macbeth*, say—would have shut us down with the awful specter of violent death. The language of *Richard II*, on the other hand, stimulates the senses. In a play that must have a lower coefficient of explicit eros (whether good or evil) than perhaps anything else in the Shakespearean canon, it's the speech that turns you on. Does it provide satisfaction? *Can* language provide satisfaction? The answer for this very young person on that particular night is apparently yes. Let us say that Shakespeare's play gave me enough sensuous stimulation so that I was able to bid farewell to my new friend in the coffee shop, indifferent to any hidden agendas, and, quite prudently, to return to Westchester with my parents at the end of the evening. Whether that would in later times always be the right choice—or the choice I actually made— is another matter. But enough about me.

Readings

The *World Shakespeare Bibliography*—an enormously useful online source—lists, under the category of "Scholarship, Criticism, History of Criticism," 55,779 items; for the individual Shakespeare works that have been featured in the present volume, a total of merely 43,838 items is tallied. Those are the dimensions of the problem.

For a solution, or at least a workaround, I turn to Plato. In the *Phaedrus*, Socrates disparages the kind of learning that arises from the reading of written text and declares it hopelessly inferior to the kind that arises out of a face-to-face encounter, such as Socrates himself dispenses, which he describes as "writing on the soul." The trouble is that generally there are not enough in-person Socrateses to go around, and their classes tend to fill up during the first hour of registration. I've been fortunate, though: When it comes to Shakespeareans, I have been blessed with many who have written on my soul as well as in print. And so, in keeping with this volume's unrepentant insistence on the first person, I offer a set of outside readings that is also a record of some extraordinary people who have produced them and, by their presence in my life, have helped produce me.

Janet Adelman

My elder in graduate school; her work blended Freudian theorization with a determination to value the emotional significances of real experience.

Suffocating Mothers: Fantasies of Maternal Origin in Shakespeare's Plays,
  "Hamlet" to "The Tempest" (London: Routledge, 1992)

Harry Berger, Jr.

One of the great polymaths, and one of the great friends; he taught me everything I know about the exercise of the individual imagination as a legitimate tool of analysis.

Imaginary Audition: Shakespeare on Stage and Page (Berkeley: University of
   California Press, 1990)
Making Trifles of Terrors: Redistributing Complicities in Shakespeare (Stanford,
   CA: Stanford University Press, 1997)

Harold Bloom

An eminence grise, always benevolent in my educational career; his larger-than-life
engagement in text was inspiring whether you agreed with the details or not.

Shakespeare: The Invention of the Human (New York: Riverhead, 1998)

Rosalie Colie

As is indicated more than once in these pages, she was in person—but also in print—
my most influential mentor. A scrupulous historian, she was also capable of limitless
and inspired freedom in interpretation.

Shakespeare's Living Art (Princeton: Princeton University Press, 1974)
Some Facets of "King Lear": Essays in Prismatic Criticism (London: Heinemann,
   1974)

Margreta deGrazia

A truly original thinker; she manages to place Shakespeare both inside his own historical moment and across time to our moment.

Hamlet without Hamlet (Cambridge: Cambridge University Press, 1997)

Lynn Enterline

She has considered the classical tradition and taken it vividly in directions—rhetoric,
gender, melancholy—where she has opened many horizons for my own work.

The Rhetoric of the Body from Ovid to Shakespeare (Cambridge: Cambridge
   University Press, 2000)
Shakespeare's Schoolroom: Rhetoric, Discipline, Emotion (Philadelphia: University
   of Pennsylvania Press, 2012)

Marjorie Garber

Her influence on my thinking dates back sixty years. A brilliant analyst of the Shakespearean text who has became a brilliant analyst of our own culture.

Dream in Shakespeare (New Haven, CT: Yale University Press, 1974)

Shakespeare after All (New York: Random House, 2004)
Shakespeare and Modern Culture (New York: Pantheon, 2008)

Stephen Greenblatt

The most honored Renaissance scholar of my generation, and deservedly so: No one can manage both the big picture and the minute evidence of artistic objects with more assurance and persuasiveness.

Shakespearean Negotiations (Oxford: Oxford University Press, 1987)
Hamlet in Purgatory (Princeton: Princeton University Press, 2001)
Will in the World (New York: Norton, 2004)

Julia Lupton

She has written on Shakespeare with a wonderful disregard for the limits of what we're supposed to talk about when we talk about Shakespeare; when she *thinks* with Shakespeare, worlds open up.

Thinking with Shakespeare: Essays on Politics and Life (Chicago: University of
    Chicago Press, 2011)

Louis Montrose

One of the first in a line of students that taught me more than I taught them; his formulations, beginning while he was still a graduate student, of the relations between lived history and poetic text remain for me definitive.

*The Purpose of Playing: Shakespeare and the Cultural Politics of the Elizabethan
    Theatre* (Chicago: University of Chicago Press, 1996)
The Subject of Elizabeth: Authority, Gender, and Representation (Chicago: University
    of Chicago Press, 2006)

Stephen Orgel

There is no aspect of early modern culture, verbal or visual, that he has not observed with brilliance and originality. For me, he is the first citizen of English early modern studies and the closest to my heart.

Impersonations: The Importance of Gender in Shakespeare's England (Cambridge:
    Cambridge University Press, 1996)
Imagining Shakespeare (London: Palgrave, 2003)
The Authentic Shakespeare and Other Problems of the Early Modern Stage (London:
    Routledge, 2002)

Peter Platt

A friend who brings to his intellectual work his human (and humane) experience combined with the ability to see many sides of a question.

Shakespeare and the Culture of Paradox (Farnham: Ashgate, 2009)
Shakespeare's Essays (Edinburgh: Edinburgh University Press, 2020)

Norman Rabkin

He intervened in a struggle to answer the question "What gives us the right to interpret Shakespeare and to claim that our interpretations count as knowledge?"—and he answered definitively.

Shakespeare and the Common Understanding (New York: Free Press, 1967)
Shakespeare and the Problem of Meaning (Chicago: University of Chicago Press, 1981)

Mary Beth Rose

Friend and intellectual co-conspirator for my wonderful Chicago years. Mothers, lovers, and families all form part of her vision of an inclusive world in early modern literature.

"Where Are the Mothers in Shakespeare? Options for Gender Representation in the English Renaissance," *Shakespeare Quarterly* 42 (1991)

Leo Salingar

A wonderfully un-Oxbridgean Oxbridgean, he exemplified the kind of work at its best that a gifted and learned close reader, attentive in particular to genre, can accomplish.

Shakespeare and the Traditions of Comedy (Cambridge: Cambridge University Press, 1974)

Susan Snyder

My mentor and example as an undergraduate; she left us too soon but left behind a set of luminous essays.

The Comic Matrix of Shakespeare's Tragedies (Princeton: Princeton University Press, 1979)
Shakespeare: A Wayward Journey (Newark: University of Delaware Press, 2002)

Richard Strier

Friend and gastronomic blood brother; his vision of a Renaissance poetic deeply steeped in theology is exactly what I always need as a corrective to my own impenitent secularism.

"Mind, Nature, Heterodoxy, and Iconoclasm in *The Winter's Tale*," *Religion and Literature* 47 (2015)

And a few other Shakespearean indispensables whom I know mostly or entirely from their writings—again, a very personal list:

C. L. Barber, Catherine Belsey, Sigurd Burckhardt, Stanley Cavell, Walter Cohen, Joel Fineman, René Girard, John Holloway, Coppelia Kahn, Murray Krieger, Ania Loomba, Gail Kern Paster, Bruce Smith, Valerie Traub

Note on Text

All quotations from Shakespeare's plays are drawn from *The Oxford Shakespeare*, general editor, Stanley Wells, though in the case of *King Lear* I have used the conventional act and scene numbers rather than those of the Quarto.

Acknowledgments

This book owes its largest debt of all to the family members and friends who appear in it; I hope I have been true to them. It owes a fundamental debt as well to the friends and colleagues whom I cite—lovingly, I hope—in the section on "Readings" at the end of the main text. Further, a special expression of gratitude to a group of persons who communicated their faith in the project when others (even I) were doubting it: Nick Barberio, André Bernard, Peter Dougherty, Miriam Kellerhals, Tom Lay, Peter Platt, Jerry Singerman. Without these wise and kind folks the book would either not have been written or not have been published.

Index

Leonard Barkan is the Class of 1943 University Professor at Princeton, where he teaches comparative literature, art history, English, and classics. His many books include *The Hungry Eye: Eating, Drinking, and European Culture from Rome to the Renaissance* (Princeton, 2021), *Berlin for Jews: A Twenty-First-Century Companion* (Chicago, 2016), *Michelangelo: A Life on Paper* (Princeton, 2010), *Satyr Square: A Year, a Life in Rome* (Farrar, Straus & Giroux, 2006), and *Unearthing the Past: Archaeology and Aesthetics in the Making of Renaissance Culture* (Yale, 1999), which won prizes from the Modern Language Association, the College Art Association, the American Comparative Literature Association, *Architectural Digest*, and Phi Beta Kappa.

Printed in the USA
CPSIA information can be obtained
at www.ICGtesting.com
JSHW072140230224
57970JS00010B/80